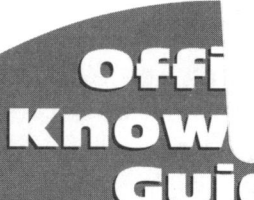

Official Know-It-All Guide™

Cruises
How to Sail in Style for Less

by
Georgina Cruz

Fell's

Frederick Fell Publishers, Inc.
2131 Hollywood Blvd., Suite 305, Hollywood, FL 33020
Phone: (954) 925-5242   Fax: (954) 925-5244
Web Site: www.FellPub.com

Fell's Official Know-It-All Guide
Frederick Fell Publishers, Inc.
2131 Hollywood Boulevard, Suite 305
Hollywood, Florida 33020
954-925-5242
e-mail: fellpub@aol.com
Visit our Web site at www.fellpub.com

Reproduction, translation, or use in any form by any means of any part of this work beyond that permitted by Section 107 or 108 of the 1976 United States Copyright Act without the permission of the copyright owner is unlawful. Requests for permission or further information should be addressed to the Permissions Department, Frederick Fell Publishers, Inc., 2131 Hollywood Blvd, Suite 305, Hollywood, FL 33020.
DISCLAIMER:
The information provided in this book is for informational purposes only. Although all reasonable efforts have been made to ensure that the information contained in this book is accurate as of the date of publication, the author and the publisher disclaim any liability with respect to the timeliness or accuracy of the information.

Library of Congress Cataloging in Publication Data

Cruz, Georgina, 1944-
   Cruises : how to sail in style for less / by Georgina Cruz.
      p. cm. -- (Fell's official know-it-all guide)
Includes index.
   ISBN 0-88391-086-1 (pbk.)
1. Ocean travel--Guidebooks. 2. Cruise ships--Guidebooks. I. Title.
II. Series.
   G550.C84 2003
   910'.2'02--dc21

                                                    2003002239

10 9 8 7 6 5 4 3 2 1
Copyright © 2003 by Georgina Cruz. All Rights Reserved.
Cover photo courtesy of Royal Caribbean International.
Graphic Design by: Elena Solis

Dedication

To my husband Humberto Cruz and my daughter Veronica Alicia Cruz,
the world's best cabin-mates in the voyage of my lifetime.

Acknowledgments

No book is ever the work of just one person. This guide would not have been possible without the assistance of the public relations departments of many cruise lines and tourist boards, which provided facts, figures and information included throughout the book.

Similarly, I owe a debt of gratitude to the hundreds of fellow passengers I've met and made friends with in my more than 25 years of cruising. Their comments and observations provided useful insights into the wonderful world of cruising long before I ever dreamed of writing a book.

"Infinity" Photo courtesy of Celebrity Cruises.

What Others Are Saying...

If you are serious about cruising, take advantage of the wealth of knowledge inside from someone who knows her stuff.
— Carolyn McGuire, associate travel Editor, Chicago Tribune

Georgina Cruz is a true cruise aficionado. Having sailed on more than 100 cruises, her expertise in the industry makes her an "Official Know-It-All" when it comes to cruising. Fells's Official Know-It-All Guide to Cruises is a fantastic resource for everyone from the first-time cruiser to the cruise connoisseur.
— Sharon Dodd, Editor, CruiseCritic.com

No one is more knowledgeable about the modern cruise liner than Georgina Cruz. Her shipboard experience is vast, and she really does her homework, then she shares her love of cruising with readers in an affable, bright and clear style. These are among the many reasons Georgina has been a valued contributor to Cruise Travel magazine for nearly two decades.
— Charles Doherty, Managing Editor, Cruise Travel magazine

As a travel editor based in San Juan, Puerto Rico, I have been reading Georgina Cruz's stories for several years and I can say they're always lively, crisp, up to date and full of useful details. Her first book is no exception. It's obviously the work of someone who enjoys traveling, who enjoys sharing with others her experiences and who is able to bring forth the specific information anyone would need to make the most of his or her trip.
Her wide-ranging book, which covers just about everything from food to itineraries to how to complain on board, from particular travel destinies to specific ships, should become a reference guide for anyone interested in cruise vacations.
— Rafael Vega Curry, Associate Editor Sunday magazines, El Nuevo Dia, San Juan, Puerto Rico

Georgina Cruz's trademarks are liveliness and accuracy

— Enrique Pizzi, Editor, Vea Magazine,
Puerto Rico

In the many years I have worked with Georgina Cruz at the South Florida Sun-Sentinel, I have found her a solid writer, very accurate and informative. She has the knack of preparing her readers for cruising, letting them in on what to expect and ways to choose the ships and itineraries that are right for them.

— Jean Allen, travel columnist and former travel Editor,
South Florida Sun-Sentinel

Georgina Cruz has been there and done that when it comes to cruising and she knows how to get the most enjoyment out of a great way to vacation.

— Phil Hartman, managing Editor,
The Ohio Motorist

Even the most ardent landlubber will take to the sea with ease after reading this essential cruise guide. The guide is fantastic, jam-packed with great information for cruisers.

—Merryn McLachlan, former Editor of the Australian Cruise Passenger

For those of us who regularly review cruise ships, Georgina Cruz is a familiar face. Now, with the knowledge she has gained from sailing on more than 100 of these floating palaces, Georgina has put together a tip-filled primer on cruising, perfect for the vast majority of Americans who have never set foot on a cruise ship.

—Jay Clarke,
Travel Writer and former Travel Editor of the Miami Herald

"Veendam" Photo courtesy of Holland America Line.

Table of Contents

Introduction	**xvii**
Chapter One: Setting Sail On Your Cruise	**21**
Misconceptions Vs. Reality	22
Booking A Cruise	27
Getting Ready To Cruise	32
Budgeting For Your Voyage	32
Dust Off Your Luggage	34
Test The Waters Tips	38
Insider's Savings Insights	40
Chapter Two: Types Of Ships	**43**
Small Ships	43
Mid-size Ships	45
Large Ships	46
How To Select The Right Ship For You	48
Test The Waters Tips	49
Insider's Savings Insights	49
Ship Sizes At A Glance Chart	50
Chapter Three: Types Of Cruise Lines	**53**
Part A - Major Cruise Lines Ahoy!	**54**
Carnival	54
Celebrity	57
Costa	59
Crystal	61
Cunard	62
Disney	64
Holland America	65
Norwegian	68
Orient	70
Princess	71

Radisson Seven Seas	73
Royal Caribbean	75
Seabourn	78
Silversea	79
Windstar	80
Part B - More Cruise Lines	**82**
Part C - Barge & River Cruises	**90**
Test The Waters Tips	92
Insider's Savings Insights	92
Chapter 4: Cruising Regions	**95**
Introducing The Caribbean Cruise	**96**
Tips For Caribbean Cruising	99
Touring Ideas For Independents At Embarkation Cities	99
Major Caribbean Ports Of Call	100
Antigua	100
Aruba	100
Barbados	101
British Virgin Islands	102
Cozumel	102
Curacao	103
Dominica	104
Dominican Republic	104
Freeport	105
Grand Cayman	105
Grenada	106
Guadeloupe	106
Key West	107
Martinique	107
Nassau	108
Ocho Rios	109
St. Barts	110
St. Croix, U.S. Virgin Islands	110

St. Kitts	111
St. Lucia	111
St. Maarten/St. Martin	112
St. Thomas/St. John, U.S. Virgin Islands	113
San Juan	114
Other Caribbean Ports	**114**
Introducing The Alaska Cruise	**115**
Tips For Alaska Cruising	**116**
Touring Ideas For Independents At Embarkation Cities	**117**
Major Alaska Cruise Ports Of Call	**119**
Juneau, Alaska	119
Ketchikan, Alaska	121
Sitka, Alaska	121
Skagway, Alaska	122
Victoria, B.C., Canada	123
Other Cruising Regions	**124**
Panama Canal	124
Mexican Riviera	125
Mediterranean	126
Northern Europe	130
New England/Canada	131
Bermuda	132
South America	132
Baja And The Sea Of Cortez	133
Hawaii	134
The South Pacific	135
Asia	136
Still Other Cruises	137
Test The Waters Tips	139
Insider's Savings Insights	139
Chapter Five: Itineraries	**141**
Preliminary Planning	141

Season/Off-Season/Shoulder Season Fares	142
Type Of Holiday You Want: Laid-back Vs. Port-Intensive	142
Sample Itineraries	143
Finding The Right Itinerary For You	150
Things To Look Out For As You Study Itineraries	151
Pre- And Post-Cruise Packages	152
Test The Waters Tips	152
Insider's Savings Insights	153
Chapter Six: Shore Excursions	**155**
Options For Touring	155
Pros & Cons Of Buying Tours Through The Line	157
Things To Ask About Ship's Tours	159
Mingling With The Locals On Ship's Tours	159
Other Worthwhile Ship's Tours	165
Tips For Touring Independently	166
When It Is Not A Good Idea To Tour Independently	167
Test The Waters Tips	167
Insider's Savings Insights	168
Chapter Seven: Shipboard Cabins	**171**
Your Cozy Home At Sea - Standard Cabins	171
Advantages Of A Veranda	174
Suites	174
Location, Location, Location	175
Test The Waters Tips	177
Insider's Savings Insights	178
Chapter Eight: Shipboard Lifestyles	**181**
Lifestyles/personal preferences accommodated aboard ship	181
Active/Social Cruiser	181
Passive/Wanna-get-away-from-it-all Cruiser	186
Special Interest Cruiser	187
* Health-conscious/spa enthusiast	187

* Gambling, anyone?	194
* Shopping, anyone?	196
* Theme Cruises for other interests	198
Complaining and Praising	198
Test The Waters Tips	200
Insider's Savings Insights	201

Chapter Nine: Culinary Delights — **205**

Food, Glorious Food!	205
Dining At Sea	206
Traditional Two Seatings or Open Seating	206
What's For Dinner? Sample Menus	208
Test The Waters Tips	223
Insider's Savings Insights	223

Chapter Ten: Cruising Solo, With A Significant Other, With The Kids, On Multi-Generational Reunions. And Cruising For Free — **227**

Singles	228
Couples	231
Families	234
Multi-generational reunions	239
Cruising For Free	242
Test The Waters Tips	243
Insider's Savings Insights	243

Appendix — **245**

Nautical Lingo	**245**
Cruise Line Addresses, Phones & Web Sites	**246**
Other Resources	**249**
Major Cruise Travel Agencies	**249**
Online Cruise Agencies	**249**
Useful Internet Sites	**250**
Your Personal Cruise Diary	**252**

xvi *"Caronia"* Photo courtesy of Cunard Line.

Introduction

So you are thinking of booking a voyage—or maybe you are just intrigued by ships and cruise vacations—and would like to know more, particularly about sailing well at a good price tag. By picking up this guide, you have steered the right course to an ocean of information about the cruise experience and its costs.

Here you will find the type of details that will enable you to make the right choices confidently and intelligently—the choices that can make the difference between merely sailing on a ship and enjoying the most magical voyage of a lifetime, and the choices that will be kind to your pocketbook. After reading through these pages, you will feel like an insider possessing the knowledge that will enable you to feel as comfortable about cruising as if you were already lounging out on deck by the pool, serenaded by a tropical band and sipping something frosty cold while gulping down the even more refreshing views of indigo waters.

It is the aim of this guide to walk you through the entire cruise experience, to ensure you feel at ease from the moment you first set foot on the gangway and hear the words "bon voyage" as well as to save you big bucks before, during and after your cruise.

There was no train American poetess Edna St. Vincent Millay would not take; with me there is no ship I would not take —and it's beginning to feel like there is no ship I have not taken. With 100+ voyages under my belt, I know ships and have a love of everything nautical—in fact, mine is an affection as strong as that one accords to relatives and some friends (well, if one is lucky to have a great family and friendships). I totally agree with marine historian John Maxtone-Graham,

Fell's Official Know-It-All: Cruises

who once confided after a lecture at sea, "If it has a smokestack and it floats, I love it!"

And not only am I passionate about cruises, but I am equally eager to share my experiences with others. This is the book I always dreamed of writing and my goal has been to make it one you'd love to read —the book you find most convenient and useful as you look at the cruise experience.

Written all over these pages you will find, in clear and simple language, information to assist you every step of the way: from selecting a travel agent and the best fare, to browsing through cruise line brochures and Web sites, to picking the right cruise line, ship, cabin and itinerary, to packing, and to what to wear when during your fabulous voyage.

On one of my early cruises, the first night of the sailing tablemates of ours came to dinner in full formal regalia (he in a tuxedo, she in a long gown and dripping in jewelry) and they were visibly embarrassed when they saw that everyone else was in pants and polo shirts, sundresses and other casual attire. It was their first cruise and they did not know that embarkation night on any ship is designated casual, as some guests have been traveling most of the day to get to the ship and some may not have even received their luggage in their cabins after boarding. Having read this guide you will not be embarrassed like that. You will, in fact, become acquainted with all aspects of life aboard ship (from the culinary delights you have no doubt already heard about, to the wacky and crazy contests (knobby knees, hairy chests, beer drinking, etc.) and deck games featured aboard ships. You will get the lowdown on how to pick shore excursions, tipping the staff, disembarkation procedures and much more. And you will learn how you can save your hard-earned vacation dollars.

We all know how important it is to stick your toe in the water before plunging right in, so I do it for you: including Test The Waters Tips in each chapter to ensure you are in the swim of things from the moment you board your ship. In other words, you will have your "sea legs" even before you set sail.

Last, but most certainly not least, we all realize that one of life's greatest pleasures is to enjoy something fully without breaking the bank, so each chapter has Insider's Savings Insights to help you sail well for less. This way you will be all smiles from the moment you get your first whiff of fresh ocean air.

Welcome aboard!

"Silver Cloud" Photo courtesy of Silversea Cruises.

Chapter: 1
Setting Sail On Your Cruise

A cruise is the travel equivalent of a piece of cake: scrumptious and easy to enjoy—as close as you can get to an effortless vacation. You leave your cares behind, like excess baggage on the pier, and you feel your worries drift away in sparkling breezes as you board the ship. How cool is that? The coolest!

Because almost magically, you have entered a new world: a pampering place where you are fed—six or more meals and snacks a day all included in the cruise ticket. In fact, I know of people who have managed to eat and nibble nine times in 24 hours on ships, and a cruise line public relations department (Royal Caribbean's) claims you can eat 15 times per day if you set your mind to it!

And there is more. You have also entered a world where you are picked up after, entertained day and night, and waited on hand and foot. Onboard, after you unpack (you just have to do it once to visit a variety of ports) the greatest effort you may have to exert might be waving a hand while you lounge by the pool to get a waiter's attention; and the most difficult dilemma to solve will be whether to order the warm apple pie a la mode or the cherries jubilee for dessert—but soon you catch on that this is one delicious dilemma very easily solved: simply order both!

And yet, the world of cruising is still a largely undiscovered world. The Cruise Line International Association (an organization created to promote the cruise product that counts as its members 23 lines representing 95 percent of the cruise capacity marketed from North America) estimates that only about 14 percent of Americans have cruised. When they do, however (and the organization projected in 2001 that 7.4 million passengers will cruise on an annual basis) they discover that a voyage is a ticket to the good life. About 90 percent who try it, say they are either extremely satisfied or very satisfied, according to CLIA surveys.

So why aren't more people taking the plunge into cruising? Let's take a look at some of the myths surrounding the cruise industry that may be keeping many -perhaps you too?-from setting sail.

* Misconception: "Cruises are expensive—just for the rich."

* Reality: Cruises attract people from all walks of life. During the quarter century that I have been cruising, I have enjoyed as dining room table mates and in conversations at the railing and around the ship, the companionship of waitresses, nurses, teachers, clerks, actors, salesmen, doctors, a countess -to name a few. If you find cruise brochure prices intimidating, you will be glad to know that they are like the sticker prices on cars -very few, if any, ever pays them! With all the discounting going on in the industry—including everything from early bird discounts to two-for-one offers—you can enjoy per day rates of $100 or less (sometimes $75 per day or less), depending on what bargains are available for the time you wish to sail. And when cruise fares are compared to the prices of a land-based resort, guess which vacation is less expensive? A cruise, because of its packaged nature: the lines reserve big blocks of seats on airlines so they get excellent fares to fly you to the ship (if you need to travel by air to the port of embarkation), they include all your meals and snacks, ground transfers (if you buy the air tickets through the cruise line), daytime activities, including sports contests, dance lessons and bridge tournaments, and

Setting Sail on Your Cruise

evening entertainment such as musical revues and variety shows. On a typical land-based resort vacation you pay extra for taxis to get you to and from the airport to the hotel; for sports activities, for evening entertainment, not to mention your meals and snacks.

* Misconception: "Most everyone gets seasick."
* Reality: With today's stabilizing systems, seasickness is rare. But if you are concerned because you have experienced motion sickness on cars, trains, buses and/or airplanes, there are several things you can do. Sail on mega-liners, these ships are so big you hardly feel any movement at all. Choose to sail in protected waters—such as Alaska's Inside Passage or coastal voyages-or go barging on a river in the U.S. or in Europe and other destinations. Bring along remedies like Dramamine and Bonine, available over the counter at your drugstore (most ships also dispense these free of charge at the reception desk). You can also check with your doctor to see whether a Transderm patch (available by prescription) is right for you. If you start feeling queasy, overcome the temptations to crawl away and lie down in your room and to stop eating; instead, go to an open deck for lots of fresh air and keep your stomach full (both these strategies work wonders).

> One of the best remedies against seasickness is eating lots of crackers and bread. These soak up stomach fluids and make you feel much better almost instantly. I have never gotten seasick—I heard of the simple and effective crackers solution from a ship's doctor at a cocktail party.

Misconception: "I will feel confined and be bored."
Reality: Today's ships, particularly mega-liners, are in a word: huuuuuge! Often you get off after a seven-day cruise without visiting some areas of the ship twice—

that happened to me when I sailed on Royal Caribbean's mega-liner ***Sovereign of the Seas***. I loved the line's hallmark Viking Crown Lounge, wrapped around the smokestack and with panoramic views of the sea and ports, and I meant to return there during the voyage, but before I knew it the cruise was practically over and I had not gone back, busy as I had been exploring and enjoying other areas of the ship. And mid-size ships and mega-liners offer an almost round-the-clock roster of activities and nighttime entertainment: things like talks on the ports of call, sports contests, dance lessons, lectures on a wide variety of topics, wine tastings, bridge tournaments, bad-hair-day and nutrition seminars in the spa, yoga and exercise classes, bingo, and more.

> Your cabin steward delivers the next day's activities and entertainment log to your stateroom the night before. Check off activities you are interested in and carry the log with you all day, so you know where to go when, to participate in all your favorites.

* Misconception: "I will get fat."
* Reality: While it is true that a cruise is as bountiful as the ocean itself when it comes to culinary delights, you do not have to put on weight if you do not want to. I weigh less now after more than 100 voyages than I did when I started cruising a quarter century ago. My secret: I have cereal for breakfast, select frequently the low-fat dishes for lunch and dinner, and skip the midnight snacks. Most ships offer light and healthy selections at all meals—one ship, the ***Norwegian Sun***, offers an alternative dining option, Pacific Heights, with an entire menu of ***Cooking Light*** recipes—the vegetarian lasagna is outstanding! Of course, if you go for the baked Alaska or Crepes Suzette for dessert, you can join the walkathon or work out in the gym the following morning.

Setting Sail on Your Cruise

> Want to burn up some extra calories aboard ship? Always take the stairs to go from one place to another!

* Misconception: "I will find the love of my life."
* Reality: While there is no denying that cruises are romantic—endless horizons, dancing under the stars, exotic ports-you may find that more often than not, single women outnumber the unattached men onboard. On a number of my voyages, I have come across a half-dozen couples that had actually met on a cruise and subsequently got married—and now they were back to celebrate an anniversary or to enjoy a romantic getaway—so it can happen. But you probably have as good a chance as of winning the lottery. So, to avoid disappointment, it is best not to count on Cupid's arrows hitting the mark during a particular sailing. Come aboard expecting to have a good time and most certainly you will; come aboard expecting to meet the love of your life and you will likely be disappointed. See the section of this guide in Chapter 10 about cruising solo.
* Misconception: "Cruising is not safe."
* Reality: Cruise lines have put in place a host of extraordinary measures to ensure your safety -on a recent cruise I was on, aboard NCL's **Norwegian Star**, for example, I learned that the security personnel at the ship's gangway is military-trained.

Immediately after the Sept. 11, 2001 attacks on America, cruise lines implemented Level III (the highest level) security measures, as cited in the U.S. Coast Guard's **Security for Passenger Vessels and Passenger Terminals** regulations, and remained at that level at this writing. As part of the security measures, the U.S. Coast Guard has added armed sea marshals to cruise ships and Coast Guard cutters often escort ships in and out of ports.

Only ticketed passengers are allowed into the embarkation points of cruise terminals. Crew re-boarding the vessel in the ports of call must show identification and passengers must produce their boarding cards. No visitors are allowed unless the visit has been pre-arranged. Hand luggage is X-rayed and you walk through airport-type screeners. Some lines, including Crystal Cruises, stopped tours of the navigational bridge post Sept. 11, 2001. Others, like Orient Lines, still offer them.

Safety standards have come a long way since the ill-fated ***Titanic*** (oh, yes, now there will be enough lifeboats for everyone onboard) and technology advances in modern mega-liners include monitoring cameras in public areas of the ship, like the spa and cabin hallways, that send images to the navigational bridge. When it comes to fire safety, ships operate under the international Safety of Life at Sea rules. These call for smoke detectors and low-level lighting for escape routes. Within 24 hours of sailing (often just before departure or shortly thereafter) there is a compulsory muster drill of all passengers. When you hear the announcement for this drill, go to your cabin, put on your lifejacket and head for your muster station (its location is generally posted on the back door of your stateroom). At the drill you will be shown the proper way to wear your lifejacket, given tips on what to do if there is an emergency that requires evacuation of the ship, and told or shown the location of your lifeboat. Make sure you (and everyone in your party if you are traveling with others) attend this muster drill—this information will come in handy in the unlikely event of an emergency (and what a fun photo opportunity to get a picture with your lifejacket on). The U.S. Coast Guard conducts inspections of ships sailing out of U.S. ports four times a year. And the Centers for Disease Control and Prevention (CDC) also inspects ships arriving at U.S. ports for water quality and food safety. Scores are issued for each ship (86 is a passing grade). Check the latest score for the ship you are considering by visiting www.cdc.gov/travel.

Setting Sail on Your Cruise

> A bit of common sense advice regarding measures you can take when it comes to safety. Do what you would normally do at a resort or hotel: don't invite strangers into your stateroom and don't open the door to your cabin unless you know the person knocking on it. If it is someone identifying themselves as ship's crew to fix or check something, do as you would at a hotel, phone reception to verify before you open the door.

So now, having debunked a half-dozen myths about cruising, we can go on, full speed ahead, to the ABCs/1-2-3s of cruising. Jump right in with me—the water's fine!

* Booking A Cruise - One way to book your cruise—the most popular—particularly when it comes to first-timers, is through a travel agent. Being able to sit face to face with an experienced agent who can make recommendations and answer your questions is great.

Look for an agent who specializes in cruises, works for a cruises-only agency, or works at the cruise desk of an all-travel agency. Such an agent is in frequent communication with the cruise lines, knows about the latest discounts and deals, and can offer you invaluable expertise on all aspects of the cruise experience, from discussing staterooms to dinner seatings to sightseeing suggestions to what is the ship's usual clientele. I booked my first cruise 25 years ago through an agent who worked on the cruise desk at an agency located near our home. She walked me through the basics: ship/cabin/itinerary selection, dinner seating time, children's facilities (we were traveling with our then four-year-old daughter) and she got us a complimentary upgrade and told us about a discount off brochure fares. She was a very good agent, but I really lucked out—I should have done more homework.

Before you pick an agent:

(1) Contact the Cruise Lines International Association (phone: 212-921-0066; Web site: www.cruising.org) and/or the National Association of Cruise Oriented Agencies (phone: 305-663-5626; Web site: www.nacoaonline.com) for recommendations on good agencies. Agencies who are members of both groups are cruise specialists. Another membership you like to see an agency have is that of the American Society of Travel Agents (visit: www.astanet.com). These three organizations check members for ethical practices. Yet another thing to look for is the letters CTC (Certified Travel Counselor) next to the agent's name on his card. Agents earn this designation by taking a course from the Institute of Certified Travel Agents.

(2) Ask questions, particularly what lines has the agent actually sailed on? What can he tell you about his firsthand experiences on those lines? Ask the agent specifically about the food, entertainment, cabins, clientele, facilities and anything else that matters to you.

(3) Does the agent ask you questions and does he seem interested in getting to know you and what you want for your vacation -or does he seem simply interested in making the sale so he can pocket his commission from the cruise line?

(4) Does the agent offer you a variety of choices? Some agents specialize in just a few cruise brands—much like auto dealers who only sell you certain cars. The agent should be presenting you with a variety of choices, not just pushing one or two ships.

Many travel agencies book big blocks of space on a ship in advance to be able to offer their clients a special group rate. Sometimes these groups also get perks like complimentary cocktail parties. Find out if your agent has a group booking that is attractive to you.

Setting Sail on Your Cruise

> Once you set sail, you can book your next cruise onboard. Most lines have a future cruises desk on each ship with incentives such as special discounts and upgrades, and if you wish, your travel agent back home will get a commission.

If you are Internet-savvy, you may opt to bypass a travel agent and take matters into your own hands researching and booking the cruise online. Most cruise lines have Web sites, packed with information about the ships, accommodations, facilities, amenities, services, itineraries, fares and more, and in many cases, you can book the cruise directly through the site. You can also visit www.uniglobe.com that allows visitors to chat with an agent live, and sites and online agencies that specialize in cruises like www.cruise411.com, www.icruise.com and www.cruise.com. Some sites, like www.allcruiseauction.com feature a half-dozen cruise auctions, plus promotions, cruise information and message boards.

In addition to the specials you find at online sites check your local newspaper's Sunday Travel Section -it is a good source of information on special fares. Other helpful resources are magazines, like **Cruise Travel**, with lots of ads of discounters, consolidators and cruise specialists, plus a variety of features, ship reviews and detailed guides with charts (contact: P.O. Box 342, Mount Morris, Ill. 61054; newsstand price is $5.99 per issue) and newsletters like **Ocean & Cruise News** (P.O. Box 92, Stamford, Conn. 06904; subscription price is $30 for 12 issues).

So, what is the best way to book a cruise -through a travel agent or online with you doing everything from research to actual booking? Well, whichever way you feel most comfortable with! I personally like a combination of both with the would-be cruiser doing lots of research online and on newspapers and magazines. Then, going to consult a travel agent, armed with information, ideas on ships and itineraries you think you might like, plus a few examples of fares that you have found that are attractive to you.

> Jot down three or four specials on ships/itineraries you are interested in and take them to an experienced travel agent and ask if he can beat the fares. He just might, and if he cannot, he may still be able to discuss their pros and cons (if any) with you.

Once you are ready to proceed with the booking, the cruise line will, of course, want your money. To secure the booking, your agent will ask for a deposit that may be a fixed amount or a percentage of the total fare, with the remainder due usually no later than two months prior to sail date.

To ensure your days in the sun, it is advisable to buy travel insurance to protect against trip cancellation, bankruptcy of the cruise line and other perils. Check to see if your existing health insurance covers you in the event you become ill while on the cruise, and that your homeowner's policy covers lost or stolen luggage (it probably does, if you have off-premise theft protection). Some travel insurance companies include:

Travel Guard International, 1145 Clark Street, Stevens Point, WI 54481; telephone: 800-826-1300; Web site: www.travel-guard.com.

Access America, 6600 W. Broad Street, Richmond, VA 2320; telephone: 800-284-8300; Web site: www.accessamerica.com.

Travelex Insurance Services, 11717 Burt Street, Suite 202, Omaha, NE 68154; telephone: 800-228-9792; Web site: www.travelex-insurance.com.

Pay for the cruise with your credit card. The credit card company can help in the event of a filing for bankruptcy by the cruise line.

You usually receive all your documents, including cruise ticket, airline ticket (if needed and purchased through the cruise line), baggage tags to attach to your luggage for delivery to your cabin from the airport or pier, transfer vouchers, and

Setting Sail on Your Cruise

boarding forms anywhere from two weeks to a month before departure depending on the cruise line. You generally also receive a shore excursions booklet outlining the tours available for purchase through the ship and a "Welcome Aboard"-type booklet with lots of practical information about shipboard life, including those all-important meal times.

Twenty-five years ago, when I sailed on my first cruise, a 10-day Caribbean voyage from Fort Lauderdale, I was amazed that the check-in clerk did not ask to see any identification. She merely took my cruise ticket and boarding form and sent me on to the ship. Well, a lot of water has flowed under that bridge.

Nowadays, you do need proper identification to board a ship. A passport or visa are not necessary if you are cruising in Alaska, Hawaii, Canada, the Caribbean, Mexico, Panama Canal, New England and Bermuda. If you do have a passport, however, bring it: it is the best identification in the world. If you do not have a passport, you do need photo identification and proof of citizenship (a certified copy of your birth certificate) if the cruise takes you outside the U.S. Airlines require photo identification on domestic flights and passport on international flights. Your travel agent and/or the cruise line can inform you on how to obtain any necessary visas when you travel to countries that require them such as Russia, Brazil and Australia. Ditto for any required vaccinations. Aliens residing in the U.S. must have their green cards (alien registration cards) and valid passports as well as any necessary visas. If a child is cruising with just one parent or with grandparents or other relatives, you may need to submit a letter of permission from the parent(s) for the child to go on the cruise (check with your agent and/or the cruise line for details). Bear in mind that documentation and visa regulations may change at any time -always ask your agent and/or the cruise line exactly what you need to bring with you for your specific case, and bring it. You can be denied boarding if you don't have the proper documentation and no refunds will be given.

Fell's Official Know-It-All: Cruises

> Always carry your cruise documents and passport or identification documents with you to quickly access them at check-in - never pack them in luggage you are planning to check. Also keep with you valuables, such as jewelry and cameras, and medications.

* Getting Ready To Cruise - Before you yell in jubilation, "I'm outtahere!" there are a few additional odds and ends to take care of in preparing for your cruise.

* Budgeting For Your Voyage. While the bulk of your expenses are included in the cruise, there are items, mostly of a personal nature, that are not covered. Here are some typical prices for these items to help you budget your money.

Typical Shipboard Incidentals

Sodas:	$1.50-$2
Beer:	$2.95-$3.95
Wine:	$10-$300/bottle
Cocktails:	$3.50-$5
Casino:	you decide
Dining in alternative venue:	free to $25
Dry cleaning/laundry:	$1-$10/item
E-Mail:	$0.50-$1.50/min.
Group babysitting:	$6-$8/hr.
Haircuts	
Men's:	$23-$29
Women's:	$52-$70
Line's logo souvenirs:	$3-$60
Massage:	$65-$249
Phone calls:	$5.95-$15.95/min.
Photos (5 x 7):	$6.95-$7.95
Ship's shore tours:	$25-$300+
Tips (per person, per day):	about $8-$10

Setting Sail on Your Cruise

> To save on shipboard expenses, look at the list of typical incidentals and see how much you can do at, or bring from, home: get your haircut before the trip, get film bought on sale back home and load your camera, and bring your own liquor to consume in your cabin (not allowed in public areas). If the ship does not have a self-service launderette, pack enough changes to avoid hefty laundry/dry-cleaning charges. Instead of phoning, use e-mail, or better yet, good, old-fashioned postcards!

Tips on Tipping

Cruise lines generally offer guests tipping guidelines in their brochures, welcome aboard literature, cabin literature and during a disembarkation talk by the cruise director.

Generally, tips are given the last evening of the cruise directly to the people (never give the tips to someone to give to somebody else) who have served you during the voyage: the dining room waiter and his assistant, the cabin steward, dining room section manager, and maitre d' (in my case, I tip the maitre d' only if he has provided a special service, such as arranging for a birthday cake). Per person, per day tips generally average about $10 on moderately priced lines.

Some lines, like Royal Olympic Cruises, pool the tips, which are then distributed among the service personnel. Others, like Norwegian Cruise Line and Carnival, automatically charge the gratuities to your shipboard account (you can, and should, adjust the amount to reflect the service you have received). Others, like Princess give you a choice: you can have the tips ($10 per person, per day) automatically charged to your account or you can tip those who served you personally on the last night of the voyage.

Still other lines, like Holland America and Windstar operate under a "no tipping required" policy, but you get a definite feeling that tips are expected. The lines do not give guests any guidelines. Passengers I have asked tell me they give about half of what they'd normally give on other ships (or about $5 per person, per day) and that is approximately what I give on these lines as well.

On ultra-deluxe lines like Silversea Cunard, Radisson Seven Seas and Seabourn, tips are included. Tips are not included on luxury line Crystal Cruises where recommended amounts are: $4 per person, per day to cabin stewardess (singles, $5 per day); $4 per person, per day to the dining room waiter, and $2.50 per person, per day to assistant waiter. Recommendation for penthouse guests only on Crystal is an additional $4.50 per person, per day for the butler.

If you are on a voyage that is longer than two weeks, consider giving half the recommended tipping amount halfway through the voyage, and the second half at the conclusion of the cruise—the staff will appreciate it (we always do and find that the service gets even better!).

Dust off your luggage —You're Going Places!

When it comes to packing, let's not put the cart before the horse. First, consider what ship you will be going on and its dress codes and then, of course, take into account where you are headed. The first consideration, the ship, is important because some vessels are definitely dressier than others. In the pack-the-tux-and-dress-to-the-nines-almost-every-night category are ultra-deluxe vessels like those of Crystal Cruises, Silversea and Seabourn. In what we could call the "come as you are" category are expedition vessels like those of Lindblad Expeditions and other small ships including some sailing vessels like those of Windjammer Barefoot Cruises. Other ships like those of Norwegian Cruise Line and Star Clippers have a dress code that makes "resort casual" appropriate every night. Most other ships call for two formal nights on seven-day cruises (dark suit or tux for the men, cocktail dress or long gown for ladies), two informal nights (jacket and tie, or sometimes

Setting Sail on Your Cruise

just jacket (no tie) for the men; pantsuits or dresses for the ladies) and three casual nights (polo shirts or button down shirts and slacks for the men, skirts or pants and blouses or sundresses for the ladies). Note that many lines request that no shorts, t-shirts and the like be worn to dinner in the ship's main restaurants even on casual nights. On 10- to 14-night voyages, there usually are three or four formal nights. The first and last nights of every cruise, regardless of length, are casual.

Cruise lines do not limit the amount of luggage you bring on board, but airlines will charge for excess baggage and cruise cabins generally do not have as much closet/drawer space as hotels and resorts, so keep those things in mind as you pack. Where you are going, is of course, the next important thing to consider. When cruising in the Caribbean and other warm waters such as the Panama Canal and Mexican Riviera, pack two bathing suits (they will come in handy if you'd like to go swimming twice the same day), a cover-up, shorts and t-shirts, light-weight pants and tops, a baseball cap or other hat and suntan lotion. For evening wear, bring two dressy outfits for the formal nights, two nice outfits (like a blazer and pants for the men; pantsuits for the women) as well as casual resort wear. Don't forget a light sweater or jacket to wear in the air-conditioned public rooms or walks on deck in the cool ocean breezes. Rain showers are usually brief in the Caribbean and other tropical areas, but it won't hurt to bring a small umbrella or raincoat.

If you are sailing in Alaska and other cold waters, like northern Europe including the Baltic, pack layers of clothes including long-sleeved shirts, sweaters and/or sweat shirts and coats/jackets that you can take off and put on depending on the weather. Throw in some raingear just in case.

Pack comfortable walking shoes for touring and a pair of rubber-soled shoes, for walking on sometimes wet decks, no matter where you are going. If your sightseeing plans include going into churches, basilicas, synagogues and mosques, pack an appropriate, conservative outfit. Pack a soft-sided, fold away bag in case you need extra room for souvenir purchases. A small carry-on bag will come in handy to bring a change of clothes. It may take a few hours after you board to receive your luggage in your cabin on embarkation day, and you can put your pajamas and toiletries in there the morning of disembarkation as you will be asked to put the rest of your luggage outside your room the night before so the crew can bring it ashore for you.

Bring your binoculars for Alaska and other scenic natural areas, like Costa Rica and the Galapagos, when you will be on the lookout for nature's wonders and wildlife.

Before you leave for the airport or port, double check that you have your cruise documents/passport or proper identification with you and tag your baggage with the tags provided by the cruise line (fill in your name, address, cabin number, etc.). The bags will be delivered to your stateroom a few hours after you board the ship - usually before dinnertime. If, in the unlikely event they are not when you return from dinner (if you are on the 6 or 6:30 p.m. early seating); or before you leave for dinner (if you are on the 8 or 8:30 p.m. late seating), contact your room steward and reception so they can look for your luggage. I must say I have never had any problems in this department.

If you are flying to meet the ship, call the airline to select your seats (cruise lines will not do this for you), and ask the airline for any special meals you may want, and reconfirm your flight.

When you get to the pier, a porter will take your bags and you will see them in your cabin a few hours later (usual tip is $1 a bag, except in New York, where it is $2 per suitcase). If you flew and purchased air through the cruise line, a representative of the line will meet you at the airport (usually in baggage claim on domestic flights; outside Customs in international flights) and will arrange for your luggage to be sent on to the ship. But, of course, you must claim your baggage from

Setting Sail on Your Cruise

the airline and bring it to, or point it out to the cruise representative. Once two women on one of my sailings simply identified themselves to the representative and went on to waiting transportation without claiming their bags and bringing them to the representative. They thought that, because their bags were tagged, that someone from the line would collect them at the airport. That is not the case, particularly that day when we had landed in Barcelona, Spain, where, as in any international destination, cruise personnel has to stay outside the baggage/customs area. The two women had to go back into the terminal to try to retrieve their luggage (hard to do because they were not supposed to re-enter the baggage/customs area once they had cleared it). The delay made them miss the first few airport-to-ship-transfers, but eventually they were able to get their bags and made it to the ship.

When you arrive at the vessel's pier, there will often be several lines for embarkation, usually arranged alphabetically. A clerk will take your cruise ticket and boarding form and check your passport (in the case of international destinations, the cruise line may keep your passport and give you a receipt for it -this is so the line can have everyone's passports ready for speedier inspection by authorities at each port of call). Your passport will be returned at the end of the cruise. You will be issued a boarding card, which is usually your room key and, when you put down a credit card, the boarding card will also become your charge card onboard ship (the last day of the cruise you will receive a statement of your charges during the voyage and you can elect to pay it with the credit card you originally gave, with cash or with traveler's checks).

Next thing you will hear is: "Smile!" and the ship's photographer will snap a photo for posterity of you sailing away on a pleasure cruise.

Test the Waters Tips

Need a passport? Apply in person for one at one of more than 4,500 passport acceptance facilities nationwide including many federal, state and probate courts, many post offices, some libraries, a number of county and municipal offices and 13 passport agencies. Fee is $60 and you will need to submit two passport-size photos with your application. You receive your passport in the mail about six weeks after application. Passport renewals can be done through the mail (cost is $40). For more information, including details on conditions required for renewal through the mail, and to download passport application forms, visit http://travel.state.gov and plan to apply early, at least two months ahead of departure and longer if you will be needing visas.

* Note that cruise lines, airlines and tour operators instruct that your passport should be valid for at least six months after the conclusion of your trip. So if you have a passport, check its expiration date.

* As soon as you get your cruise documents, check them over for accuracy. For example, check that your cabin number is correct, and if you purchased air, make sure your name is spelled correctly on the air tickets so as not to run into a problem with the airline. Make sure the agent and/or line has included sufficient bag tags for your luggage; a boarding form for you to fill out (prior to check-in at the pier) with your name, address, phone number, emergency phone number, cabin number, and similar information.

* If you are going through a travel agent, select one you can develop a rapport with. If you can work with the same agent repeatedly you will save tons of time as he will already know your likes and dislikes.

* Are you celebrating a special occasion on your cruise? Tell the agent to notify the cruise line. The line may surprise you with a cake presented by singing waiters at your dining room table or with some other amenity.

Setting Sail on Your Cruise

* All good things must come to an end, and so does a cruise. Disembarkation is easy. If you are paying your bill with the credit card you presented at check-in you will get a statement in your cabin; check it over and if it is O.K., you need do nothing—it will get charged to your account. If you want to pay with cash, travelers' checks or a different credit card go to the purser's desk/reception to do so the last evening of the cruise. The last night of the voyage is also the time you give tips to the dining room staff and cabin steward (about $8-$10 per day per person on mainstream lines). Some lines, like Norwegian Cruise Line and Carnival, automatically charge the gratuities to your shipboard account (you can adjust them up or down at reception). Your cabin steward will give you colored luggage tags to be put on to your bags. The bags themselves need to be placed outside your cabin, usually between 10 p.m. and midnight to be retrieved by the crew and brought ashore. If you have sailed outside the U.S., your steward will also bring you a Customs Declaration form (the same form that airlines distribute to international passengers, to be filled out one per family). Post Sept. 11, 2001, U.S. citizens ending their cruise at a U.S. port, need to clear immigration upon arrival like non-U.S. citizens and green-card holders. If disembarking in a foreign country, U.S. citizens will, of course, have to go through that country's passport control (sometimes at a lounge onboard ship—bring your passport with visa, if a visa is required).

If you are disembarking in the U.S. you will clear U.S. Customs at the pier; if your cruise is ending in a foreign country, you will clear U.S. Customs when you enter the U.S. Fill out your Customs form truthfully -much better to pay duty than a hefty fine. Standard allowance for U.S. citizens is $400 per person in duty-free goods (including one carton of cigarettes or 100 cigars—note that Cuban cigars are not allowed in the U.S.) and one liter of alcohol (must be over 21 years old). If you go over the limit, you must list individual items on the Customs declaration form. Green-card holders and non-U.S. residents staying no more than 72 hours in the U.S. enjoy the same allowance.

If your cruise visits certain countries your allowance goes up. Take the U.S. Virgin Islands: you can bring back $1,200 duty-free if your cruise calls there. Puerto Rico is even better, since that island is a commonwealth of the U.S.; everything you buy there pays no duty. Goods produced and acquired in Mexico and Canada are also duty-free. If you visit Antigua, Aruba, the Bahamas, Barbados, British Virgins, Grenada, Guadeloupe, Jamaica, St. Lucia and St. Kitts your allowance is $600 and two liters of alcohol. Your cruise director will go over customs details (including items like meats, fruits, Cuban cigars, etc. that are not permitted to be brought into the U.S.). If you want to obtain additional information before you sail, visit the U.S. Customs Service Web site at www.customs.treas.gov/travel/travel.htm.

Insider's Savings Insights

* Get your feet wet by checking out some cruise Web sites. An excellent one with lots of information on cruises, ship reviews, advice, news as well as deals from the cruise lines is www.CruiseCritic.com (access with keyword CruiseCritic on America Online).

* When there are empty cabins close to departure time, cruise lines run sales. Check with the line, travel agents specializing in cruise vacations, consolidators and short-notice agencies like Moments' Notice at 888-241-3366 (Web site: www.moments-notice.com); Vacations to Go (800-338-4962; Web site: www.vacationstogo.com); Last Minute Travel Services (800-527-8646; Web site: www.lastminutetravel.com); and World Wide Cruises (800-882-9000; Web site: www.wwcruises.com). If you are flexible and can get your foot out the door quickly, you will enjoy savings -sometimes of up to 75 percent off brochure prices. Here are some sample fares available from World Wide Cruises on selected 2002 sailings: seven-day Southern Caribbean voyages on NCL's **Norwegian Majesty** from $540 (up to 70 percent off published rates); seven-day Alaska cruises on Holland America

Setting Sail on Your Cruise

ships on selected dates from $599 (up to 70 percent off from brochure rates); selected Orient sailings on Princess from $899 (up to 70 percent off published rates).

* Ask your agent if his agency is offering any incentives for you to book -sometimes this might be a free bus to the pier or a bottle of champagne sent to your cabin or dining room table; once an agent offered us a free dinner for two at a nice local restaurant if we booked a cruise.

"*Silver Wind*" Photo courtesy of Silversea Cruises.

Chapter: 2
Types of Ships

Size matters, particularly when it comes to ships. If a vessel is like a magic carpet whisking you from one exotic corner of the globe to another, you must decide how big you want that carpet to be: an area rug (small, yacht-like vessel), a room-sized carpet (mid-size ship) or wall-to-wall carpeting (a large ship).

Choose the right ship for you and presto! You are on your way -feeling right at home- to the vacation of your dreams.

To help your decision process, here is a description of each ship size (also refer to this guide's Chapter Three - Types of Lines, for additional insights about amenities and services that are signatures of each cruise line).

* Small Ships - Intimate and yacht-like, this type of ship accommodates fewer than 500 passengers in a clubby ambience. Facilities aboard these vessels (tonnage: 10,000 Gross Register Tons, or GRT, or less) generally include a lounge/showroom, a main dining room, and informal buffet-style restaurant (that may double up as an alternative bistro for dinner) a small spa or gym, a pool/Jacuzzi, and sunbathing area with bar service, a modest library/e-mail facility, perhaps a small casino, and reception/shore excursions desks.

Grouped under the umbrella of small ships are a variety of vessels, including expedition ships, informal and homey, generally with accommodations for fewer than 100 passengers and equipped with the basics for comfortable exploration (not with such facilities as a casino or spa, but with zodiacs (motorized inflatable craft) to make quick landings to explore such exotic faraway areas of the planet like the Galapagos). The ships of Lindblad Expeditions fit into this category.

Other vessels in the small ship category include river boats and barges that are like floating inns usually with good cuisine, comfortable accommodations, and included shore activities to help you explore the French countryside, the Rhine River, the Nile and other exotic locales. Riverboats usually accommodate 100-200 passengers. Barges generally carry fewer than two dozen people. The barges of French Country Waterways and the riverboats of KD River Cruises fit into this category.

Small ships may or may not have a doctor onboard, but they usually stay close to land so in an emergency, medical help is available quickly. If this is a concern with you, ask about medical facilities on the ship you are contemplating to take (mid-size and large ships have hospitals usually staffed by a doctor and nurse who post daily office hours and who are available to treat emergencies).

Also grouped in this category are romantic sailing ships like those of Star Clippers (moderately-priced) and those of Windstar Cruises (luxury), and yacht-like vessels like those of Seabourn and Silversea (all-suite and ultra-deluxe). These ships carry fewer than 500 guests.

On small vessels, passengers inevitably run across each other often—and on occasion, "cliques" of guests, who associate only with each other, may develop. The staff generally knows many passengers by name from the first evening at sea. Shipboard life on small ships is more unregimented than the lifestyle on larger vessels, generally featuring open seating in the dining room (seating at unassigned tables, with passengers coming to the dining room when they wish within a block of time allotted for meals).

There are few organized onboard daytime activities and evening entertainment may consist of small-scale musical shows (maybe four singers/dancers and local folkloric groups brought onboard to entertain in one or more of the ports on deluxe and ultra-deluxe ships) and/or a piano player. On moderately priced expedition vessels and sailing ships, entertainment

Types of Ships

may consist of a piano player or other musician, an occasional local folkloric group and such activities as stargazing.

Accommodations range from nautical-themed cabins on sailing vessels to lavish suites on such ultra-deluxe vessels as Silversea's **Silver Whisper** and the **Seabourn Legend**.

> Small, yacht-like ships do not feature the non-stop rosters of activities found on large ships. Passengers are pretty much left to entertain themselves and they are happy to do so.

* Mid-size Ships - These vessels accommodate from 500 to about 1,000 passengers. For the most part, the existing fleet in this size category consists of vintage, classic vessels like Cunard Line's **Caronia**, launched in 1973, and Orient Lines' **Marco Polo** built in 1965, as the cruise lines increasingly in recent years have been building more profitable large ships (they need just one captain, one cruise director, one head chef, etc.) to serve twice the number of passengers or more) and yacht-like vessels to appeal to certain niches (such as guests looking for an exclusive, ultra-deluxe experience, and people wanting to sail on an expedition to the far corners of the planet). One exception was Renaissance Cruise Line, a line that launched eight mid-size ships in three years beginning in 1998 and went bankrupt in 2001 -perhaps because of it?

An in-between category (tonnage: 10,000 to 40,000 GRT), mid-size vessels have more facilities than yacht-like ships, but less than mega-liners. They usually offer one restaurant or two, about a half-dozen bars and lounges, a showroom, a disco/observation lounge, a casual (buffet-style) eatery, library/Internet Café, casino, card room, spa/gym, pool/Jacuzzi area with lounge chairs, promenade for walking/jogging and medical facilities. Some ships in this category may feature children's clubrooms. Life aboard most of these vessels is traditional with two assigned dinner seatings, usually at about 6 p.m. and 8 p.m., a roster of organized activities and themed evenings (50s & 60s Evening, Pirates' Night, Country & Western Hoedown, etc.). Other after-dark entertainment consists of musical revues, variety, a piano player and/or duos and trios in the lounges. A DJ plays favorites in the disco until the wee hours. Onboard ambience is usually relaxed with few lines at reception and buffets, and fewer chances to come across that friendly couple you met at the terminal while waiting to embark than if you were on a small ship, but more opportunities to meet again by chance than if you were on a large ship. The staff in reception/guest relations and at your favorite lounge may get to know you by the second or third day of the voyage.

Accommodations feature inside (windowless) cabins and outside (windowed) cabins and suites. Ships that fit within this size category include Costa Cruises' **CostaRiviera** and **CostaAllegra**.

> If you are concerned about feeling confined on a cruise, your worries will dissolve in the waters you sail if you book a large ship -these mega-liners and ultra-liners are like floating towns with acres of deck space and tons of public rooms.

* Large Ships - The granddaddies of them all (tonnage: more than 40,000 GRT), large ships accommodate more than 1,000 passengers. In recent years, this category begs to be divided, like apparel for better fit, into large or mega-liner (40,000 to 100,000 GRT) and extra-large, or ultra-liner, if you will (more than 100,000 GRT) with the launching of behemoths like Princess Cruises' **Grand Princess** (109,000-ton, 2,600-passengers), Carnival's **Carnival Destiny** (101,353-ton, 2,642-passengers), and Royal Caribbean's **Voyager of the Seas** (138,000-ton, 3,114-passengers, along with sister ship **Explorer of the Seas**, the biggest ships in the world). To put it into every day perspective, extra-large ships (or ultra-liners) like Royal Caribbean's **Voyager of the Seas**, as an example, has the following mind-boggling features/characteristics: an interior promenade the length of one-and-a-half football fields, rock-climbing wall and ice-skating rink, and the vessel is twice as wide as Broadway in New York, twice the size of the largest aircraft carrier ever built, and rises higher than a 20-story skyscraper from the sea. Wow!

Types of Ships

Large ships have everything under the sun: two or more main dining rooms (or a multi-level restaurant); alternative restaurants; casual, buffet-style eatery; pastry shop/café; spas and gyms that would make some land-based health clubs mud-green with envy; library; Internet Café; resort deck with pools, Jacuzzis, bar and stage for the steel band to serenade you with "Yellow Bird" and other tropical tunes; a variety of bars and lounges (sometimes more than a dozen); proscenium theaters; cinema; a casino rivaling Vegas gaming houses; lobby with reception area/shore excursions desk/bank; acres of open decks including promenades and jogging tracks; and a wide variety of accommodations including cabins with balconies, mini-suites and lavish suites—some of palatial dimensions and amenities. There is so much onboard you begin to wonder if they will be issuing compasses along with cabin keys!

> If sailing on a mega-liner, keep the ship's pocket-sized deck plan, available from reception, with you always for the first few days. It will come in handy until you know your way around your big ship.

Some of the giants in the extra-large or ultra-liner subdivision of this size category of ship not only give you everything under the sun, but the moon and stars as well. They may offer things like a wedding chapel for nuptials, renewal of vows and other ceremonies; rock-climbing wall; ice-skating rink; in-line skating rink; miniature golf; full-size basketball court, and other incredible features.

Some large ships offer traditional dining seatings (those of Royal Caribbean, for example); others offer open seating (Norwegian Cruise Line's Freestyle Cruising) and still others offer a combination of both (Princess Cruises' Personal Choice program, where you can pick traditional dinner seating or open seating). Life aboard offers a non-stop schedule of activities and entertainment with evening pursuits including Broadway and Vegas-style musical revues, variety entertainment, themed nights, disco, movies in the cinema and cabin television, and music in the lounges.

How To Select The Right Ship For You

Selecting the ideal vessel for you is a breeze once you do your homework. Begin by reading the next chapter in this guide about the major cruise lines. Be inquisitive, asking the following questions of yourself and, when appropriate, of others (the rest of your party if you are traveling with others, your travel agent, and/or the cruise line):

* What kind of cruise experience do you want? An intimate, unstructured voyage on a yacht-like vessel? A floating city sailing on a mega-liner or ultra-liner with two or three thousand fellow passengers and lots of facilities and activities? Or something in between on a mid-size ship?

The more you love big land-based resorts and big city life with its multiple dining and entertainment options, the bigger the ship you can choose.

* What facilities are important to you? If you would like to continue the exercise regimen that you follow at home, or start a new one, or indulge in exotic spa treatments, select a ship with a big health club including gym, spa and personal trainers. If you have an appetite for varied culinary delights, choose a vessel with a variety of alternative dining venues, and so on.

* Where do you want to go and for how long? Check out this guide's chapter on itineraries and pick a ship that takes you to your dream ports.

* Go over the cruise line's brochures and Web sites with a fine-tooth-comb-checking deck plans, in particular, for facilities and amenities. Consult a travel agent who specializes in cruises. Travel agents' expertise and advice is free and can be invaluable.

> Your travel agent may be able to refer you to past passengers of the ship you are considering. Past passengers are good, independent resources who can tell you about the shipboard lifestyle and answer any questions you may have.

Types of Ships

Test the Waters Tips

* When going over cruise line brochures, pay more attention to deck plans and to sections with factual information (like tonnage, number of passengers, cabin dimensions, etc.) than to mere photos. Brochure photos are taken to show the most attractive angles of staterooms and other facilities.

* If you are sailing with children, check deck plans to make sure there are playrooms and particularly, a shallow or splash pool for their use. Ask the agent or the cruise line to describe in detail the children's facilities and programs.

* If you are concerned about becoming seasick, select a mega liner or ultra-liner. These giants usually give you a smoother ride.

* If you worry about being bored on a cruise, select a large ship -they have an almost round-the-clock roster of activities.

Insider's Savings Insights

* In recent years, cruise lines have unleashed a wave of new ships, with 14 entering service in 2002 and dozens more on order for delivery within the next five years. In difficult times, such as the aftermath of the Sept. 11, 2001 attack on America, cruise lines have to resort to deep discounts to fill their ships, creating waves of discounts and deals, such as two-for-one offers, free air upgrades, free land packages. This aggressive pricing should continue for at least through 2003, according to Colin Veitch, president and CEO of Norwegian Cruise Line (although it may be in varying degrees as the industry has recovered faster than most observers expected). Also, since lines with many mega-liners and ultra-liners have more berths to fill (therefore harder to sail full in difficult times and off-season periods), it may be easier to find the most attractive last-minute deals on them.

Ships at a Glance

Ship: Wilderness Discoverer Line: Alaska's Glacier Bay Tours & Cruises/Voyager Cruise Line Tonnage: 85 Passengers: 88	Ship: Nantucket Clipper Line: Clipper Cruise Line Tonnage: 1,471 Passengers: 102
Ship: Wind Spirit Line: Windstar Cruises Tonnage: 5,350 Passengers: 148	Ship: Star Flyer Line: Star Clippers Tonnage: 2,298 Passengers: 170
Ship: Song of Flower Line: Radisson Seven Seas Tonnage: 8,282 Passengers: 180	Ship: Silver Cloud Line: Silversea Cruises Tonnage: 16,800 Passengers: 296
Ship: Caronia Line: Cunard Tonnage: 24,492 Passengers: 665	Ship: Zenith Line: Celebrity Tonnage: 47,255 Passengers: 1,374
Ship: Veendam Line: Holland America Tonnage: 55,451 Passengers: 1,266	Ship: Norwegian Sun Line: Norwegian Cruise Line Tonnage: 77,104 Passengers: 2,002
Ship: Disney Magic Line: Disney Cruise Line Tonnage: 83,000 Passengers: 2,400	Ship: Carnival Triumph Line: Carnival Tonnage: 101,509 Passengers: 2,758
Ship: Golden Princess Line: Princess Cruises Tonnage: 109,000 Passengers: 2,600	Ship: Voyager of the Seas Line: Royal Caribbean Tonnage: 138,000 Passengers: 3,114

"Zaandam" Photo courtesy of Holland America Line.

Chapter: 3
Types of Cruise Lines

All cruise lines are, of course, not created equal. Say that we were to compare them to people—well, you would immediately note that some are youthful, others mature; some flashy, others sedate; some stick to a home base, others roam the world.

This chapter is, in essence, a chance for you to enjoy a quick "rendezvous" with major cruise lines (Part A) so you can begin to get to know their personalities: interesting tidbits about them, plus vital things like what cruise experience does each line offer, who is it good -or not good—for, who is likely to be onboard sharing it with you, what the line's price category is, where do its ships go, and what special services, amenities and accommodations you will find onboard its vessels.

Also listed in Part A of this chapter are noteworthy facilities and services—unless otherwise noted, each line offers the staples you do expect to find on any ship like pool deck, casino, show lounge, main dining rooms, and fitness centers.

Parts B & C of this chapter include additional cruise lines and cruising alternatives like river and barge cruises.

Regarding pricing, cruise line brochure fares are seldom, if ever, the actual price passengers pay-due to tremendous competition, a veritable tsunami of new ships whose berths need to be filled up (during 2002, 14 new vessels entered service) as well as the post-Sept. 11 discounting feeding frenzy that is likely to continue in varying degrees at least through 2003. So I do not quote you the brochure prices, but instead, I group the lines into three price categories:

Budget (less than $200 per day),
Moderate ($200-$300 per day) and
Luxury ($300-$900 per day)

And, perhaps what you may find most useful of all as a guideline, I also include an estimate of what you may actually pay during crisis/difficult times and/or when, close to sail date, the lines are forced to discount to fill their ships (what I call "hot water" periods). These bottom-of-the-barrel rates are generally cruise-only (with airfare, if needed, being extra). The Deals & Discounts section in each line's profile in Part A of this chapter lists the line's customary specials such as early bird discounts and two-for-one offers. Armed with this knowledge, and your local Sunday newspaper's Travel Section, you can be a well-informed consumer when you consult a travel agent or online agencies and auction sites. For cruise lines addresses, telephones and Web sites, and other useful reference information, check this guide's Appendix.

Part A —Major Cruise Lines Ahoy!

Carnival Cruise Lines

About The Line: Glitz galore! A cruise industry giant, once known as the bargain-basement-emporium of cruising, Carnival has in recent years enhanced its menus and food presentation as well as its cabin amenities—adding a basket of name-brand products including shampoo, conditioner, deodorant, shavers and even candy.

Kind Of Cruise: party, family, resort/playground.

Fleet: **Carnival Conquest, Carnival Destiny, Carnival Legend, Carnival Pride, Carnival Spirit, Carnival Triumph, Carnival Victory, Celebration, Ecstasy, Elation, Fantasy, Fascination, Holiday, Imagination, Inspiration, Jubilee, Paradise, Sensation. Carnival Glory (2003).**

Kind Of Ships: Modern mega-liners and ultra-liners.

Types of Cruise Lines

Good For: Anyone wanting to have some fun and more than a few belly laughs. Families. Fitness buffs. Fresh air enthusiasts will love the non-smoking **Paradise** (when good Americans die they may go to Paris as Oscar Wilde pointed out -but this toned-down, more sedate Carnival ship is where good American non-smokers go when they want to live it up: the air everywhere is sparkling and pure!).

> The *Paradise* is the world's only non-smoking ship. Passengers must sign an agreement that they will not smoke onboard ship and transgressors face severe penalties, including disembarkation and return home at their own expense.

Price Category: Budget/mass market. May be able to get in for less than $100 a day (sometimes even less than $75 a day) in "hot water" periods.

Cruise Experience: They don't call them "Fun Ships" for nothing; if you are ready to paaaarty, these are the ships for you.

Who's Sharing It With You: Average age is the low 40s. There are lots of young singles, families with children, couples of all ages, seniors attracted to the low fares -people from all walks of life, many cruising for the first time.

What's There For You: Glitzy, sometimes eye-popping-décor; Vegas-style revues and casinos; excellent spas/fitness centers; lots of food including a 24-hour pizzeria and two late-night buffets; Internet cafes; children's facilities and programs; areas for topless sunbathing; vacation guarantee (if a guest is dissatisfied with the cruise while on board the guest can disembark at the first non-U.S. port and receive a refund for the unused portion and reimbursement for air transportation to the ship's homeport); one smoke-free ship (*the Paradise*).

Favorite Haunts: Themed libraries, Joe's Stone Crabs alternative restaurant on the **Carnival Spirit**, the fun water slides.

Whatever You Do, Don't Miss The… Wacky games like the Knobby Knees Contest and the Hairy Chest Contest (in a version of this latter contest, a woman is blind-folded and she has to identify her husband by feeling a bunch of guys' hairy chests). On the Knobby Knees Contest a woman "judges" each fellow's knees, usually by feeling them—what can I tell you: they are hilarious.

Look Elsewhere If… You prefer gracious to glitzy.

Accommodations: There is a wide range from inside (no window) cabins to staterooms with views, veranda cabins and suites. Standard cabins are a good, comfortable size. Suites tend to be smaller than similar accommodations on lines like Celebrity.

Itineraries: Alaska, Bahamas, Bermuda, Canada, Caribbean, Europe, Hawaii, Mexican Riviera, Panama Canal.

Deals & Discounts: Super Savers (early booking discounts); children's fares; AARP discounts; pre-post cruise packages; air add-ons including transfers.

Ships at a Glance

Ships	
Carnival Conquest: Built: 2002 - Tonnage: 110,000 - Length: 952 ft. - Guests: 2,974 - Crew: 1,100.
Carnival Destiny: Built: 1996 - Tonnage: 101,353 - Length: 893 ft. - Guests: 2,642 - Crew: 1,050.
Carnival Legend: Built: 2002 - Tonnage: 84,000 - Length: 960 ft. - Guests: 2,124 - Crew: 920.
Carnival Pride: Built: 2001 -Tonnage: 84,000 - Length: 960 ft. - Guests: 2,124 - Crew: 920.
Carnival Spirit: Built: 2001 - Tonnage: 84,000 - Length: 960 ft. - Guests: 2,124 - Crew: 920.
Carnival Triumph: Built: 1999 - Tonnage: 102,000 - Length: 893 ft. - Guests: 2,758 - Crew: 1,100.
Carnival Victory: Built: 2000 - Tonnage: 102,000 - Length: 893 ft. - Guests: 2,758 - Crew: 1,100.
Celebration: Built: 1987 - Tonnage: 47,262 - Length: 733 ft. - Guests: 1,486 - Crew: 670.
Ecstasy: Built: 1991 - Tonnage: 70,367 - Length: 855 ft. - Guests: 2,040 - Crew: 920.
Elation: Built: 1998 - Tonnage: 70,367 - Length: 855 ft. - Guests: 2,040 - Crew: 920.
Fantasy: Built: 1990 - Tonnage: 70,367 - Length: 855 ft. - Guests: 2,040 - Crew: 920.
Fascination: Built: 1994 - Tonnage: 70,367 - Length: 855 ft. - Guests: 2,040 - Crew: 920.
Holiday: Built: 1985 - Tonnage: 46,052 - Length: 727 ft. - Guests: 1,452 - Crew: 669.
Imagination: Built: 1995 - Tonnage: 70,367 - Length: 855 ft. - Guests: 2,040 - Crew: 920.
Inspiration: Built: 1996 - Tonnage: 70,367 - Length: 855 ft. - Guests: 2,040 - Crew: 920.
Jubilee: Built: 1986 - Tonnage: 47,262 - Length: 733 ft. - Guests: 1,486 - Crew: 670.
Paradise: Built: 1998 - Tonnage: 70,367 - Length: 855 ft. - Guests: 2,040 - Crew: 920.
Sensation: Built: 1993 - Tonnage: 70,367 - Length: 855 ft. - Guests: 2,040 - Crew: 920.

Types of Cruise Lines

Celebrity Cruises

About The Line: Do you want to be Pampered with a capital P, but at moderate prices? Celebrity Cruises has been doing that since its creation in 1989. You won't believe what your money buys: warm, attentive service; gourmet cuisine; beautiful ships with museum-quality art collections; world-class (truly!) spas; great activities/entertainment package - undeniably one of the best values afloat.

Kind Of Cruise: Resort, romantic, family, gourmet, fitness.

Fleet: **Century, Galaxy, Horizon, Mercury, Zenith, Millennium, Infinity, Summit, Constellation.**

Kind Of Ships: Classy, large ships.

Good For: Family vacationers, those in the mood for romance, gourmands, spa/fitness enthusiasts.

Price Category: Moderate. May be able to sail for less than $150 per day (sometimes less than $100 per day, and occasionally even less than $75 per day) in "hot water" times.

Cruise Experience: Elegant and sophisticated, this is a premium quality product at moderate prices (great value for your vacation dollar, with some outstanding features as world-class spas and crème de la crème cuisine and alternative dining).

Who's Sharing It With You: Most passengers are 40-60; middle and upper-middle class. Most have seen some of the world.

What's There For You: Arguably the best floating spas in the industry, the 25,000 sq. ft. AquaSpa on the **Millennium, Infinity, Constellation** and **Summit** are more extensive than those on five-star land resorts like The Breakers of Palm Beach and Raffles Hotel in Singapore. The AquaSpas on Millennium-Class vessels include a café serving delicious low-calorie dishes by the spa's pool and complimentary thalassotherapy pool with airbeds. Innovations like exterior glass elevators and music libraries are also featured on the Millennium-Class ships. Excellent menus created by Michelin-starred Chef Michel Roux fleet-wide and superb alternative dining venues themed to great ocean liners of the past on the Millennium-Class ships (fee is $25 and worth every penny); museum-quality art collections; Broadway-style revues; Internet cafes (in-cabin Internet access in newest ships); children's facilities and programs; culinary demonstrations and wine tasting.

Favorite Haunts: The Cova Café Milano (charming tea/coffee house) with harp music - great for people watching from its atrium tables. The lobby with its grand onyx staircase and silk lanterns on the Millennium-Class ships.

Whatever You Do, Don't Miss The... Big, wonderful thalassotherapy pool in the AquaSpa -with its airbeds, neck/shoulder pipes and jet stations-it is like enjoying a head-to-toe massage. Whenever I'm on a Celebrity ship, my companions, if they are looking for me, know to look there first.

Accommodations: Excellent - tastefully decorated and spacious. Lavish suites with attentive butlers whom you desperately wish you could take home with you at the end of the cruise.

Look Elsewhere If... You think you would prefer an intimate, small ship experience.

Itineraries: Alaska, Bermuda, Caribbean, Europe, Hawaii, Panama Canal, South America.

Deals & Discounts: Early booking discounts represent savings of up to 50 percent on cruise-only fares. Combine two itineraries and you receive a special rate. Children's fares. Pre- and post-cruise packages. Air add-ons including transfers.

Ships at a Glance

Ships

Century:	Built: 1995 - Tonnage: 70,606 - Length: 807 ft. - Guests: 1,750 - Crew: 853.
Constellation:	Built: 2002 - Tonnage: 91,000 - Length: 964 ft. - Guests: 1,950 - Crew: 999.
Galaxy:	Built: 1996 - Tonnage: 77,713 - Length: 858 ft. - Guests: 1,870 - Crew: 909.
Horizon:	Built: 1990 - Tonnage: 46,811 - Length: 682 ft. - Guests: 1,354 - Crew: 645.
Infinity:	Built: 2001 - Tonnage: 91,000 - Length: 964 ft. - Guests: 1,950 - Crew: 999.
Mercury:	Built: 1997 - Tonnage: 77,713 - Length: 860 ft. - Guests: 1,870 - Crew: 907.
Millennium:	Built: 2000 - Tonnage: 91,000 - Length: 964 ft. - Guests: 1,950 - Crew: 999.
Summit:	Built: 2001 - Tonnage: 91,000 - Length: 964 ft. - Guests: 1,950 - Crew: 999.
Zenith -	Built: 1992 - Tonnage: 47,225 - Length: 682 ft. - Guests: 1,374 - Crew: 645.

Types of Cruise Lines

What is important to you when it comes to a vacation? Impeccable service? Great nightlife? Gourmet dining? Select a cruise line that offers those features.

Costa Cruise Lines

About The Line: This line offers new and traditional ships with one common denominator: Italian-style cruising -ambience and service with an Italian accent.

Kind Of Cruise: Family, party, resort/playground.

Fleet: ***CostaAllegra, CostaAtlantica, CostaClassica, CostaEuropa, CostaMarina, CostaRiviera, CostaTropical, CostaVictoria.***

Kind Of Ships: Classic ships and modern large ships.

Good for: Families, fun-seekers, fitness buffs.

Price Category: Budget/mass market. May be able to get in for less than $100 per day during "hot water" periods (maybe even for less than $75 per day).

Cruise Experience: Italian-style service and ambience. With all the pasta, pizza, gelato and espresso it's almost like taking a trip to Italy, even when you are sailing in the Caribbean.

Who's Sharing It With You: A good number of Europeans are onboard in Europe; most passengers are American in the Caribbean.

What's There For You: Alternative dining on some ships; main dining rooms, pizzeria and pastry cafes in all vessels; children's programs; activities including Italian language lessons.

Favorite Haunts: The Ristorante Magnifico by Zeffirino—of Genoa, Italy fame - (Frank Sinatra was a regular at Zeffirino's restaurant whenever he was in Genoa) is the delicious alternative dining venue on the CostaAtlantica (fee is $18.75, one free pass for suite occupants), and on the same ship, Café Florian, inspired on the 18th century Venetian café of the same name.

Whatever You Do, Don't Miss The… Roman Bacchanale (toga party -it was great fun during our sailing, with most everyone coming to the dining room wrapped up in their sheets) and the Festa Italiana (like an Italian street festival with Venetian mask-making, pizza dough tossing contest and more!

Accommodations: A variety of comfortable accommodations—spacious and well designed— are available on most ships.

Look Elsewhere If... You are turned off by a European-style vacation and numerous daily announcements in five languages.

Itineraries: Caribbean, Europe, South America, transatlantic.

Deals & Discounts: Advance booking "Andiamo Fares" (10-20 percent off). Seniors discounts. Discounts when combining two cruises. Children's fares. Air add-ons and air/sea packages (sometimes including free hotel stays in Europe).

Ships at a Glance

Ships

CostaAllegra - Built: 1992 - Tonnage: 28,500 - Length: 616 ft. - Guests: 820 - Crew: 450.
CostaAtlantica: Built: 2000 - Tonnage: 85,000 - Length: 959 ft. - Guests: 2,114 Crew: 920.
CostaClassica: Built: 1991 - Tonnage: 53,000 - Length: 718 ft. - Guests: 1,308 Crew: 650.
CostaEuropa - Built: 2002 - Tonnage: 54,000 - Length: 798 ft. - Guests: 1,494 Crew: 670.
CostaRiviera: Built: 1963 - Tonnage: 30,000- Length: 700 ft. - Guests: 974 - Crew: 500.
CostaRomantica: Built: 1993 - Tonnage: 53,000 - Length: 718 ft. - Guests: 1,356 - Crew: 610.
CostaTropicale: Built: 1981 - Tonnage: 36,674 - Length: 660 ft. - Guests: 1,022 Crew: 550.
CostaVictoria: Built: 1996 - Tonnage: 76,000 - Length: 817 ft. - Guests: 1,928 - Crew: 800.

Crystal Cruises

About The Line: Japanese-owned, Los Angeles-based Crystal Cruises is in a niche of its own: a large ship, luxury line, with a glamorous ambience and carrying a third of the passengers of other vessels its size.

Kind of Cruise: Upscale and sophisticated, gourmet, romance.
Fleet: **Crystal Harmony, Crystal Symphony, (Crystal Serenity, 2003).**
Kind Of Ships: Modern, ultra-deluxe large ships.
Good For: Gourmands, learners, spa enthusiasts, and romantics.
Price Category: Luxury. May be able to sail for about $375 per day, maybe less.
Cruise Experience: Elegant and stylish with two traditional dinner seatings in the main dining room, where service is impeccable and the food delicious. Plus an entertainment package that features Broadway- and Vegas-style revues, variety, a **cappella** ensembles, folkloric presentations, themed teas and enrichment lecturers.

Who's Sharing It With You: Affluent, well-traveled Americans mostly in their 40s to 70s who like to dress to the nines for dinner on formal nights and who enjoy the entertainment/amenity choices of these large luxury ships.

What's There For You: Outstanding programs including Computer University@Sea and Crystal Visions Enrichment Lecture Series; superb alternative dining venues; in-room Internet access; gentlemen hosts who dance with unescorted ladies; excellent Broadway-style revues.

Favorite Haunts: The Crystal Plaza, atrium lobby, a marvel of marble, glass-sculpture, waterfall, lights and staircases. The Palm Court, airy and light and filled with greenery - reminiscent of a Somerset Maugham novel setting. The Vista tri-level observation lounge. The two chic outdoor pools, one with retractable roof and the spa recently redone according to the principles of Feng Shui.

Whatever You Do, Don't Miss The... Special themed teas, including the out-of-this-world Mozart Tea. Offered once during each voyage, the Mozart Tea features classical musicians in period costumes and such delights as Vienna Sacher cakes, Black Forest cakes, apple tortes with streusel, Napoleon and Linzer slices, and chocolate fondue to dip fresh strawberries that have dark and white chocolate stems (Yum! Yum! I've always felt this is the epitome of the good life at sea!).

Accommodations: Comfortable, though some are a bit compact. The lavish Crystal Penthouses are among the best at sea.

Look Elsewhere If…You prefer your luxury in small ships or if you do not feel at ease in an ultra-deluxe, sophisticated ambience.

Itineraries: World roaming vessels. World cruise.

Deals & Discounts: Advance purchase discounts of up to 30 percent. Past passenger club savings. Children's fare. Air add-ons and pre-, post-cruise packages.

Ships at a Glance
Ships

> Crystal Harmony: Built: 1990 - Tonnage: 49,400 - Length: 791 ft. - Guests: 940 - Crew: 545.
>
> Crystal Symphony: Built: 1995 - Tonnage: 51,044 - Length: 781 ft. - Guests: 940 - Crew: 545.

Cunard Line

About The Line: This venerable cruise line whose "queens" were the pride of the golden age of the grand ocean liners, operates two aging vessels, but is in the midst of Project **Queen Mary**, billed as the largest, grandest ship afloat, scheduled to debut in 2003.

Kind Of Cruise: Luxury, gourmet, romance, nostalgic.

Fleet: ***Caronia, Queen Elizabeth 2***

Kind Of Ships: Large and mid-size classic vessels of a certain age.

Good For: Discerning travelers, learners, gourmands, romantics.

Price Category: Luxury. May be able to sail for less than $250 per day during "hot water" periods.

Cruise Experience: British ambience both on the legendary **Queen Elizabeth 2** and the ***Caronia***—so much so if you are on a transatlantic crossing on the **QE2**, it feels like

Types of Cruise Lines

you are in England already from the minute you board -what with such amenities as a floating Harrods and an authentic British pub. Wonderful, attentive service. Elegant, formal ambience. Three classes on **QE2** transatlantic runs with dinner in the superb grills reserved only for passengers who book the highest accommodation categories.

Who's Sharing It With You: Seasoned, well-heeled, generally mature travelers: Americans, British, and while in Europe in particular, a good number of Germans and other Europeans.

What's There For You: Enrichment lectures; movie theater; gentlemen hosts who dance with unescorted ladies; launderette. On **QE2**, a floating Harrods, florist, pub, library with full-time librarian, children's playrooms/nursery with British nannies; on **Caronia**, concierge, bookstore, library, children's counselors during school holidays.

Favorite Haunts: Cunard memorabilia shop, the library with its full-time librarian, and the Queen's Ballroom—a true ballroom— on the QE2. The intimate Tivoli Italian restaurant alternative dinner venue on the **Caronia**.

Whatever You Do, Don't Miss… Sampling the lagers at the Victorian-style Golden Lion British Pub on the QE2 while you enjoy a game of darts, or a classical concert in the pleasant Garden Lounge on the **Caronia**.

Accommodations: Wide range of categories on both ships including, on the **Caronia**, four categories for singles and 151 cabins in various categories for singles on the **QE2**. Wonderful duplex apartments on **Caronia**; luxurious, two-level suites with balconies on **QE2**.

Look Elsewhere If… You prefer a casual, let's-party-all-night-long ambience.

Itineraries: Roaming the world. World cruise.

Deals & Discounts: Advance booking; past passenger discounts, savings when combining two (or more) sailings. Pre- and post cruise packages; air packages with transfers.

Ships at a Glance

Ships

Caronia: Built: 1973 - Tonnage: 24,492 - Length: 628 ft. - Guests: 677 - Crew: 400.

QE2: Built: 1969 - Tonnage: 70,327 - Length: 963 ft. - Guests: 1,778 - Crew: 1,015.

Disney Cruise Line

About The Line: Disney came on the cruise scene in 1998. Its two vessels are no Mickey Mouse ships (although the Big Cheese himself is often spotted aboard). The vessels are traditional and nostalgic (the ***Magic*** has Art Deco interiors, the ***Wonder***, Art Nouveau), but with ultra-modern touches like rotation dining and world-class spas. Disney's debut with the ***Magic*** was not magical (long lines at embarkation, cabin cardkeys that would not open doors, no cruise director, to name a few problems) but by the time the ***Wonder*** came on line in 1999 Disney had its act together -and a marvelous one it is.

Kind Of Cruise: Family-oriented, resort/playground.
Fleet: ***Disney Magic, Disney Wonder***.
Kind Of Ships: New mega-liners.
Good For: Families, fitness buffs, and believe it or not, adults too, with separate adults-only areas both on the ships and on the private island.
Price Category: Moderate. May be able to get in for about $100 per day (sometimes less) in "hot waters".
Cruise Experience: Family-oriented voyages with magical "theme park-like" touches including frequent appearances by the popular Disney characters (for instance, Mickey Mouse and Minnie Mouse host the welcome aboard cocktail party, along with the captain). Cruises can be combined with Walt Disney World stays.
Who's Sharing It With You: People of all ages and from all walks of life. Lots of families.
What's There For You: Wonderful restaurants including one, Animator's Palette, which changes color magically as you dine (you rotate, along with your wait staff, from one restaurant to another during your cruise). Arguably the industry's best private island experience -the ship docks at a pier so you can get off and back on during the day without having to wait for launches to take you to and from the ship; family beach and adults-only beach on private island; adults-only areas on the ships including the spa, a pool, and nighttime entertainment district; outstanding children's facilities and programs (kids' areas measure a whopping 13,000 sq. ft. and there are some 30 counselors onboard); launderette.
Favorite Haunts: The adults-only entertainment district, including a great comedy club, on both ships.

Types of Cruise Lines

Whatever You Do, Don't Miss... Getting a massage in a cabana opening to the sea on the adults-only beach on Disney's private island.

Accommodations: Cabins are comfortable, attractively decorated and feature practical divided baths (the toilet is separate from the rest of the bathroom) so two people can use them at once (a boon for families). Many cabins have third and fourth berths, also to cater to the line's family clientele.

Look Elsewhere If... You do not like Disney parks and characters and if you want to gamble aboard on your cruise (there are no casinos onboard).

Itineraries: Bahamas, Caribbean

Deals & Discounts: Early booking discounts. Children's fares. Air add-ons including transfers. Pre-and post-cruise packages.

Ships at a Glance

Ships

Disney Magic: Built: 1998 - Tonnage: 83,000 - Length: 964 ft. - Guests: 1,750 - Crew: 964.

Disney Wonder: Built: 1999 - Tonnage: 83,000 - Length: 964 ft. - Guests: 1,750 - Crew: 964.

Holland America Line

About The Line: This line's motto could be "tradition, tradition!" It has a glorious history dating back to 1871 and by golly, from the minute you board, you are aware that you are in good hands and that they very much know what they are doing. This is an excellent value for your vacation dollar with a variety of extras such as a souvenir logo canvas bag, scrumptious hand-made chocolates and delicious cookies in the evening in one of the lounges (the Explorer Lounges), hot hors d'oeuvres at cocktail time in the lounges, freshly-made popcorn in the cinema (its aroma leads me to the cinema every afternoon when I sail on HAL ships), alternative Italian specialty restaurant and other delightful details that are all included in the cruise fare.

Kind Of Cruise: Gracious resort, family.

Fleet: ***Amsterdam, Maasdam, Noordam, Prinsendam, Rotterdam, Ryndam,***

Statendam, Veendam, Volendam, Zaandam, Zuiderdam, Oosterdam (2003).

Kind Of Ships: Modern large vessels.

Good for: Mature travelers looking for a traditional, gracious cruise, yet with all the modern conveniences; families.

Price Category: Moderate. May be able to sail for less than $150 a day (sometimes less than $100) in "hot water" periods.

Cruise Experience: Gracious, traditional and sedate, with outstanding, friendly service by an Indonesian and Filipino staff, extensive menus, excellent no-fee Italian alternative restaurant.

Who's Sharing It With You: Mostly people in their 50s and up, often well-traveled. Recently, the line has been attracting more families with children due to enhanced facilities for them, particularly in the Caribbean during school holidays. In the summer of 2001, for instance, Holland America reported that more than 12,000 children cruised with their families on its ships.

What's There For You: Beautiful vessels graced with antiques, art, nautical artifacts and lots of fresh flowers. Excellent Lido buffet -one of the most varied afloat with dozens of cold and hot dishes including such niceties as graham crackers for breakfast, and yogurt not only available for breakfast but for lunch too (I like it as a light dessert at lunch sometimes!). Broadway-style revues and variety. Internet cafes. Gracious touches like a call to dinner by a uniformed steward playing chimes throughout the public areas. Excellent private island. Hot hors d'oeuvres at cocktail time. Delectable, lavish Royal Dutch High Tea (that will have you feeling like royalty). Self-service launderette. University At Sea program enables health care professionals such as doctors, nurses, dentists, pharmacists, chiropractors and veterinarians to earn continuing education credits.

Favorite Haunts: The lovely, ocean-view libraries with comfortable chairs and writing desks. The elegant atriums with colossal sculptures, fountains or other artifacts.

Whatever You Do, Don't Miss The... Hand-made chocolates in the ships' Explorers Lounge and dinner in the alternative restaurant featuring delectable Italian cuisine.

Accommodations: Comfortable cabins, among the most spacious in this price category in the industry.

Look Elsewhere If...You want a party-till-you-drop atmosphere.

Types of Cruise Lines

Itineraries: Alaska, Canada, Caribbean, Europe, Hawaii, New England, Mexico, South America. World cruise.

Deals & Discounts: Early booking savings. Children's rates. Air add-ons. Pre-and post-cruise packages.

Ships at a Glance

Ships

Amsterdam: Built: 2000 - Tonnage: 61,000 - Length: 780 ft. - Guests: 1,380 - Crew: 593.
Maasdam: Built: 1994 - Tonnage: 55,000 - Length: 720 ft. - Guests: 1,266 - Crew: 602.
Noordam: Built: 1983 - Tonnage: 33,930 - Length: 704 ft. - Guests: 1,214 - Crew: 566.
Prinsendam: Built: 1988 - Tonnage: 38,000 - Length: 673 ft. - Guests: 758 - Crew: 450.
Rotterdam: Built: 1997 - Tonnage: 59,652 - Length: 780 ft. - Guests: 1,316 - Crew: 593.
Ryndam: Built: 1994 - Tonnage: 55,000 - Length: 720 ft. - Guests: 1,266 - Crew: 602.
Statendam: Built: 1993 - Tonnage: 55,000 - Length: 720 ft. - Guests: 1,266 - Crew: 602.
Veendam: Built: 1996 - Tonnage: 55,000 - Length: 720 ft. - Guests: 1,266 - Crew: 602.
Volendam: Built: 1999 - Tonnage: 63,000 - Length: 780 ft. - Guests: 1,440 - Crew: 600.
Zaandam: Built: 2000 - Tonnage: 63,000 - Length: 780 ft. - Guests: 1,440 - Crew: 600.
Zuiderdam: Built: 2002 - Tonnage: 85,000 - Length: 951 ft. - Guests: 1,848 - Crew: 800.

It is, of course, not just about the cheapest fares, but about value for your money. If a line gives you extras like free alternative dining and enrichment programs with distinguished lecturers at no additional charge—and you enjoy those features—that might be the best value for you.

Norwegian Cruise Line

About The Line: This pioneering line -it literally invented modern cruising with its ship, **Sunward** in 1966-is innovative. Through the years, it pioneered private islands and introduced the first Internet Café afloat. Its latest innovation is "Freestyle Cruising," a boon to freedom-loving people everywhere as it allows you, among other things, the freedom to dine with whomever and whenever you choose at a variety of dining venues.

Kind Of Cruise: Party, resort/playground, family, sports/activities.

Fleet: ***Norway, Norwegian Dream, Norwegian Majesty, Norwegian Sea, Norwegian Sky, Norwegian Sun, Norwegian Star, Norwegian Wind, Norwegian Dawn.***

Kind Of Ships: Large vessels, including one vintage liner.

Good for: Families, singles, fitness and sports enthusiasts, revelers.

Price Category: Moderate. May get in for less than $100 per day, maybe less than $75 per day in "hot waters" periods.

Cruise Experience: Casual and laid-back. The line's "Freestyle Cruising" means you can enjoy dinner whenever and with whomever you choose from 5:30 p.m. to midnight in all the ships' restaurants. Dress code makes "resort casual" attire always appropriate (there is one optional formal night in one of the restaurants for those who like to dress up). Gratuities ($10 per person, per day) are automatically charged to shipboard accounts and guests may adjust up or down. Disembarkation is leisurely.

Who's Sharing It With You: People of all ages and walks of life -the lion's share being middle class. Lots of honeymooners, lots of families with kids particularly during school holidays.

What's There For You: Plenty of freedom due to the line's "Freestyle Cruising," excellent alternative restaurants -and a fabulous variety of them including ethnic eateries, particularly on two of the line's newest ships, the ***Norwegian Star*** (10 restaurants and alternative dining venues) and ***Norwegian Sun*** (nine dining rooms/alternative restaurants) designed and built specifically for "Freestyle Cruising" and both launched in 2001. Full productions of Broadway shows or Broadway-style and Vegas-style revues. Sports program. Internet cafes (in-cabin Internet access on newest ships).

Favorite Haunts: Le Bistro and other alternative restaurants; "Lifestyle" areas for cultural and other learning on the ***Star*** and ***Sun***.

Types of Cruise Lines

Whatever You Do, Don't Miss The... Chocoholics Buffet, a scrumptious spread with every item being made of chocolate -yum! The Dive In program is a fabulous way to get your feet wet (I learned to snorkel with this program in the Bahamas 24 years ago) if you would like to explore the waters you sail on (they even have a program in Alaska —brrrrr!- if you go on it, take photos: they'll never believe you back home).

Accommodations: There are at least 10 cabin categories on all NCL ships, with some having close to 20. Cabins are comfortable and good-sized. The Sea's staterooms are smaller than those on other ships.

Look Elsewhere If... You like a traditional, structured travel experience and small ships.

Itineraries: Alaska, Asia, Australia, Bahamas, Caribbean, Europe, Hawaii, New England, New Zealand, Panama Canal, South America.

Deals & Discounts: Early booking savings including free two-night pre- or post-cruise hotel stay in Europe. Two-for-ones. Children's fares. Senior discounts on selected ships/cruises. Air add-ons with transfers. Pre-, post-cruise packages.

Ships at a Glance

Ships

Norway: Built: 1960 - Tonnage: 76,049 - Length: 1,035 ft. - Guests: 2,032 - Crew: 920.	
Norwegian Dawn: Built: 2002 - Tonnage 91,000 - Length: 965 ft. - Guests: 2,300 - Crew: 1,100.	
Norwegian Dream: Built: 1992 - Tonnage: 46,000 - Length: 754 ft. - Guests: 1,726 - Crew: 863.	
Norwegian Majesty: Built: 1992 - Tonnage: 38,000 - Length: 680 ft. - Guests: 1,462 - Crew: 570.	
Norwegian Sea: Built: 1988 - Tonnage: 42,000 - Length: 700 ft. - Guests: 1,504 - Crew: 630.	
Norwegian Sky: Built: 1999 - Tonnage: 80,000 - Length: 853 ft. - Guests: 2,002 - Crew: 750.	
Norwegian Star: Built: 2001 - Tonnage: 91,000 - Length: 965 ft. - Guests: 2,300 - Crew: 1,100.	
Norwegian Sun: Built: 2001 - Tonnage: 80,000 - Length: 853 ft. - Guests: 2,002 - Crew: 750.	
Norwegian Wind: Built: 1993 - Tonnage: 46,000 - Length: 754 ft. - Guests: 1,726 - Crew: 614.	

Orient Lines

About The Line: Ever wanted to go to the far corners of the world without sacrificing comfort and graciousness? Orient Lines is for you—with mid-size, classy ships that whisk you away to faraway places with fine cuisine and refined ambience. This line, which enjoys a loyal following (there were 640 repeaters on a recent Crown Odyssey cruise I took from Singapore to Australia, is an excellent value for your money).

Kind Of Cruise: Light adventure, educational.
Fleet: ***Crown Odyssey, Marco Polo***
Kind Of Ships: Classic, mid-size vessels.
Good For: Learners, explorers, people bit by the wanderlust bug, but who wish to sail in comfort in a good-sized vessel.
Price Category: Moderate. May be able to sail for less than $150 per day in "hot water" periods.
Cruise Experience: Destination-intensive cruises in a gracious ambience. Friendly and attentive crew. Alternative dining. Top-notch lecturers enrich the voyage with talks about the areas visited. Gentlemen hosts dance with unescorted ladies and attend social functions. Onboard folkloric presentations by local groups like the Darwin Aboriginal Show in Darwin, Australia and numerous local entertainers.
Who's Sharing It With You: Mostly well-traveled, middle-aged people (middle and upper-middle class) who want to explore far away places and learn about them in comfort in classy, classic mid-sized ships. A good representation of Europeans. Younger passenger rosters in the Mediterranean.
What's There For You: Refined interiors. Folkloric presentations in some ports of call; gentlemen hosts (except in Mediterranean voyages); traditional two dinner seatings; alternative dining.
Favorite Haunts: Raffles, the alternative dining spot on the ***Marco Polo***; the observation lounge and the indoor pool/Mandara-operated spa on the ***Crown Odyssey***.
Whatever You Do, Don't Miss The… Local entertainment brought on board, enrichment lectures, and the Filipino Crew Show presented once during each voyage (it's specta-crew-lar!).

Types of Cruise Lines

Accommodations: Cabins are attractive with varied sizes and configurations—and almost 70 percent are outside on the ***Marco Polo***. The ***Crown Odyssey*** offers 18 categories—more than 75 percent are outside—with the smallest being a roomy 154 sq. ft.

Look Elsewhere If… You want a non-stop party atmosphere.

Itineraries: Worldwide including Antarctica.

Deals & Discounts: Advance booking savings. Air add-ons with transfers. Since these are cruise-tours, pre- and post-cruise hotel stays, transfers, and sightseeing are included in the fares.

Ships at a Glance
Ships

Crown Odyssey	Built: 1988 - Tonnage: 34,242 - Length: 614 ft. - Guests: 1,052 - Crew: 470.
Marco Polo	Built: 1965 - Tonnage: 22,080 - Length: 578 - Guests: 850 - Crew: 350.

Princess Cruises

About The Line: The hit TV series, "The Love Boat" of the 1970s and 80s was filmed on Princess ships and to this day -is that series still in reruns? I have a feeling it will always be! And it will always retain a romantic aura about it, even though the two original ships on the series, the ***Island Princess*** and the ***Pacific Princess***, have left the fleet. Princess celebrates Valentine's Day with a big themed sailing each year. This line is a major player in Alaska and the Caribbean.

Kind Of Cruise: Family, resort/playground, romantic.

Fleet: ***Crown Princess, Dawn Princess, Golden Princess, Grand Princess, Ocean Princess, Regal Princess, Royal Princess, Sea Princess, Sun Princess. Coral Princess and Star Princess.*** The line acquired two former Renaissance Cruises ships (R3 and R4) in August of 2002 and renamed them Tahitian Princess and Pacific Princess, the latter replacing its aging vessel by the same name).

Kind Of Ships: Modern mega-liners and ultra-liners, and two mid-size ships.

Good For: Family vacationers, people in the mood for romance, spa/fitness buffs.

Price Category: Moderate. May be able to get in for $150 per day and less than $100 per day (maybe less than $75 per day) during "hot waters" periods.

Cruise Experience: Gorgeous ships, beautifully decorated. An abundance of cabins with verandas. "Personal Choice" program lets you decide if you want one of two traditional dinner seatings or open seating from 5:30 p.m. to midnight. Alternative dining including pizzerias with finger-licking-good calzones and pizzas (my favorite is the pizza margherita). A variety of activities and entertainment onboard and excursions ashore including the New Waves snorkeling and scuba diving program (this is the only line where you can get scuba certification during the cruise).

Who's Sharing It With You: Mostly people in their 40s and up (slightly younger in the Caribbean, older on longer, exotic itineraries) from the middle classes and upper middle classes. Lots of families in the summer and school holidays.

What's There For You: Broadway-style and Vegas-style revues, museum-quality art collections, a variety of sports activities, children's facilities and programs, pastry café, 24-hour dining, self-service launderette. Wedding chapels (you can get legally married by the captain) on **Grand Princess, Golden Princess** and **Star Princess** (and the chapels are equipped with "wedding cams" so friends back home can "virtually" attend).

Favorite Haunts: The clubby, nautically-themed Wheelhouse Bar on **Grand Princess**, the British Colonial-inspired Bengal Bar on **Regal Princess** -both great convivial places for pre-dinner cocktails or after-dinner drinks and conversation.

Whatever You Do, Don't Miss The... Daily pasta specials for dinner (Delicioso!) and the Champagne Waterfall during one of the formal nights.

Accommodations: One of Princess' trademarks is an abundance of verandas. There is a wide stateroom variety -**Grand Princess** alone, for instance, has an incredible 35 cabin categories!

Look Elsewhere If... On land vacations you prefer inns to big resorts.

Itineraries: Africa, Alaska, Australia, Bermuda, Canada/New England, Caribbean, Europe, Hawaii, Mexican Riviera, New Zealand, Orient, South America.

Types of Cruise Lines

Deals & Discounts: Early booking savings. Children's fares. Air add-ons with transfers. Pre- and post-cruise packages.

Ships at a Glance

Ships

Ships
Coral Princess: Built: 2002 - Tonnage: 88,000 - Length: 965 ft. - Guests: 1,950 - Crew: 961.
Crown Princess: Built: 1990 - Tonnage: 70,000 - Length: 811 ft. - Guests: 1,590 - Crew: 696.
Dawn Princess: Built: 1997 - Tonnage: 77,000 - Length: 856 ft. - Guests: 1,950 - Crew: 900.
Golden Princess: Built: 2001 - Tonnage: 109,000 - Length: 951 ft. - Guests: 2,600 - Crew: 1,100.
Grand Princess: Built: 1998 - Tonnage: 109,000 - Length: 951 ft. - Guests: 2,600 - Crew: 1,100.
Ocean Princess: Built: 1999 - Tonnage: 77,000 - Length: 856 ft. - Guests: 1,950 - Crew: 900.
Regal Princess: Built: 1991 - Tonnage: 70,000 - Length: 811 ft. - Guests: 1,590 - Crew: 696.
Royal Princess: Built: 1984 - Tonnage: 45,000 - Length: 757 ft. - Guests: 1,200 - Crew: 520.
Sea Princess: Built: 1998 - Tonnage: 77,000 - Length: 856 ft. - Guests: 1,950 - Crew: 900.
Star Princess: Built: 2002 - Tonnage: 109,000 - Length: 951 ft. - Guests: 2,600 - Crew: 1,100.
Sun Princess: Built: 1995 - Tonnage: 77,000 - Length: 856 ft. - Guests: 1,950 - Crew: 900.
Tahitian Princess: Built: 1999 - Tonnage: 30,227 - Length: 594 ft. - Guests: 688 - Crew: 373.
Pacific Princess: Built: 1999 - Tonnage: 30,227 - Length: 594 ft. - Guests: 688 - Crew: 373.

Radisson Seven Seas Cruises

About The Line: Radisson Hotels International steered a course into cruising in 1992 and in 1995, its line, Radisson Diamond Cruises merged with Seven Seas Cruise Line to form the present ultra-deluxe line.

Kind Of Cruise: Luxury, romantic, gourmet.

Fleet: **Paul Gauguin, Radisson Diamond, Song of Flower, Seven Seas Mariner, Seven Seas Navigator. Seven Seas Voyager (2003)**.

Kind Of Ships: Small and mid-size ultra-deluxe ships.

Good For: People with discriminating tastes, gourmands, learners, romantics.

Price Category: Luxury. May be able to get in for about $300 per day in "hot waters" (and there are two-for-ones and other specials during these times).

Cruise Experience: Sophisticated, ultra-deluxe ambience, with impeccable service and delectable cuisine.

Who's Sharing It With You: Affluent, well-traveled guests, in their mid-40s and 50s and older. On the **Paul Gauguin** in Tahiti, there are a good number of honeymooners in their 30s.

What's There For You: Open seating dining. Alternative dining. Well-appointed cabins. Enrichment lectures. Nightclub, cabaret and musical entertainment in the lounges. Book/video library. Computer terminals for e-mailing. Internet Café and computer classes on the **Seven Seas Mariner**. Gentlemen hosts on select sailings. Children's activities in Alaska and the Baltic.

Favorite Haunts: The Grill alternative dining venue on the **Radisson Diamond**, the Vista Lounge forward observation lounge on the **Seven Seas Navigator**.

Whatever You Do, Don't Miss… Some of this line's intriguing shore excursions that let you in to places you might not normally have access to: perhaps private palazzos while in Venice, an artist's home/studio in Croatia.

Look Elsewhere If… You think you would prefer the ultra-liner experience.

Accommodations: All-outside staterooms and suites.

Itineraries: Worldwide. World cruise.

Deals & Discounts: Early booking discounts. Two-for-ones and other specials. Air add-ons. Pre- and post-cruise packages.

Types of Cruise Lines

Ships at a Glance
Ships

Paul Gauguin: Built: 1998 - Tonnage: 18,800 - Length: 513 ft. Guests: 320 - Crew: 206.
Radisson Diamond: Built: 1992 - Tonnage: 20,295 - Length: 420 ft. - Guests: 354 - Crew: 192.
Seven Seas Mariner: Built: 2001 - Tonnage: 50,000 - Length: 675 ft. - Guests: 700 - Crew: 354.
Seven Seas Navigator: Built: 1999 - Tonnage: 30,000 - Length: 500 ft. - Guests: 490 - Crew: 313.
Seven Seas Voyager: Built: 2003 - Tonnage: 46,000 - Length: 708 ft. - Guests: 720 - Crew: 360.
Song of Flower: Built: 1986 - Tonnage: 8,282 - Length: 409 ft. - Guests: 180 - Crew 157.

Royal Caribbean International

About The Line: A breeze of fresh air at sea, this line is as pleasing to American tastes and as wonderful as apple pie and the girl next door. Its ships are beautifully decorated with a contemporary feel and outstanding public areas graced with multi-million-dollar art collections. It counts among its roster the reigning biggest ships in the world.

Kind Of Cruise: Family, resort/playground, party, spa-fitness.

Fleet: ***Viking Serenade, Nordic Empress, Sovereign of the Seas, Legend of the Seas, Rhapsody of the Seas, Monarch of the Seas, Majesty of the Seas, Grandeur of the Seas, Enchantment of the Seas, Splendour of the Seas, Vision of the Seas, Radiance of the Seas, Voyager of the Seas, Explorer of the Seas, Adventure of the Sea. Brilliance of the Seas, Navigator of the Seas.***

Kind Of Ships: Mega-liners and ultra-liners.

Good For: Families, fitness buffs, people wanting an active, fun vacation.

Price Category: Moderate. May be able to get in for about $100 per day, maybe even less than $75 per day during "hot water" periods.

Cruise Experience: Like floating Hyatt Hotels with dramatic atriums dripping in marble, brass, fountains, greenery and glass elevators. Lots of activities and entertainment. Traditional two-seating dinner, and alternative dining venues. Great themed spas/solariums.

Who's Sharing It With You: Most passengers are in their 40s, middle-class and upper middle-class, some first-timers, many repeaters. Lots of families particularly during school holidays. Older guests in longer voyages.

What's There For You: Viking Crown observation lounges, many smokestack-wrapped with panoramic views—where I invariably toast at least one sunset at sea. Great private island experiences. Children's programs and facilities. Internet centers; in-cabin Internet access on newest vessels.

Favorite Haunts: The themed Solariums with pools covered by retractable glass domes. The atriums where there is (live and player piano) music all day long and most of the night.

Whatever You Do, Don't Miss…Trying the ice-skating rink and rock climbing wall on some of this line's vessels.

Accommodations: Early Royal Caribbean ships used to have such tiny cabins, you were tempted to ask your companion to leave every time you had to change for dinner. That is no longer the case, with new ships featuring comfortable accommodations—153 sq. ft. in standard cabins in the Vision-Class ships, for example.

Look Elsewhere If… On land, you prefer intimate accommodations to big resorts.

Itineraries: Alaska, Australia, Asia, Bahamas, Caribbean, Europe, Mexico, Panama Canal, South America.

Deals & Discounts: Early booking savings (Breakthrough Fares) that provide up to 40 percent discounts -the earliest bird catches the biggest savings. Children's fares. Senior discounts fleet wide at various times. Air add-ons with transfers. Pre- and post cruise packages.

Types of Cruise Lines

Ships at a Glance

Ships

Adventure of the Seas: Built: 2001 - Tonnage: 142,000 - Length: 1,020 ft. - Guests: 3,114 - Crew: 1,180.
Brilliance of the Seas: Built: 2002 - Tonnage: 90,000 - Length: 962 ft. - Guests: 2,100 - Crew: 859.
Enchantment of the Seas - Tonnage: 73,817 - Length: 916 ft. - Guests: 1,950 - Crew: 760.
Explorer of the Seas: Built: 2000 - Tonnage: 142,000 - Length: 1,020 ft. - Guests: 3,114 - Crew: 1,180.
Grandeur of the Seas: Built: 1996 - Tonnage: 73,817 - Length: 916 ft. - Guests: 1,950 - Crew: 760.
Legend of the Seas: Built: 1995 - Tonnage: 69,130 - Length: 867 ft. - Guests: 1,804 - Crew: 720.
Majesty of the Seas: Built: 1992 - Tonnage: 73,941 - Length: 880 ft. - Guests: 2,354 - Crew: 822.
Monarch of the Seas: Built: 1991 - Tonnage: 73,941 - Length: 880 ft. - Guests: 2,354 - Crew: 822.
Navigator of the Seas: Built: 2002 - Tonnage: 142,000 - Length: 1,020 ft. - Guests: 3,114 - Crew: 1,180.
Nordic Empress: Built: 1990 - Tonnage: 48,563 - Length: 692 ft. - Guests: 1,600 - Crew: 671.
Radiance of the Seas: Built: 2001 - Tonnage: 90,000 - Length: 962 ft. - Guests: 2,100 - Crew: 859.
Rhapsody of the Seas: Built: 1997 - Tonnage: 78,491 - Length: 915 ft. - Guests: 2,000 - Crew: 765.
Sovereign of the Seas: Built: 1988 - Tonnage: 73,192 - Length: 880 ft. - Guests: 2,278 - Crew: 840.
Splendour of the Seas: Built: 1996 - Tonnage: 69,130 - Length: 867 ft. - Guests: 1,804 - Crew: 720.
Viking Serenade: Built: 1982 - Tonnage: 40,132 - Length: 623 ft. - Guests: 1,512 - Crew: 612.
Vision of the Seas: Built: 1998 - Tonnage: 78,491 - Length: 915 ft. - Guests: 2,000 - Crew: 660.
Voyager of the Seas: Built: 1999 - Tonnage: 142,000 - Length: 1,020 ft. - Guests: 3,114 - Crew: 1,180.

Chapter Three

Seabourn Cruise Line

About The Line: Atle Brynestad, a Norwegian industrialist, founded this line in 1987 with a goal of cradling its guests in the lap of luxury as they explore the world. It has succeeded!

Kind Of Cruise: Exclusive, luxury, gourmet, romantic.

Fleet: ***Seabourn Legend, Seabourn Pride, Seabourn Spirit.***

Kind Of Ships: Yacht-like, ultra-deluxe vessels.

Good For: Those who demand the very best, gourmands, romantics.

Price Category: Luxury. May be able to sail for about $300 per day with specials during "hot water" periods.

Cruise Experience: Elegant, sophisticated voyages to every corner of the world.

Who's Sharing It With You: Well-heeled, well-traveled guests with discriminating tastes generally in their 50s and older.

What's There For You: Impeccable, attentive service, superb cuisine, luxurious accommodations, water sports marina, enrichment programs, small gym, exclusivity, may get to rub elbows, like I did, with royalty. There are no children's facilities, but staff will plan some activities for young sailors when they are onboard.

Favorite Haunts: The observation lounges with their floor-to-ceiling windows and elegant, understated décor.

Whatever You Do, Don't Miss… Enjoying dinner served course by course impeccably in the intimate setting of your suite—very impressive!

Accommodations: All-suite.

Look Elsewhere If… You prefer big, five star resorts to intimate deluxe inns, or if you are not comfortable in ultra-deluxe settings and/or dressing up (these ships are dressy).

Itineraries: Seabourn ships roam the world.

Deals & Discounts: Early booking savings. Children's fares. Air-add-ons with transfers. Pre- and post-cruise packages. During the post-Sept. 11, 2001 crisis, Seabourn was flying guests free to Europe and Asia embarkation ports and offering 45 percent discounts.

Types of Cruise Lines

Ships at a Glance

Ships

Seabourn Legend: Built: 1992 - Tonnage: 10,000 - Length: 439 ft. - Guests: 204 - Crew: 145.
Seabourn Pride: Built: 1988 - Length: 439 ft. - Guests: 204 - Crew: 145.
Seabourn Spirit: Built: 1989 - Length: 439 ft. - Guests: 204 - Crew: 145.

Silversea Cruises

About The Line: Can you get used to Limoges china, Christofle silverware, Frette bed linens and the softest down pillows? Fine enrichment programs from Le Cordon Bleu and National Geographic? Welcome aboard!

Kind Of Cruise: Luxury, gourmet, romantic.
Fleet: *Silver Cloud, Silver Wind, Silver Shadow, Silver Whisper.*
Kind Of Ships: Modern small ships.
Good For: Learners, romantics, gourmands, those who demand the very best.
Price Category: Luxury. Lowest per diems generally average about $500.
Cruise Experience: The crème de la crème at sea. Refined interiors, impeccable service, gourmet cuisine, open-seating dining, luxurious all-suite accommodations. As all-inclusive a cruise as you can find: beverages (including select wines and spirits) airfare (economy class included, upgrades to business class are available at extra cost), transfers, tips are all covered in your ticket price. It was a great feeling, on my sailing, not having to be concerned with signing checks each time I ordered a drink at the bar or wine with dinner.

Who's Sharing It With You: Seasoned, affluent guests —attorneys, bankers, doctors, dentists, lawyers—maybe a countess or two-in their 40s and over, with the bulk generally over 50.

What's There For You: Enrichment program including superb guest lecturers and chefs. Alternative dining most evenings—on our Mexican Riviera sailing, a guest chef from Mexico presented a true fiesta of Mexican dishes plus such events as tequila tastings. Bvlgary boutique. Book/video library. Self-service launderette. There are no children's facilities.

Favorite Haunts: The bars and lounges.

Whatever You Do, Don't Miss The... Silversea Signature event—a complimentary shore activity—perhaps an authentic fiesta in a town near Puerto Vallarta or a private concert at the ruins in Ephesus.

Look Elsewhere If... You are uncomfortable in ultra-sophisticated and ultra-elegant environments, or if you are traveling with children.

Accommodations: Luxurious all-suite, nearly 75 percent with verandas on the older ships, nearly 85 percent on the newer ones.

Itineraries: Worldwide. World cruise.

Deals & Discounts: Fifteen percent discount when final payment is made six months in advance of sail date. Pre-, post-cruise packages.

Ships at a Glance

Ships

Silver Cloud: Built: 1994 - Tonnage: 16,800 - Length: 514 ft. - Guests: 296 - Crew: 210.
Silver Wind: Built: 1994 - Tonnage: 16,800 - Length: 514 ft. - Guests: 296 - Crew: 210.
Silver Shadow: Built: 2000 - Tonnage: 25,000 - Length: 597 ft. - Guests: 388 - Crew: 295.
Silver Whisper: Built: 2001 - Tonnage: 25,000 - Length: 597 ft. - Guests: 388 - Crew: 295.

Windstar Cruises

About The Line: Its slogan, 180-degrees from the ordinary, comes alive when you stand out on deck and watch its four triangular sails unfurl like whispers to the wind. And you thank your lucky stars!

Kind Of Cruise: Romantic with a capital R, soft adventure, gourmet.

Fleet: **Wind Song, Wind Spirit, Wind Star, Wind Surf.**

Kind Of Ships: Chic, deluxe sail-cruisers.

Good For: Romantics, dreamers, gourmands, water sports enthusiasts.

Price Category: Luxury. May be able to sail for less than $250 per day during "hot water" periods.

Types of Cruise Lines

Cruise Experience: Luxurious, relaxed, unregimented, romantic sailings to some of the world's most beautiful ports. Menus by celebrity chefs Joachim Splichal and Jeanne Jones. Resort casual dress code.

Who's Sharing It With You: Mostly couples ranging from honeymooners to retirees -the majority in their 30s-60s, generally professionals looking for a quality, laid-back getaway.

What's There For You: Beautiful, exclusive sail-cruisers to whisk you away to exotic ports. Open bridge policy. Water sports platform with sailboats, windsurfers, snorkeling gear, scuba diving, water-skiing. Comfortable, nautical-themed accommodations with great baths. Spa on the **Wind Surf** only. No children's facilities.

Favorite Haunts: The water sports platform. The lounge. The spa on **Wind Surf**.

Whatever You Do, Don't Miss The… Pool barbecue in the Caribbean including grilled lobster tails, and the Mediterranean Night in the Mediterranean with a lavish buffet of regional specialties -including a bounty of salads and pastas, focaccia, olive loaf and other breads, main dishes and desserts—the flan was my favorite.

Accommodations: Excellent cabins with portholes and other nautical touches and great baths. Suites with "his" and "hers" baths on the **Wind Surf**.

Look Elsewhere If… You like to dress up to the nines and prefer large resort vacations.

Itineraries: Australia, Florida Keys/Bahamas/Caribbean, Central America, Far East, Greek Isles, Mediterranean, New Zealand.

Deals & Discounts: Early booking savings of up to 50 percent. Frequent two-for-one specials. Air add-ons with transfers. Pre- and post-cruise packages.

Ships at a Glance

Ships

Wind Song	Built: 1987 - Tonnage: 5,350 - Length: 440 ft. - Guests: 148 - Crew: 88.
Wind Spirit	Built: 1988 - Tonnage: 5,350 - Length: 440 ft. - Guests: 148 - Crew: 88.
Wind Star	Built: 1986 - Tonnage: 5,350 - Length: 440 ft. - Guests: 148 - Crew: 88.
Wind Surf	Built: 1990 - Tonnage: 14,745 - Length: 617 ft. - Guests: 308 - Crew: 163.

Fell's Official Know-It-All: Cruises

Part B —Other Cruises & Cruising Alternatives

Haven't found your match yet? Don't despair. Here are more cruise lines for you to consider, including some alternative cruising choices such as sailing vessels and expedition ships.

American Canadian Caribbean Cruise Line

This budget, small ship line enjoys a following among seasoned travelers, mostly 40-70 years old. Ships feature homey ambience and interesting itineraries in the U.S., Caribbean, Central America and the Amazon.

Ships at a Glance

Ships

Grand Caribe - Built: 1997 - Tonnage: 99 - Length: 182 ft. Guests: 100 - Crew: 20.
Grande Mariner - Built: 1998 - Tonnage: 99 - Length: 182 ft. — Guests: 100 - Crew: 20.
Niagara Prince - Built: 1994 - Tonnage: 95 - Length: 175 ft. — Guests: 84 - Crew: 15.

If you would like to enjoy a voyage without going too far away from terra firma, book a river cruise or a coastal voyage.

Clipper Cruise Line

This small ship line (price category: moderate-plus) attracts mostly upper middle class, well-traveled, mature passengers lured to the learning-tone of the voyages enriched by onboard naturalists, historians and other lecturers and to the destination-intensive itineraries in the Caribbean, Central and South America, Antarctica, Europe, New England/Canada, Great Lakes, West Coast, Mexico, Alaska and Asia.

Types of Cruise Lines

Ships at a Glance

Ships

Clipper Adventurer - Built: 1975 - Tonnage: 4,364 - Length: 330 ft. Guests: 122 - Crew: 79.
Clipper Odyssey - Built: 1989 - Tonnage: 5,200 - Length: 338 ft. Guests: 120 - Crew: 72.
Nantucket Clipper - Built: 1984 - Tonnage: 1,471 - Length: 207 ft. Guests: 102 - Crew: 32.
Yorktown Clipper - Built: 1988 - Tonnage: 2,354 - Length: 257 ft. Guests: 138 - Crew: 40.

Club Med

This line has one moderately-priced sail-cruiser, the ***Club Med 2*** (sister to Windstar's ***Wind Surf***) which it operates as if it were one of its land-based village resorts: easy, laid-back ambience with a French accent. Your fellow passengers are generally in their 30s to 60s, mostly couples—many from France and other European countries. The ship sails in the Caribbean in the winter and in the Mediterranean in the summer with transatlantic repositioning voyages in between.

Ships at a Glance

Ships

Club Med 2: Built: 1992 - Tonnage: 14,000 - Length: 613 ft. - Guests: 392 - Crew: 181.

Cruise West

A small-ship line whose prices usually hover just above the moderate price range, but sometimes drop below it, Cruise West offers a chance to enjoy nature close up. It attracts well-traveled, well-educated guests, mostly middle-aged and retired folks who enjoy an intimate ship experience that takes them to out-of-the-way places large ships cannot reach. Itineraries are featured in Alaska, Canada, the Pacific Northwest, California and the Sea of Cortez.

Ships at a Glance

Ships

Spirit of Alaska - Built: 1980 - Tonnage: 97 - Length: 192 ft. - Guests: 78 Crew: 21.
Spirit of Columbia: Built: 1979 - Tonnage: 98 - Length: 143 ft. — Guests: 78 Crew: 21.
Spirit of Discovery: Built: 1976 - Tonnage: 94 - Length: 166 ft. — Guests: 84 Crew 21.
Spirit of Endeavour: Built: 1985 - Tonnage: 95 - Length: 217 ft. - Guests: 102 Crew: 30.
Spirit of Glacier Bay: Built: 1971 - Tonnage: 97 - Length: 125 ft. - Guests: 52 Crew: 16.
Spirit of '98: Built: 1984 - Tonnage: 96 - Length: 192 ft. - Guests: 96 - Crew: 23.
Spirit of Oceanus: Built: 1991 - Tonnage: 1,263 - Length: 295 ft. - Guests: 114 Crew: 59.

Fred Olsen Lines

American passengers are in the minority on this line's **Black Watch, Bramar** and **Black Prince**, as these three ships (the first two mid-sized, the last one, small -the **Black Watch** and **Black Prince** are vintage vessels) attract a large British clientele to its European itineraries. Cruises are also featured in the Caribbean, Africa, and other destinations. Fares are in the moderate range.

Ships at a Glance

Ships

Black Prince: Built: 1966—Tonnage: 11,200—Length: 465 ft.—Guests: 517 Crew: 200.
Black Watch: Built: 1972 — Tonnage: 28,492 - Length: 630 ft. - Guest: 892 Crew: 330.
Bramar: Built: 1994 - Tonnage: 19,089 - Length: 537 ft. - Guests: 733 Crew: 300.

Types of Cruise Lines

First European Cruises

With its classic mid-size and new large ships, this moderately priced line attracts a largely European clientele including many families during school holidays. Cruises are offered in the Mediterranean and Caribbean.

Ships at a Glance
Ships

Azur: Built: 1971 - Tonnage: 15,000 - Length: 465 ft. - Guests: 800 - Crew: 330.
European Vision: Built: 2001 - Tonnage: 58,600 - Length: 823 ft. - Guests: 1,500 - Crew: 711.
Flamenco: Built: 1972 - Tonnage: 17,000-Length: 535 ft. - Guests: 850 - Crew: 350.
Mistral: Built: 1999 - Tonnage: 47,900 - Length: 708 ft. - Guests: 1,200 - Crew: 470.

Glacier Bay Cruise Line

This line presents three small ships and one catamaran-style vessel with price tags that average a little higher than moderate, but often hit the beginning-moderate range. With naturalists onboard and included shore excursions they are a good no-nonsense choice (cabins tend to be small and modest) for exploring Alaska. Passengers' ages range from 30 to 80 - the bulk being 40-70 years old. Itineraries are offered in Alaska in the summer and the Sea of Cortez in the winter.

Ships at a Glance
Ships

Wilderness Adventurer: Built: 1984 - Tonnage: 89 - Length: 157 ft. Guests: 72 - Crew: 24.
Wilderness Discoverer: Built: 1992 - Tonnage: 95 - Length: 169 ft. Guests: 72 - Crew: 24.
Wilderness Explorer: Built: 1969 - Tonnage: 98 - Length: 112 ft. Guests: 34 - Crew: 13.
Executive Explorer: Built: 1986 - Tonnage: 98 - Length: 98.5 ft. Passengers: 49 - Crew 20.

Lindblad Expeditions

Homey and comfortable, Lindblad Expeditions vessels are small ships that take you to exotic locales of the planet like the Galapagos and Antarctica. The focus of these cruises is not bingo, but binoculars. An expedition leader and a staff of naturalists are onboard to lead the program, to give recaps each day, present videos and slide shows on the destination. A fleet of zodiacs is available for quick landings and exploration (kayaks are also available, and in the Galapagos a glass-bottom boat). All shore activities are included in the fare. Your fellow passengers are mostly in their 40s to 70s, care passionately about the environment, and are happier exploring than partying. Prices are in the moderate-plus category, but when you conclude your cruise you go away with an excellent knowledge of the region you visited.

Ships at a Glance

Ships

Sea Bird: Built: 1982 - Tonnage: 100 - Length: 152 ft. - Guests: 70 - Crew: 23.
Sea Lion: 1981 - Tonnage 100 - Length: 152 ft. - Guests: 70 - Crew: 23.
Polaris: Built: 1960 - Tonnage: 2,214 - Length: 238 ft. - Guests: 80 - Crew: 27.
Endeavour: Built: 1966 — Tonnage: 3,132 — Length: 293 ft. - Guests: 110 Crew: 52.
Sea Voyager - Built: 1982 - Tonnage: 1,195 - Length: 174 ft. - Guests: 60 Crew: 23.

P & O Cruises

Venerable, very British, P & O features modern large ships and one classic mid-size vessel (*Victoria*) in the luxury category. Most guests are British from a broad age and income spectrum drawn to its worldwide port-intensive itineraries.

Ships at a Glance

Ships

Arcadia: Built: 1989-Tonnage:63,524-Length: 811 ft.-Guests: 1,475-Crew: 650
Aurora: Built: 2000 - Tonnage: 76,000 - Length: 886 ft. - Guests: 1,850 Crew: 417.
Oriana: Built:1995-Tonnage:69,000-Length: 855 ft. - Guests: 1,806-Crew: 760.
Victoria: Built:1966-Tonnage: 28,000-Length: 660 ft.-Guests: 746 Crew: 436.

Types of Cruise Lines

Regal Cruises

This line operates only one ship, a vintage mid-size vessel, in the budget category. Leave the expectations of glamour, if you have any, at the pier for this is a modest experience. Sailings to the Bahamas, Caribbean, Panama Canal, New England/Canada are offered out of Port Manatee, Fla. and New York.

Ships at a Glance

Ships

Regal Empress: Built: 1953 - Tonnage: 21,909 - Length: 612 ft. - Guests: 925 Crew: 396.

Royal Olympic Cruises (or Royal Olympia Cruises)

This budget/moderate Greek line operates a mostly vintage fleet that provides comfortable environments with a Greek accent (including cuisine specialties and dancing on Greek Night). Cruising regions include Greek Isles, Mediterranean, Central America, and Caribbean.

Ships at a Glance

Ships

Odysseus: Built: 1962 — Tonnage: 12,000 - Length: 483 ft. - Guests: 448 Crew: 200.
Olympia Countess: Built: 1976 - Tonnage: 18,000 - Length: 537 ft. Guests: 840 - Crew: 350.
Olympia Explorer: Built: 2001 - Tonnage: 25,000 - Length: 590 ft. Guests: 840 - Crew: 260.
Olympia Voyager: Built: 2000 - Tonnage: 25,000 - Length: 590 ft. Guests: 840 - Crew: 260.
Stella Solaris: Built: 1953 - Tonnage: 18,000 - Length: 544 ft. Guests: 620 - Crew: 320.
Triton: Built: 1971 - Tonnage: 14,000 - Length: 486 ft. - Guests: 620 Crew: 315.
World Renaissance: Built: 1966 - Tonnage: 12,000 - Length: 492 ft. Guests: 457 - Crew 235.

Sea Cloud Cruises

These luxury sailing vessels are elegant, la crème de la crème in sailing ships (the Sea Cloud was a wedding present from magnate E. F. Hutton to Marjorie Merriweather Post, the cereal heiress). Theirs is a discerning clientele attracted by the posh, intimate sailing experience in Europe, the Caribbean and South America.

Ships at a Glance

Ships

Sea Cloud: Built: 1931 — Tonnage: 2,532 - Length: 360 ft. - Guests: 69 Crew: 60.

Sea Cloud II: Built: 2001 - Tonnage: 3,849 - Length: 384 ft. - Guests: 96 Crew: 57.

Arriving at a port of call, say in the Greek Isles or the Caribbean, under sail is a breathtaking, poetically breezy experience.

Star Clippers

People who want to experience true sailing vessels (not computerized sailer-cruisers) at moderate prices need look no further than this line with its fleet of three traditional sailing ships. The lifestyle is casual, relaxed and laid-back for you and your fellow passengers who are generally in their 30s and 40s, a soft-adventure-loving sort—many Americans, some from Europe and other parts of the globe. Every day the captain presents "story-time" with information about the ports and the day's activities. The water sports are free, so jump right in there, and you can help the crew raise and lower the sails. Itineraries include Caribbean, Mediterranean, Greek Isles, Asia.

Ships at a Glance

Ships

Star Clipper: Built: 1991 - Tonnage: 2,298 - Length: 360 ft. - Guests: 170 - Crew: 70.

Star Flyer: Built: 1992 - Tonnage: 2,298 - Length: 360 ft. - Guests: 170 - Crew: 70.

Royal Clipper: Built: 1999 - Tonnage: 5,000 - Length: 439 ft. - Guests: 224 - Crew: 100.

Types of Cruise Lines

Windjammer Barefoot Cruises

This grab-a-towel-let's-go-to-the-beach classic sailing vessels line is laid-back with some cruises paaarty-hearty, others more sedate. Special interest sailings include singles and gay, nude on occasion. Prices are in the budget/low moderate category for the most part; amenities on the minimal end of the scale. Note: there are no hot showers on ***Flying Cloud***. Itineraries include off-the-beaten path idylls in the Caribbean and Bahamas.

Ships at a Glance
Ships

Amazing Grace: Built: 1955 - Tonnage: 1,585 - Length: 248 ft. - Passengers: 96 - Crew 40.
Flying Cloud: Built: 1935 - Tonnage: 400 ft. - Length: 208 ft. - Guests: 66 Crew: 25.
Legacy: Built: 1959-Tonnage: 1,165-Length: 294 ft. - Guests: 122 - Crew: 43.
Mandalay: Built: 1923-Tonnage: 420-Length: 236 ft. - Guests: 72-Crew 28.
Polynesia: Built: 1938-Tonnage: 430-Length: 248 ft. - Guests: 126-Crew: 45.
Yankee Clipper: Built: 1927 - Tonnage: 327 - Length: 197 ft. - Guests: 64 - Crew: 29.

World Explorer Cruises

World Explorer operates a classic liner (budget/low moderate category) that attracts a seasoned, mature clientele interested in learning about nature and in its port-intensive soft-adventure programs with an accent on the educational. Onboard ambience is friendly and informal and there is an outstanding library—with about 16,000 titles—many on Alaska where the ship summers. Other itineraries include Semester At Sea programs and Caribbean/Central America.

Ships at a Glance
Ships

Universe Explorer: Built: 1957 - Tonnage: 23,500 - Length: 617 ft.— Guests: 731 Crew: 330.

Part C — Barge & River Cruises

Perhaps you would prefer to sail down the Rhine, or navigate the Nile or the Yangtze? Intimate river boats and barges can get you there in a comfortable setting and at a slow pace so you can savor the sights of the countryside you travel in and soak in the culture. Shore excursions -perhaps a trip by mini-bus to a nearby castle, walking tours in medieval cities, and bike tours-are generally included in the fare.

> Barge cruises on European canals are leisurely—their pace is so slow that passengers can get off for a walk or ride in bikes alongside (bikes are usually provided) and meet up with the barge a ways up the canal.

Here is a selection of companies that offer barge and riverboat cruises:

ABERCROMBIE & KENT: This upscale travel firm operates cruises on European rivers, the Yangtze, the Nile and the Amazon. European river holidays (passenger capacity on the boats ranges from six to 102) are available in a wide variety of programs—perhaps take in tulip time in Holland, explore the Upper Loire Valley or the regions of Burgundy and Champagne in France, or take in the sights along the Shannon River in Ireland, to name a few.

FRENCH COUNTRY WATERWAYS: Hotel barges in Burgundy, the Upper Loire Valley, Champagne and Alsace-Lorraine. Talk about an intimate way to explore the countryside: the company's five barges hold eight or 18 passengers. Six-night cruises are offered from the end of March to the beginning of November each year to explore the countryside dotted with vineyards, medieval villages and pastures. In addition to accommodations aboard the barge, meals onboard, all tours, use of bicycles and transfers, the programs include one dinner ashore at a two-star or three-star Michelin restaurant.

Types of Cruise Lines

GLOBAL QUEST (formerly OdessAmerica): This company's vessels sail in Europe including Russia and the Ukraine, Galapagos and South America and East Africa/Indian Ocean. Their Europe By River program features a dozen boats, each accommodating 150-200 guests.

KD RIVER CRUISES OF EUROPE: One of the oldest river boat companies, KD River Cruises of Europe operates a dozen boats (passenger capacity ranges from 100 to 200) on 25 itineraries including cruises on the Rhine, Elbe, Moselle, Seine, Saone and Danube Rivers and the Rhine-Main-Danube Canal. Itineraries are also featured on Russian waterways between Moscow and St. Petersburg.

ORIENT EXPRESS CRUISES: This company, of Orient Express trains fame, operates The Road to Mandalay which has been offering deluxe river boat cruises in Myanmar since 1996—a wonderful way to explore really exotic locales in comfort and luxury. The boat features such facilities as a pool, sun deck, dining room and several bars including an observation lounge.

PETER DEILMANN CRUISES: This company operates river boats on the Danube, Elbe, Rhine, Moselle, Rhone, Saone, Po and other European rivers. Its 10 river-boats accommodate 75 to 200 passengers each, depending on the boat. The company also markets a barquentine and an ocean liner.

SEA CLOUD CRUISES: In addition to two sailing ships, this company operates two luxury riverboats, the River Cloud and River Cloud II, that sail on the Dutch and German waterways: the Rhine, Main, Moselle and Danube and Italy's Po River. The boats accommodate 90 passengers.

SWAN HELLENIC CRUISES: Guest speakers lead these river cruises in central Europe. The line operates the boat Swiss Crystal (100 passengers) on the Main and Danube Rivers.

Chapter Three

REGAL CHINA CRUISES: Yangtze River cruises with cultural enrichment including mah-jongg, tai chi, crafts (such as kite-making), Chinese entertainment and more. The line, a Sino-American venture, operates three boats accommodating 250 guests each.

VICTORIA CRUISES: Yangtze River sailings with lectures about China and the Yangtze as well as narration about the sights are featured by Victoria Cruises. The company, a Chinese-American venture is New York-based. It operated a dozen boats in 2001 and plans to be running 14 riverboats by the end of 2002. The boats accommodate from 140 to 179 guests each.

Test the Waters Tips

* Spend a good number of hours going over a variety of cruise line brochures—as many as you can get your hands on (your travel agent should have a good supply)—paying special attention to deck plans and cabin sketches and looking over the photos for clues of the age of the ship's clientele and its dress codes. This activity can be informative, not to mention great for daydreaming too!

* If you have access to the Internet, or have friends or relatives who do, spend sometime browsing through cruise Web sites (for cruise line Web sites, see this guide's Appendix).

* When venturing into exotic seas, select a cruise line that has established a presence in those waters through a number of years: their land programs and shore excursions will tend to be better than those of a newcomer line that has just begun sailings there.

Insider's Savings Insights

* Three months after the Sept. 11 tragedies, during a mere 15 minutes of browsing Internet sites like www.CruiseCritic.com and www.moments-notice.com, I found the following bargains: Two-night party cruise on NCL's Norway, from $79 per person, double occupancy; seven-night Alaska cruise on Royal Caribbean's **Legend of the Seas**, from $299 per person, double; seven-night Eastern Caribbean voyage on NCL's **Norwegian Sky** from $319; buy one cruise on NCL, get another one free for yourself or immediate family—and so on.

Types of Cruise Lines

* Most lines offer past passenger clubs (most are free, some may charge a fee, and you are eligible for membership after your first cruise). These clubs give you perks (that may include a cocktail party hosted by the captain for returning passengers and discounts for repeaters generally listed in a newsletter or magazine). Depending on the line, you may receive shipboard credits to spend in the spa or the shops onboard. Membership may be automatic or you will probably receive an invitation to join towards the end of your cruise and/or receive an enrollment form at home. There may be past passenger "reunion cruises" featuring special perks and discounts—Orient Lines is one of the lines that offer these reunions that may include a dinner during the land portion of the cruise-tour and a cocktail party with the captain. Among the best past passenger programs are those offered by Crystal, Cunard, Seabourn and Silversea.

* Your cruise is coming to an end and you enjoyed it. Well, you can book the next one right on board at a discount as many lines offer Cruise Consultants on their ships that can take care of the details (and if you so desire, in many cases you can arrange for your travel agent back home to receive a commission).

"*Mercury*" Photo courtesy of Celebrity Cruises.

Chapter: 4
Cruising Regions

Let's think of the world as a juicy mandarin orange, each segment a plump cruising region ready to be enjoyed. But unlike a mandarin, whose segments have pretty uniform flavors, cruising regions have their own distinct character.

Where do you dream of going? With today's worldwide cruise itineraries, chances are excellent that there is a voyage that takes you there. Perhaps there is more than one area of the world that you want to explore. My parents, from whom I inherited my wanderlust, were insatiable when it came to travel. On several occasions, I remember fondly, they filled out little pieces of paper with destinations' names, mixed them in a bag and fished two out for their twice yearly vacations—thus leaving the decision of where to go to chance. For those who prefer to make their own choices, I describe the most popular cruise destinations below. To contact Tourism Offices worldwide for additional information on ports you find intriguing, visit www.towd.com.

We can begin with the area of the world, the Caribbean Sea, that most people associate with cruising—where, in fact, modern-day cruising as we know it had its beginnings in 1966 when Norwegian Cruise Line launched its **Sunward** on short sailings to the Bahamas. It is one of my favorites, as I was born on one of its islands where each summer I went swimming in warm, calm, aquamarine waters so much, dried saltwater was like my second skin.

Introducing the Caribbean Cruise

Close your eyes and conjure up images of a tropical paradise: turquoise waters, talcum-powder sands, palm fronds swaying in the balmy breezes. That is the delightful picture most people associate with the Caribbean, the world's most popular cruising region. Once a seasonal destination attracting North Americans who wanted to escape the northern latitudes' bitter cold winters, the Caribbean is now a year-round playground for everyone from the North, South, East and West: families wanting to share school holidays with their children, couples and singles looking for fun, footloose and fancy-free getaways.

The Caribbean's attractions include picture-postcard-perfect beaches; more beaches; lush rain forests; cascading waterfalls; superb water sports; fabulous duty-free shopping; more beaches; cultural riches from a varied European and African heritage evident in an array of cuisines, languages, architecture; art and crafts; and, yes, you guessed it: more beaches! Hon, please, pass the banana daiquiri and the Bain de Soleil!

Lines that cruise the Caribbean include American Canadian Caribbean, Carnival, Celebrity, Costa, Crystal, Cunard, Disney, Holland America, Norwegian, Princess, Radisson Seven Seas, Royal Caribbean, Royal Olympic, Seabourn, and Silversea. For additional information on Caribbean ports of call, visit www.caribbean.com or www.caribbeantravel.com. Major ports of embarkation for Caribbean cruises are Miami, Fla.; Fort Lauderdale, Fla.; San Juan, Puerto Rico; Tampa, Fla.; and Cape Canaveral, Fla. Since these major ports of embarkation are in and of themselves popular tourist destinations in their own right, you may wish to plan to tour before and/or after your cruise independently, via ship's tours, or through a pre- or post-cruise package from the cruise lines (generally including transfers and sightseeing). After our first Caribbean cruise out of Fort Lauderdale, my husband commented that Fort Lauderdale was better, or as nice, as all our ports of call, but many of our fellow passengers were missing it by flying straight home. Pity.

Here are some touring/activity ideas that are ideal for independent cruise passengers at embarkation cities. All information is current as of the time this book was written but some details such as telephone numbers can be subject to change without notice.

Cruising Regions

MIAMI, FLA. —If you have just a few hours: Spend time at the shops and restaurants of Bayside Marketplace, 401 Biscayne Blvd. (a stone's throw from the Port of Miami).

If you have longer: Take a short taxi ride over to South Beach and take in its historic Art Deco district. Or to feel as if you have left the country without needing to go through passport control, head for Miami's Little Havana neighborhood (roughly situated on Southwest Eighth Street between 4th and 27th Avenues) where you can sample Cuban sandwiches (my favorite are the "medianoches": ham, pork, Swiss cheese, pickles, mustard on toasted bread) black bean soup and other culinary specialties, and purchase guayaberas (Spanish-style embroidered safari shirts) and hand-rolled cigars. Or take in the dolphin and whale shows at the Miami Seaquarium, 4400 Rickenbacker Causeway (305-361-5705), or bask in the Renaissance splendor of the palace of Vizcaya, 3251 South Miami Avenue, Coconut Grove (305-250-9133). For information on Miami, call the Greater Miami Convention & Visitors Bureau at 800-753-8448.

FORT LAUDERDALE, FLA. —If you have just a few hours: Walk around the quaint Las Olas Boulevard district with its boutiques, sidewalk cafes and restaurants, and the Las Olas Riverfront, a shopping/entertainment complex, both in the heart of Fort Lauderdale, or go for a stroll on the Fort Lauderdale Beach Promenade.

If you have longer: Enjoy the excellent collection at the Ft. Lauderdale Museum of Art, 1 Las Olas Blvd.—ask whether they have docent-led tours during your visit (954-763-6464) or take a water taxi ride or sightseeing cruise along the Venice of America's canals. For information about Fort Lauderdale, contact the Greater Fort Lauderdale Convention & Visitors' Bureau at 954-765-4466.

SAN JUAN, PUERTO RICO —If you have just a few hours: Take a stroll in Old San Juan—I always head for this historic section that is like an open-air museum with cobblestone streets dating back to Spanish Colonial times, shady plazas, shops, art galleries, restaurants and great views of the harbor.

If you have longer: Go to lush El Yunque rainforest for a hike on its trails, and/or make a splash at Luquillo Beach with its beautiful spans of sugar-white sands. For information, call the Puerto Rico Tourism Company at 800-866-7827 and read more about San Juan in the Caribbean Ports Of Call section that follows in this guide.

TAMPA, FLA.
-If you have just a few hours: Explore quaint Ybor City, Tampa's historic Latin Quarter with restaurants (I love the black bean soup), nightclubs and shops, or visit the Florida Aquarium, 701 Channelside Drive, 813-273-4000.

If you have longer: Enjoy a fun day at Busch Gardens Tampa Bay, a 335-acre Africa-themed park (with fearsome roller coasters) and zoological gardens (813-987-5171). And/or take in the Salvador Dali Museum in St. Petersburg (1000 Third St., St. Petersburg, 813-823-3767) with a superb collection of the great surrealist master. For information on Tampa, call the Tampa Convention & Visitors Bureau at 800-44-TAMPA.

CAPE CANAVERAL, FLA.
-If you have just a few hours: Get a bite to eat or enjoy a libation at one of the restaurants and bars near the port.

If you have longer: What are you doing to do next? Go to Walt Disney World! In Lake Buena Vista this top attraction (I have gone more than 300 times and counting!) has four major themed parks, the Magic Kingdom, Epcot, Disney-MGM and Animal Kingdom and three water-themed parks as well as shopping/dining/nightclub complexes. Call 407-W-DISNEY. To feel like an astronaut, head for the Kennedy Space Center, State Road 405 E., Titusville, 321-449-4322.

> Touring independently in some ports like San Juan and Nassau is very easy. In San Juan, historic Old San Juan is within walking distance of the main cruise terminal. The heart of town is also within walking distance in Nassau and beautiful Paradise Island is a quick taxi or boat taxi ride away from the pier.

Tips for Caribbean Cruising

* Don't feel as if you have to explore every nook and cranny of Caribbean islands, so you wind up exhausted in the tropical heat and humidity. Plan some beach time or visit botanical gardens, forests and parks at each port to cool off.

* This fabled sea has a fascinating history. Take time to explore fortresses (El Morro in the Old San Juan section of San Juan, Puerto Rico, a highlight of many shipboard tours, for example) and historical-themed attractions (like Pirates of Nassau Museum, within walking distance of the pier on George and Marlborough Streets in Nassau -this last one is an excellent rainy day option, which we enjoyed while getting out of a tropical shower one afternoon).

* Enjoy the tastes of the Caribbean, perhaps having lunch ashore to savor such delights as fried flying fish in Barbados, conch fritters in the Bahamas, black bean soup in Puerto Rico, jerk chicken in Jamaica, margaritas (some almost fish-bowl-size) in Cozumel. Or, if you are on a budget and wish to take full advantage of your already-paid-for-great-meals aboard ship, maybe enjoy just a snack of fresh, exotic, mouthwatering tropical fruits like mangoes, papayas, pineapple and soursop (yum, yum, yum and yum!) bought at fruit stands, markets and grocery stores all over the islands.

* If you tour independently and hire an un-metered taxi, agree both on a fare and length of touring time before you get on, and always pay only upon your return to the ship.

* It is generally a good idea to visit accessible, nearby beaches, on the island's main resort areas. If you venture off-the-beaten path to a remote beach always arrange for your taxi driver to wait for you there (and pay when you get back to the pier).

> Itineraries that feature a private island experience offer a relaxing day at the beach with music, games, barbecue and water sports —often becoming the highlight of the cruise for many passengers. Disney, Holland America, Princess, Norwegian and Royal Caribbean are among the lines that have private islands/beaches in the Caribbean.

Fell's Official Know-It-All: Cruises

Major Caribbean Ports of Call

Here are quick-and-easy Caribbean port profiles. Prices quoted are approximate and can be subject to change from time to time, so it is always better to check:

ANTIGUA - About the port: You want to go to the beach, you say? Well, you are in the right place! You'll find 365 beaches in Antigua—yep, one for each day of the year. History buffs will enjoy Nelson's Dockyard National Park near English Harbour, a highlight on organized tours, a short taxi ride from the cricket-loving capital of St. John's.

Language: English.

Money matters: Currency is Eastern Caribbean dollars but the U.S. dollar circulates freely. Ask if prices you are quoted or read on signs are in U.S. or EC dollars.

Great shore excursions: A panoramic drive including Nelson's Dockyard is $39. The Jolly Roger Cruise ($38) is a relaxing, fun-loving West Indian party with the ship anchored in a lovely cove for swimming, beachcombing -and get ready and start limbering up as there's a limbo contest with a bottle of Antiguan rum going to the winner! If you are looking for a quintessential Caribbean beach experience this tour will not disappoint.

Ideal for independents: The duty-free shopping near the docks at Heritage Quay and Redcliffe Quay. Fares for taxi tours will run you approximately $20 per hour for up to four participants.

ARUBA - About the port: Cleanliness, friendliness and Dutch-style architecture in ice cream colors welcome you to Oranjestad, Aruba's capital. The charms of this Dutch island are many: great ribbons of sand next to aquamarine seas, particularly Palm Beach; divi divi trees bent by the trade winds and always pointing towards the leeward coast; good shopping in a range of malls and shaded walkways extending from L.G. Smith Boulevard (including Dutch Delft pottery) -not to mention that because it is situated below the hurricane belt, it gets minimal rainfall (less than 30 inches a year).

Language: Dutch and Papiamento, but English is widely spoken.

Money matters: They will take your dollars everywhere.

Great Shore Excursions: The Atlantis submarine takes you for a 50 min. dive for $79.

Cruising Regions

An off-road safari drive (bumpy in places) is a caravan-style excursion to see the sights including the 100-foot-long Natural Bridge ($95). A town and countryside drive is $32. Plus your choice of an assortment of boat trips, snorkeling/diving programs.

Ideal for independents: There is a wharf-side market with stalls that provide a feast of colors near the harbor. Shop in the boutiques of the Seaport Marketplace and then relax in the shade in adjacent Queen Wilhelmina Park. Take a taxi to one of the beach resorts (approximately $10-$15).

> Independents can rent a car in most of the islands in the $40-$70 range per day, with specials for lower rates often available on weekends and in the off-season. Driving on some islands is on the left, and some roads may be over mountainous terrain—always ask about local regulations and road conditions on the route you plan to take before you set off.

BARBADOS

About the port: As sweet as the local honey, British-influenced Barbados follows the civilized custom of afternoon tea (try it with a bit of the island's honey). Bajans, as the locals are called, are courteous and friendly and love cricket. And the island has still other great attractions—from intriguing caves to coves to shops in Bridgetown, the capital.

Language: English.

Money matters: The Barbados dollar, but the U.S. dollar is accepted at most stores.

Great shore excursions: A Harrison's Cave (an incredible cave with stalagtites, stalagmites and underground lake) and Flower Forest tour ($56) combines two of the most popular attractions on the island. A Best of Barbados and Heritage Rum Distillery Tour is $39. A Mountain Biking adventure is $59; a horseback riding tour runs $84.

Ideal for independents: Take a taxi to the Francia Plantation ($20) an example of a "Great House" and see its collection of old maps and antiques and chat with the residents, who are descendants of the original owners. Admission is $4.

BRITISH VIRGINS - About the port: The British Virgins, a yachtsman's paradise, are laid-back and secluded when compared to the U.S. Virgin Islands. The largest of the group is Tortola; the biggest attraction is The Baths at Virgin Gorda. Ships bring passengers ashore on launches.

Language: English.

Money matters: The U.S. dollar is the official currency (even though these are the British Virgin Islands).

Great shore excursions: A Full Day To Virgin Gorda And The Baths, where you can swim and relax in this scenic enclave of turquoise waters, picturesque boulders and grottoes ("This is heaven," a passenger once exclaimed), costs $78 from Tortola and includes lunch (bring your camera!). A Sage Mountain And Botanical Gardens program taking in the rainforest at Sage Mountain is $29.

Ideal for independents: Walk over to Road Town, the capital of Tortola, from the launch pier to browse for British goods in its shops. If you dare, sample the potent rum drinks at Pusser's Road Town Pub.

COZUMEL - About the port: A staple on seven-day Western Caribbean cruises, this tiny island off the Yucatan Peninsula was considered the ancient Mayans' Eden, from where their legends tell they went on to populate the mainland. Modern tourists also think it is paradise.

Language: Spanish; English spoken in shops, restaurants and other tourist places.

Money matters: The currency is the peso, but the U.S. dollar circulates freely.

Great shore excursions: Chichen Itza by plane takes participants on a 45-minute flight to the great Mayan city of Chichen Itza ($250-plus) founded in 445 A.D. and mysteriously abandoned two centuries later. Participants get to see panoramic views of the city from the air, then explore the site which is dominated by the Temple of Kukulcan pyramid and contains a Ceremonial Ball Court, Observatory (the Mayans were great astronomers) and numerous other structures. The tour generally includes boxed lunches and beverages—we picnicked within sight of the pyramid! Wear lightweight, loose clothing; and bring bottled water, a hat and suntan lotion, as the heat can be intense. Tours to the seaside Mayan ruins in Tulum on the Yucatan ($75-plus); and to the less imposing San Gervasio Mayan ruins on

Cruising Regions

Cozumel ($40-plus) are also offered, plus boat tours, folkloric shows and snorkeling/diving adventures to world-famous Palancar Reef.

Ideal for independents: Walk around the town of San Miguel where you will find lots of shops and restaurants. Take a taxi to the island's beaches or Chankanaab Lagoon, a natural aquarium ($8).

CURACAO

About the port: Get your camera ready as your ship arrives in Willemstad, the capital of Curacao—the entrance is one of the most picturesque in the Caribbean with Dutch-style gabled houses in sorbet colors and red-tile roofs flanking the port channel. Our entrance was made even more impressive by several friendly people waving their arms (their whole arms, not just polite hand waves) as a warm welcome to our ship. Another not-to-be-missed treat here is the island's orange-flavored liqueur.

Language: Dutch, but English is widely spoken.

Money matters: Dollars are accepted most everywhere.

Great shore excursions: A tour to the Hato Caves (a collection of grottoes with stalagtites, stalagmites, pools and petroglyphs) and the Liqueur Factory (where your taste buds can become acquainted with the local liqueur made from orange peels) costs $41. An Ostrich Encounter and Island Experience takes you to an ostrich farm and the Curacao Herb Gardens for $42. A canoe safari is $62, and an array of city tours including a tourist trolley, snorkeling/diving and boat excursions is offered.

Ideal for independents: Curacao is easy to tour on foot. Conduct your own walking tour, enjoying the Queen Emma Pontoon Bridge and the nearby floating market filled with schooners selling fish, fruits and vegetables from Venezuela, as well as the crafts market across the street.

> Most ships have Sail-Away Parties upon departure from Caribbean ports and everyone goes up on deck to enjoy steel band music and tropical drinks in the fresh breezes. Folks, it just does not get much better than this!

DOMINICA

-About the port: Calling all birdwatchers and nature lovers! Eco-tourism, not development is king here, as this is an unspoiled island where Mother Nature reigns supreme. The capital is Roseau—where most ships that visit these waters call-and the island has lush rainforests, rare bird life and a Carib Reservation, where Carib Indians, who along with the Arawaks were the island's original inhabitants, live. Portsmouth, where some ships call, is convenient due to its proximity to Cabrits National Park.

Language: English.

Money matters: The Eastern Caribbean dollar is the currency, but U.S. dollars are widely accepted.

Great shore excursions: Nature tours exploring the island's national parks run about $40.

Ideal for independents: From Roseau you can walk to the Old Market Square, in olden days the site of slave auctions, and behind it, the Public Market Place by the Roseau River, a bustling market on Saturday mornings. The Dominica Museum, also within walking distance, chronicles the island's history (admission is $2).

DOMINICAN REPUBLIC

-About the port: Ships call at Santo Domingo, the capital, rich in history (the New World's first capital and Columbus' own beloved city), and at Catalina Island for the world-famous resort of Casa de Campo.

Language: Spanish.

Money matters: Currency is the peso, but U.S. dollars are widely accepted.

Great shore excursions: From Catalina Island, you can join tours to Casa de Campo to enjoy horseback riding ($72); horseback riding and kayaking ($135) and golf at the famous Teeth of the Dog course ($250); a tour to Altos de Chavon Village and Folk Show is $46; or join a full-day tour (with lunch) to Santo Domingo for $99. If your ship calls at Santo Domingo, you can take advantage of walking tours of the historic Old Town (cost is approximately $25).

Ideal for independents: Cabs from the pier in Santo Domingo to the Old Town run about $10 -you can visit the Cathedral dating back to 1514 where it is claimed that Columbus is buried (Seville, Spain makes the same claim).

Cruising Regions

FREEPORT - About the port: Freeport/Lucaya is the port of call on Grand Bahama Island, only 60 miles from the U.S. coast.

Language: English.

Money maters: The Bahamian dollar, but the U.S. dollar, of equal value, circulates freely.

Great shore excursions: Tours to the International Bazaar and the Garden of the Groves run about $25 -but you can easily cover both on your own.

Ideal for independents: A taxi to the International Bazaar on East Mall Drive and East Sunrise Highway, where you will find 100 shops and a Straw Market, costs approximately $10. Taxis are metered. Botanical garden lovers may wish to check out The Garden of the Groves (Midshipman Road and Magellan Drive) an 11-acre enclave with waterfalls, flowering plants and trees. Admission is $9.95.

GRAND CAYMAN -About the port: Often referred to as the "Switzerland of the Caribbean" George Town, the capital of Grand Cayman, has more than 500 banks. Nearby Seven Mile Beach is a tropical paradise where you can count 10 or so shades of blue in the generally calm waters on any given day. This is a tender port -ships bring their passengers ashore on launches.

Language: English.

Money matters: The U.S. dollar circulates freely.

Great shore excursions: Tours to Stingray City (with snorkeling, $30; and in combination with an island tour that makes a stop at the eerie rock formations of Hell where you can get your postcards postmarked from "Hell," $55) are one of the Caribbean's most memorable adventures (the stingray encounter, that is). In shallow waters on Grand Cayman's North Shore, dozens of stingrays (who have been fed for years by the locals) come up to the visitors who can feed them (it felt like a vacuum cleaner sucking off the food on my extended hand) and even pet them as they brush past their legs. Just watch where you are going, so as not to step on a stingray—that would be a real no-no. Other shore excursions include the Atlantis Submarine ($79), island tour with visits to the Turtle Farm, Seven Mile Beach and Hell ($40) and a variety of party boats, snorkeling/diving tours.

105

Ideal for independents: Arrange for a tour of the island and afterwards have the driver drop you off at the Hyatt Regency Grand Cayman on Seven Mile Beach for some R&R of the best kind on its sugar sands and balmy waters. An island tour for four costs approximately $40 an hour.

> Sunrise...sunset! How memorable it is to enjoy them both during your cruise! Toast a sunset on a day at sea at least once -perhaps out on deck while watching the ship's wake. A good time to enjoy a sunrise is the last morning of the cruise when you have to get up early anyway to get ready to disembark.

GRENADA
-About the port: The "Spice Island" of Grenada (you can pick up inexpensive packages or baskets of nutmeg, cinnamon, cloves and other dried spices to take back home as souvenirs) has one of the Caribbean most scenic ports, St. Georges—be on deck, camera in hand, for your arrival, to snap some pictures of the pretty pastel buildings and brightly-colored boats tied up in the Carenage. History buffs will remember the 1983 U.S. invasion of Grenada.

Language: English.

Money matters: Currency is the Eastern Caribbean dollar, but the U.S. dollar is welcome everywhere.

Great shore excursions: The island tour hitting the highlights, including beautiful Grand Anse Beach (a frequent entry in Top 10 Beaches lists) runs about $30. Glass-bottom boat/snorkeling trips are $30-$40.

Ideal for independents: There is an incredible stretch of palm-dotted white sand beach with your name on it! Grab a towel and head, via water taxi ($4), to Grand Anse Beach to claim your day in paradise.

GUADELOUPE
- About the port: French Guadeloupe, less visited than also French Martinique, is comprised of two islands that give it a distinct butterfly shape: Basse-Terre, where the capital Pointe-A-Pitre, where ships call is located, and Grande-Terre.

Language: French—Some English is spoken in the shops.

Money matters: U.S. dollars are accepted.

Great shore excursions: Island tours run about $30.

Ideal for independents: The center of Pointe-a-Pitre is adjacent to the pier, so you can browse in the shops, and enjoy the local flavors at one of the restaurants.

KEY WEST

-About the port: What can I say, you'll simply love Key West. Ninety miles from Cuba, the "Last Key" in the Florida chain is friendly, accessible and filled with attractions.

Language: English.

Money matters: Since Key West is in the U.S., the currency is, of course, the U.S. dollar.

Great shore excursions: A Boat and Kayak Eco-Adventure in the rich waters of Florida Bay costs $59.

Ideal for independents: Key West is an independent traveler's dream. You can walk from the pier to the Hemingway House (907 Whitehead Street; admission is $8), where the Nobel laureate penned many of his acclaimed novels including **Death in the Afternoon, For Whom The Bell Tolls, The Snows of Kilimanjaro**; the Mel Fisher Maritime Museum, 200 Greene Street ($6.50), where the famous treasure hunter set up his treasures recovered from sunken Spanish galleons; enjoy the shops and watering holes on Duval Street, including Sloppy Joe's, one of Hemingway's favorites at 201 Duval Street; visit Harry Truman's Little White House (111 Front Street; $7.50); take in the exhibits at the Audubon House (205 Whitehead Street; $6), among other attractions. The Old Town Trolley ($18) is a good way to hit the attractions with on-and-off privileges all day. If your ship stays in port past sunset, take in the carnival-like ambience of the Sunset Celebration at Mallory Square.

MARTINIQUE

-About the port: Can't afford to go to France this year? Think again. When you come to Martinique, you are in France—it is a "departement" of France-there are gendarmes on the streets and French perfumes and Lalique crystal in the shops of Fort-de-France, the capital. Known as the "Isle of Flowers," Martinique has exuberant blooms including anthuriums, bougainvillea, royal Poinciana, and hibiscus as well as lush foliage.

Other points of interest include gray-sand beaches and a volcano, Mt. Pelee, which erupted in 1902 killing 30,000 people.

Language: French. Some English is spoken in the tourist areas.

Money matters: The U.S. dollar is accepted.

Great shore excursions: A Tour to St. Pierre, the town destroyed by the eruption of Mt. Pelee, includes a visit to the Musee Volcanologique that chronicles the disaster with exhibits and artifacts (I found this small museum very moving), and is $59.

Ideal for independents: Spend some time shopping—c'est magnifique! Visit La Savane park, with its pretty gardens adjacent to the International Pier in Fort-de-France (your ship may be docked there or at the main harbor, a short cab ride from the center of Fort-de-France). Also worthwhile is the Musee Departemental de la Martinique, 9 rue de la Liberte, with exhibitions about the island's history. Admission is $3.30. Other island highlights include the church of Balata (inspired in Paris' Sacre Coeur Church in Montmartre); Trois-Ilets, birthplace of Josephine, wife of Napoleon and empress of France, and La Pagerie, where a museum is dedicated to her.

NASSAU

-About the port: Nassau, on New Providence Island, is the British colonial-flavored capital of the Bahamian archipelago of 700 islands. A visit here can be a day at the beach: the surrounding waters are drop-dead gorgeous, particularly on Paradise Island across from Nassau.

Language: English.

Money matters: The currency is the Bahamian dollar, but U.S. dollars circulate freely.

Great shore excursions: An America's Cup Challenge program on a racing yacht costs $89; a Harbor Cruise and Discover Atlantis Golf Package is $56; a Stingray Snorkel and Beach Break where you encounter southern Atlantic stingrays is $42; a Dolphin Encounter is $94 (where you can go for a swim with the dolphins, but the dolphins are captive, which may turn some people off, including me).

Ideal for independents: This is a perfect set-up for independent sightseeing. A short walk from the pier is Rawson Square, the city's focal point, and the Straw Market with every imaginable item from bedroom slippers to dolls made of straw, as well as the shops of Bay Street. Take a horse-drawn carriage to see the sights to a clip-clop tune (about $10 per person; always check on the rate before you get on the carriage). For about $25 an hour you can get a taxi tour of the highlights including the Queen's Staircase, 66 steps carved out of limestone in honor of Queen Victoria, and Fort Fincastle, built by the British in the 18th century. Take a taxi or water taxi to the beaches of Paradise Island ($2) where the mega-resort Atlantis is located.

OCHO RIOS

-About the port: Want to go to Jamaica? No problem, mon! Your vessel will probably take you to Ocho Rios. This port on Jamaica's Northern Shore is where most cruise ships dock. Enjoy a visit to what could arguably be called the Caribbean's quintessential cascade, breathtakingly beautiful Dunn's River Falls.

Language: English.

Money matters: The Jamaican dollar, but they will take your U.S. dollars everywhere. Always ask about prices that may be in Jamaican dollars.

Great shore excursions: A tour to Dunn's River Falls, a 600-ft. cascading waterfall in a lush tropical setting, is a must. You can climb the falls with the help of a local guide (he and the participants hold hands to make a chain as they ascend). The guide will also snap a photo of you for posterity. Bring your bathing suit and rubber-soled shoes and be prepared to slip a few times to the choruses of laughter of the other climbers. No matter, your reward will be getting soaked in the fresh, babbling waters—how cool is that? This tour usually also includes island highlights like Fern Gully rainforest and the Shaw Park Botanical Gardens (approximately $35). Tours also combine Dunn's River Falls with Brimmer Hall Plantation (a real working plantation) for $56; or with the Prospect Hall Plantation Great House for $45. The Rose Hall Great House tour (reputedly the largest Great House in the Caribbean and former home of the "witch" Annie Palmer) costs $59 and includes a beach stop and buffet lunch. I would pass on the River Rafting on the Martha Brae tour ($49). The last time I did it, the mosquitoes were ferocious and people approached us to sell us drugs.

Ideal for independents: The Ocean Village Shopping Centre is a mile's walk from the pier at Ocho Rios. On your way there and back, you may be accosted by people offering to give you "a braid" (do your hair in cornrow braids) and by insistent vendors.

> If you have shopping on your mind, choose a cruise that takes you to St. Thomas in the U.S. Virgin Islands, the undisputed Caribbean queen of shops.

St. Barts
- About the port: This tropical hideaway's real name is St. Barthelemy. Favorite pastimes include bathing in its more than a dozen beautiful coves and shopping for French perfume and designer labels in Gustavia, where ships anchor and disembark passengers via launches.

Language: French, but English is spoken in shops and tourist places.

Money matters: The U.S. dollar is accepted.

Great shore excursions: Island tours visiting some of the island's villages and beaches runs about $25.

Ideal for independents: The shops of Gustavia are a short walk from the tender pier. Or spend your day at the beach perhaps at the Baie of St. Jean, where you can enjoy water sports or at secluded Marigot (note you may encounter topless sunbathing on St. Bart's beaches and coves). Taxis are cheap and plentiful.

ST. CROIX
-About the port: More sedate than St. Thomas, this U.S. Virgin Island boasts beautiful beaches and nearby Buck Island, an underwater wonderland with marked trails maintained by the National Park Service. Only small ships can dock at Christiansted, the capital, where shopping is a highlight; most ships dock at Frederiksted, a small town 17 miles from Christiansted.

Language: English

Money matters: Currency is the U.S. dollar.

Great shore excursions: Buck Island National Park Snorkeling is $59 including complimentary sodas. A Cruzan Rum Factory and Botanical Garden program costs $36 and includes a complimentary rum beverage. A Carambola Golf Course Package runs $90-$120. There is also an array of boat trips, snorkeling/scuba programs, and tours to Great Houses.

Ideal for independents: Air conditioned buses take passengers from Frederiksted to Christiansted (fare is $1). Taxis will charge about $20 (negotiate the fare before you get on, as cabs are un-metered). Once in Christiansted you can explore on foot -spend some time at Fort Christiansvaern, maintained by the National Park Service.

ST. KITTS -About the port: Laid-back Basseterre, where the ships call, is highlighted by the Brimstone Hill Fortress, a 300-year-old fort on a 40-acre hill 780 feet above sea level. Its first cannons were mounted in 1690 while the French and the British fought for St. Kitts. The next two centuries saw the completion of the structure, among the largest of its type in the New World and often called the "Gibraltar of the West Indies."

Language: English.

Money matters: Currency is the Eastern Caribbean dollar, but the U.S. dollar is accepted.

Great shore excursions: A Brimstone Fortress And Gardens tour costs $39; Beach Horseback Riding is $55; Nature Kayaking is $60.

Ideal for independents: Go for a stroll in Basseterre, enjoying its British colonial architecture, the market and shops. Arrange for an island tour ($55-$60) to explore Brimstone Hill Fortress.

ST. LUCIA -About the port: Lovely, lush St. Lucia, is considered by many visitors the most scenic island in the Caribbean. One of its highlights are the two cone-like green mountains of Gros Piton and Petit Piton that rise straight up more than 2,500 ft. from the indigo sea—our ship cruised by them on a Fourth of July and to mark the holiday, waiters paraded by with complimentary champagne flutes (a fabulous combination). When your ship does scenic cruising in St. Lucia, plan to be on deck and get your camera ready!

Language: English.

Money matters: The Eastern Caribbean dollar, but the U.S. dollar is accepted widely and most shops and restaurants give you prices in U.S. dollars.

Great shore excursions: A Forest And Sulfurous Hiking Adventure is a two-and-half-mile hike near the town of Soufriere with time to luxuriate in a pool of warm sulfuric water, rumored to be good for the skin, costs $69. Land And Sea To Soufriere takes you to see the Pitons and Sulfur Springs, a drive-in volcano where you can see the bubbling pools of lava ($72). A Horseback Adventure is $69.

Ideal for independents: Most ships dock at Castries, which is a short cab ride or walk from the center of town. You can explore Fort Charlotte, within walking distance of the center of town, to see its cannons and the panoramic view of the harbor.

ST. MAARTEN/ST. MARTIN

-About the port: A case of "split personality" island-style! Roughly about one half of this 37-square-mile island is Dutch (St. Maarten), the other French (St. Martin). So when you go shopping here, you can pick up French perfumes and fashions on one side of the island; Dutch Delft pottery and crystal on the other —the Dutch side, by the way, has more shops and casinos; the French side has the best restaurants and art galleries for my taste.

Language: On St. Maarten, Dutch; on St. Martin, French. People in the shops, restaurants and tourist areas speak English.

Money matters: The U.S. dollar is accepted in both the Dutch and French sides of the island.

Great shore excursions: A 12-meter Racing Regatta on an America's Cup yacht will set you back $81 but what a thrill it is! A Pinel Island Snorkeling Tour (excellent snorkeling) costs $36; Shipwreck Cove Snorkeling is $46; a Lagoon Kayaking program is $69. A Beach Rendezvous with lunch at Orient Beach, often called the French Riviera of the Caribbean, costs $49 (note that certain parts of Orient Beach are clothes optional).

Ideal for independents: Your ship will probably dock at Phillipsburg in the Dutch side —most do. You will find a tourist office in the terminal with a supply of brochures and maps. You can take a launch from the new pier to Front Street in Phillipsburg, where you will find a multitude of shops. Or spend the day at Great Bay Beach or Little Bay Beach, both near Phillipsburg. On the French side, the open-air market in the harbor at Marigot is bustling with activity in the mornings, and sidewalk cafes (croissants and café au lait, anyone?) art galleries and shops beckon visitors.

ST. THOMAS/ST. JOHN
-About the port: Often referred to as "the shopping center of the Caribbean," St. Thomas in the U.S. Virgin Islands is a highlight of most typical seven-day Eastern Caribbean cruises. Shops—lots and lots of them—are housed in Danish warehouses with red-tiled roofs, and line the waterfront offering a pirate's booty of goods. When you are done shopping you can cool your tired feet in Magens' Bay Beach (I often do), a heart-shaped idyll that consistently makes Top 10 Beaches of the World lists. Neighboring St. John is an emerald isle two-thirds National Park-kind of a Peter Pan's Never Never Land, with its spectacular Trunk Bay almost a Mermaid's Lagoon.

Language: English.

Money matters: U.S. dollar is the currency.

Great shore excursions: Virgin Islands By Helicopter gives you a bird's eye view of the gorgeous panoramas of St. Thomas and St. John ($97)—our pilot swooped down daringly in places making for a thrilling ride. Kayaking the Marine Sanctuary ($66) offers participants a chance to get close to nature. There is also a wide array of party boat cruises, snorkeling/scuba programs, and a St. John Safari/Snorkeling in Trunk Bay ($48). Island Tours ($34) take you to see sights including The Mountaintop (home of the banana daiquiri) with panoramic views of the island.

Ideal for independents: Shop till you drop, either in town ($4 by cab) or at the Havensight Mall by the cruise ship pier! Go to Coral World Marine Park (next to Coqui Point Beach—great for snorkeling, and there are changing rooms/lockers in the park) to take in its aquariums, touch tanks, and air-conditioned underwater observation tower. Admission is $18 for adults, $9 for kids. The Paradise Point Tramway ($10 adults, $5 for children) takes you from the Havensight Mall to Paradise Point (697-ft. high) for views of Charlotte Amalie, St. Thomas' capital.

SAN JUAN, PUERTO RICO

-About the port: Puerto Rico is a Commonwealth of the U.S. so though it could feel to Americans like a foreign country—we are actually really home. The capital of San Juan offers a varied palette of attractions to visitors beginning with the historic fortress of El Morro Castle built by the Spanish to protect the city against pirate attack -it has impressive cannon galleries and panoramic views of the port (park rangers from the National Park Service give tours inside the fortress).

Language: Spanish, but English is widely spoken.

Money matters: Currency is the U.S. dollar

Great shore excursions: An El Yunque Rainforest Tour, with its jungle-like tropical vegetation, waterfalls and hiking trails is $28; combined with lunch and a dip at Luquillo Beach it is $58. A city tour with Bacardi Rum Distillery (including a complimentary rum drink) costs $26. A San Juan Nightlife Tour visiting a nightclub for a show and drink runs about $38.

Ideal for independents: This is another special set-up for independents, as sweet as the "piraguas" (snow cones with tropical flavors) and the fresh fruits sold by vendors in the streets of Old San Juan. Most cruise ships dock precisely at the edges of Old San Juan (with a tourist office with free maps and brochures at its entrance). This is the city's historic district, dating back from the 16th century, adorned with cobblestones, brought in as ballast by Spanish galleons, and by old-fashioned gas lamps. Spend a half-day checking out its churches (including the Cathedral where Ponce de Leon, of Fountain of Youth fame, is buried), art galleries, shops, restaurants, and feeding the pigeons in its plazas and parks—particularly Pigeons Park (Parque de las Palomas) with its views of the harbor.

More Caribbean Ports

In addition to the variety of ports already described, the Caribbean, like a bottomless pirate's treasure chest, has a seemingly never-ending wealth of islands, each a jewel unto itself. To name a few more: seldom-visited, pastoral Anguilla; Bonaire, sitting pretty atop a coral reef with excellent snorkeling and diving; the exotic San Blas Islands of Panama where the women embroider many-layered, colorful mola cloth in designs suitable for framing (once you buy one, it's like eating potato chips, you can't stop: I wind up with

Cruising Regions

four); unspoiled St. Vincent; Trinidad with superb bird watching, and the Grenadines with a bounty of some 100 islands including the jet-set idyll of Mustique. Enjoy! Enjoy! Enjoy!

Introducing the Alaska Cruise

Aaah, Alaska! It is on most travelers' wish lists for a trip of a lifetime. And it's easy to understand why. Its early inhabitants, the Aleuts used to call it "Alyeska" or "The Great Land"—I like to refer to it as the WOW! (notice, all capitals) Land. Here in this larger-than-life region where beauty reigns in ice-blue glaciers; serrated, snow-capped mountains; unspoiled bays; pristine forests and a rich wildlife, the Creator chose to work, as it were, on a really biiiiig canvas.

Here are just a few superlatives of this natural wonderland from the Alaska Division of Tourism:

* The world's largest marine highway, the Inside Passage, stretches for more than 1,100 miles from Bellingham, Washington to Skagway, Alaska.

* The State of Alaska is one-fifth the size of all the rest of the U.S. put together, with more than 1,400 miles north to south, and 2,400 miles east to west. To put it in everyday life perspective, if everyone in Manhattan moved to Alaska, they would each have 125 acres.

* Alaska has the tallest peak in North America—Mount McKinley, soaring to 20,320 ft. high. And of the 20 highest peaks in the U.S., 17 are in Alaska.

* Alaska has the largest national forest in the country, the Tongass National Forest with more than 16 million acres.

* When it comes to wildlife, the region is unrivaled: it enjoys the highest concentration of brown bears in the world, on Admiralty Island, and the largest gathering of eagles in the world in the Chilkat Bald Eagle Preserve near Haines, with about 4,000 of these majestic birds coming here each winter.

* More than 50 major glaciers, 1,000 islands and 10,000 miles of shorelines are found in Southeast Alaska alone.

Typically, the most popular Alaska cruises are seven-day Inside Passage sailings roundtrip from Vancouver or Seattle, and seven-day Gulf of Alaska or Route of the Glaciers voyages from Vancouver to Seward or vice-versa. The first is often combined with land packages to explore Canada; the second one is usually extended with packages to the interior of Alaska including Denali National Park for wildlife viewing and panoramas of Mt. McKinley.

> A pre- or post-cruise package in Alaska is an excellent idea as its interior is as spectacular as its coast.

Cruise lines that offer Alaska voyages include Alaska's Glacier Bay, American Safari, Carnival, Celebrity, Clipper, Cruise West, Crystal, Holland America, Lindblad, Norwegian, Princess, Radisson Seven Seas, Royal Caribbean.

Tips for Alaska Cruising

* Shipboard life on Alaska cruises is sightseeing-intensive, and with some 18 hours of sunlight you will be able to enjoy the sights well into the night. Like pioneer explorer John Muir you may not be able to tear yourself away from the railing, and when you do, you will probably want to head to the ship's observation lounge—binoculars in hand—to take in the spectacle of enormous chunks of ancient ice breaking off glaciers ("calving") and landing with thunderous claps into the water; pristine forests and snowcapped mountains; and to spot the wildlife: perhaps a harbor seal, floating on an Aqua-Velva-blue iceberg; puffins and other birds; and the grandest sights of all: orcas and humpback whales. During my last Alaska cruise we came across a big pod of orcas in the Inside Passage and whale-watched from the ship for about an hour; and I signed up for a whale-watching excursion out of Juneau, where we encountered a half-dozen humpbacks. What can I say? Magnificent sights!

* Don't forget to pack your camera and plenty of film, the aforementioned binoculars, layers of clothing, comfortable shoes and rain gear in case you run into bad weather.

* Although Alaska's coast is spectacular and its ports frontier-friendly and quaint, plan to take tours that take you to explore the equally dramatic interior, and if your time and budget allow, book a pre- or post-cruise package offered by such lines as Royal Caribbean,

Cruising Regions

Celebrity, Holland America and Princess to explore the wonders beyond the coast such as Denali National Park, where wildlife includes bears, caribou and moose. An example of a popular Alaska land package combined with a seven-night Gulf of Alaska (Glacier Route) cruise on Royal Caribbean (priced from $2,249 with early booking in 2001 brochures, the ones available at this writing) includes two nights in Fairbanks, one night in Talkeetna and one night in Denali National Park. Land travel is via motor coach and on Royal Celebrity Tours' The Wilderness Express Train, superb glass-domed train cars with a la carte fine dining. I took this type of program on Celebrity Cruises in 2001 and found it to be an excellent way to enjoy Alaska's coast and interior.

* Since there are extended sunlight hours, booking a cabin with a window or veranda is a wonderful splurge to enjoy the almost non-stop scenery.

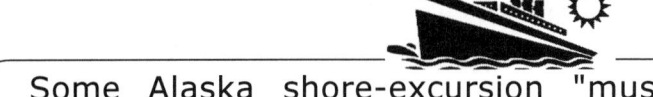

> Some Alaska shore-excursion "musts" include a whale-watching tour, helicopter flightseeing with a walk on a glacier and/or dog sledding, a floatplane trip to Misty Fjords and a salmon bake.

Touring Ideas for Independents at Major Embarcation Cities

VANCOUVER, BRITISH COLUMBIA, CANADA - This is the charming port—surrounded by mountains and water—that most ships depart from on seven-day Inside Passage sailings and seven-day Gulf of Alaska/Route of the Glaciers voyages. Ships usually dock at beautiful, sail-evocative Canada Place near the city's historic heart.

If you have just a few hours: I always go for a walk in quaint Gastown (a short stroll from the pier) with its cobblestone streets and gaslights, a steam clock, shops, cafes, street entertainment and restaurants.

If you have longer: Visit Chinatown to sample Chinese cuisine, browse in its shops and take in the serene Dr. Sun Yat-sen Garden (578 Carral Street, 604-689-7133). Or spend a leisurely afternoon mixing with the locals in the city's playground, Stanley Park, with 1,000 acres of gardens, nature trails, a totem pole park and more, a short drive north of the city. For information on Vancouver, call Tourism British Columbia at 800-663-6000.

SEWARD, ALASKA
-This is the port of embarkation and disembarkation (for Anchorage) for those on seven-day Gulf of Alaska/Route of the Glaciers cruises.

If you have just a few hours: Pick up a walking tour map at one of the tourist information booths (there is one at the pier and another one at the old Alaska Railroad car at the corner of Third Avenue and Jefferson Street). Visit the Alaska SeaLife Center at the waterfront (1000 Rail Way) or take in the Seward Museum, Third Avenue and Jefferson Street.

If you have longer: Go for a boat tour on Resurrection Bay; visit Kenai Fjords National Park (these are the two main attractions in Seward); or take in a dogsled demonstration (I love the dogs!) and ride at Iditarod Dogsled Tours ($39; a cab there is $10) on Old Exit Glacier Road, 800-478-3139. For additional information on Seward and other Alaska ports, contact the Alaska Division of Tourism, P.O. Box 110801, TIA, Juneau, AK 99811-0801; 907-465-2010; www.travelalaska.com.

ANCHORAGE
-Your ship most likely embarks or disembarks you in Seward where most Gulf of Alaska/Route of the Glacier cruises begin or end and transfers you by bus to Anchorage.

If you have just a few hours: Enjoy the art collection and historical exhibits at the Anchorage Museum of History and Art, 121 West Seventh Avenue. Or join a historic tour ($5) given by Alaska Historic Properties June-August (907-274-3600).

If you have longer: Visit the Alaska Native Heritage Center, 8800 Heritage Center Drive (admission: $19.95). And/or get out of town to take in the landscapes and wildlife of the Chugach Mountains and/or Turnagain Arm to Portage Glacier. For information on Anchorage and other Alaska ports contact the Alaska Division of Tourism, P.O. Box 110801, TIA, Juneau, AK 99811-0801; 907-465-2010; www.travelalaska.com.

Cruising Regions

SEATTLE -Small ships were the main users of Seattle as a port of embarkation, until Norwegian Cruise Line based one of its ships there recently.

If you have just a few hours: Head for Pike's Place Market (First Avenue between Pike and Pine Streets) and enjoy its shops, restaurants and art galleries. And take in the 600-ft. Seattle Space Needle, 203 Sixth Avenue, North), the symbol par excellence of Seattle, I spent a half-hour enjoying the panoramic views of the city from its observation deck during my visit. Admission is $9.

If you have longer: Visit the popular Seattle Aquarium, 1483 Alaskan Way, in the Seattle Waterfront ($8) and/or go to the Seattle Art Museum, 100 University Street, to enjoy its collection of native art. For travel information on Seattle, call the Seattle Convention & Visitors Bureau at 206-461-5800.

SAN FRANCISCO -"Why would anyone want to live anywhere else?" our daughter asked after a visit to San Francisco, so impressed was she by its beauty. And small wonder: The City By The Bay, of Golden Gate Bridge, Lombard Street, TransAmerica Pyramid and cable cars fame, is a pretty-as-a-picture place -a marvelous port of embarkation for an Alaska cruise. It is a small jewel of a city, only seven-miles by seven-miles, so you can see a lot of the sights on foot.

If you have just a few hours: Chow down on the chowder at Fisherman's Wharf and shop till you drop at Pier 39, then cross the street and sample the chocolates at Ghirardelli Square. Hop on the Powell & Market Streets cable car for a wheeee! roller-coaster-like ride on the city's hills ($2).

If you have longer: Visit quaint bayside Sausalito (I enjoyed browsing in its shops and art galleries) and take in the majestic redwoods at Muir Woods. For additional information on San Francisco, call the San Francisco Convention & Visitors Bureau at 415-974-6900.

Major Alaska Cruise Ports of Call

JUNEAU, ALASKA -About the port: Alaska's capital, Juneau is the premier port of call because of its multitude of tour/activity options. No roads lead to Juneau, it can be reached only by boat or plane -since it is sandwiched between a backdrop of green mountains and the water.

Language: English.

Money matters: This being Alaska, the U.S. dollar is, of course, the currency.

Great shore excursions: There is a wide array of excursions/activity by land, air and water including sport fishing, Mendenhall Glacier float trips, nature walks, helicopter flightseeing, sea kayaking, and gold panning. Two of the absolute best are the following: a Whale Watching Tour ($99) that takes you to Auke Bay to look for humpback whales (on two occasions we saw several of these awesome creatures diving to reveal their powerful flukes (tails) as gracefully as Spanish dancers flicking their fans and even breaching—jumping clear out of the water. And a Glacier Panorama & Dog Sled Ride by helicopter ($359) is fabulous as well - although admittedly expensive-but it is a once-in-a-lifetime opportunity to combine helicopter flightseeing, a landing on a glacier and a dog sled ride on a glacier (for sure, you will have everyone's attention at the office water cooler when you tell them about this puppy).

Ideal for independents: The pier is within walking distance of the Red Dog Saloon, with its sawdust-strewn floor. The Mt. Roberts Tramway (a pass good all day is $19.75) is conveniently located right at the cruise ship docks. Last time we were there, we spotted a black bear cub from its restaurant window. There are nature trails, shops, a theater and on clear days, great views. For a taste of Alaska, try the Gold Creek Salmon Bake ($28) and all-you-can-eat feast of truly scrumptious honey-glazed salmon, salads, barbecued ribs, baked beans, rice pilaf, corn bread, beverages and blueberry cake. A folk singer entertains and before or after you eat, and you can view the Salmon Creek and waterfall (where in spring salmon spawn). Complimentary buses take you to the Gold Creek Salmon Bake from a stop by the Mt. Roberts Tramway on the docks.

Your ship will sell you tickets to the Mt. Roberts Tramway in Juneau, usually for a dollar or a couple of dollars more than if you just stroll there yourself and buy your own tickets.

Cruising Regions

KETCHIKAN, ALASKA
-About the port: The word Ketchikan is derived from the Indian "Kach Khanna" which means "spread winds of a prostrate eagle." It had its beginnings as an Indian fish saltery and grew to become the largest salmon-canning center in the world. With the 1898 gold rush to the Klondike, Ketchikan became a supply base for miners. Ships usually dock right in town in its beautiful harbor adorned by green mountains and houses on stilts. Totem poles are big here - and Ketchikan claims to be the "totem pole capital of the world." I have found it pays to have an umbrella and/or raincoat here: it has rained all three times I have visited.

Language: English.

Money matters: Currency is the U.S. dollar.

Great shore excursions: A Totem Bight State Park and Town Tour is $31; a trip to the Saxman Native Totem Village to watch master carvers at work costs $45; a Misty Fjords Floatplane Adventure to the 2.3-million-acre Misty Fjords natural wonderland is $195 (our trip was awesome: somehow reminding me of the flightseeing scene in the film *Out of Africa*); an Alaska Bear Watch to Neets Creek via floatplane is $247.

Ideal for independents: The Southeast Alaska Visitors Center (50 Main Street, a block from the cruise ship pier) has exhibits depicting the local history and Indian life. Dolly's House on Creek's Street, a brothel until the 1950s is now a museum (admission is $4).

SITKA, ALASKA
-About the port: Situated on Baranoff Island, Sitka was once the capital of Russian America and served as headquarters for the Russian-American Company's fur and other trade operations. Its Russian roots are evident in the onion-domed St. Michael's Russian Orthodox Cathedral and the New Archangel Russian dance troupe (an all-woman group, because the men would not join them when they began the company, and later, once the women were established and the men came knocking, the ladies would not welcome them in anymore). Sitka's combination of Russian history and native culture make it a fascinating port of call. Most ships bring passengers ashore on launches.

Language: English.

Fell's Official Know-It-All: Cruises

Money matters: Currency is the U.S. dollar.

Great shore excursions: Sport fishing is $172; a Sea Kayaking Adventure is $94; a Sea-Life Discovery Semi-Submersible is $75; a Sea Otter Wildlife Quest runs $104; a Bike And Hike Adventure is $65; a Silvery Bay Cruise & Salmon Hatchery Tour costs $39; a Sitka Historical Tour runs $34 and stops at St. Michael's Russian Orthodox Cathedral.

Ideal for independents: Pick up a free map and brochures at the Sitka Convention & Visitors Bureau at the dock in the Centennial Building and walk, take a free shuttle, or a short cab ride to town from the dock. Visit St. Michael Russian Orthodox Cathedral -which was rebuilt in 1966 after a fire. Take in a performance of the New Archangel Dancers at the Centennial Building ($6). Shop for the ubiquitous, cute Russian nesting dolls.

> A variety of pre- or post-cruise (on Gulf of Alaska/Route of the Glaciers voyages) feature a visit to Denali National Park on game-spotting bus tours. If you spot bear, moose, caribou, Dall's sheep, and the "mountain is out" (meaning Mt. McKinley is visible) it's called a "grand slam." We did, and it was truly an incredible, unforgettable day.

SKAGWAY, ALASKA

-About the port: Skagway was born as a jumping off point for prospectors during the Gold Rush days of 1898. Some 100,000 gold-crazed adventurers passed through here leaving in their wake a colorful town with wooden sidewalks, beer halls and brothels.

Language: English.

Money matters: Currency is the U.S. dollar.

Great shore excursions: The priest who said Sunday Mass on our latest voyage recommended The White Pass Scenic Railway ($93) to the congregation (!). And no wonder, most in the congregation were saying "Amen" after going on this narrow-gauge railroad that takes visitors on a scenic ride past such landmarks as Bridal Veil Falls, Inspiration Point and Dead Horse Gulch. A Klondike Bicycle Tour is $80; Chilkoot Horseback Riding

Cruising Regions

is $124; a Haines Wilderness Kayak Adventure & Cruise costs $154.

Ideal for independents: Pick up a free walking tour map at the Skagway Convention & Visitors Bureau (Broadway and Fifth Avenue) and stop for a libation at the Red Onion Saloon (Broadway and Second Avenue, formerly a saloon/brothel) both within walking distance of the pier.

> Skip the ship's Skagway city tour (generally about $30) as the park rangers in the Klondike Gold Rush National Historic Park (which encompasses most of the town) give free guided walking tours.

VICTORIA, BRITISH COLUMBIA, CANADA

-About the port: Pretty as a picture, with flowers everywhere, Victoria is a charming port on Alaska cruises departing from Seattle and San Francisco. If you love flowers, don't leave without visiting beautiful, 130-acre Butchart Gardens.

Language: English.

Money matters: Currency is the Canadian dollar (CAN$1 = .63 U.S., at this writing—this fluctuates, of course). The U.S. dollar is accepted in some stores.

Great shore excursions: A City Tour With Butchart Gardens with its formal English, Italian, Japanese and other gardens costs about $70. A City Tour with High Tea costs $70-$75.

Ideal for independents: Take a shuttle from Ogden Point, where cruise ships dock, to the Inner Harbor and from there you can, buy an ice cream cone (like we did) and walk around this pretty town and/or stop for tea at the opulent Empress Hotel.

> Plan to be out on deck most of the day if your ship takes you to Glacier Bay, the highlight of an Alaska voyage with 18 ice-blue glaciers including the impressive Margerie and Johns Hopkins Glaciers, so you can experience glacier "calvings" with big chunks of ice breaking off the face of the glacier. Other highlights: puffins and other birds (there are 430 species in Alaska).

Other Cruising Regions

Well, let's see, we still have lots of other segments of that juicy mandarin orange which is the world and its cruising regions. Here are some other popular ones:

Panama Canal Cruises

Considered by many the Eighth Wonder of the World, the Panama Canal is a marvel of engineering. Most passengers are up on deck, in the ship's observation lounge (or in their own private verandas if they are lucky to have them) since dawn's early light and many stay riveted in their positions for most of the nine hour or so Panama Canal transit as the ship negotiates a series of elevator-like locks (whose sides are so close to the ship it seems you can reach out and touch them). The vessel is raised 85 feet from sea level in the locks and then lowered back to sea level again.

The Panama Canal transit seasons are in the spring and fall as the cruise lines reposition their ships from the Caribbean to Alaska (spring) and from Alaska to the Caribbean (fall). The Canal is also featured in some Caribbean itineraries in the winter. Ports of call on Panama Canal voyages include Caribbean islands like Aruba, Curacao, and the San Blas Islands; Central American countries such as Costa Rica (an eco-tourist's delight) and Nicaragua; and Mexican Riviera enclaves such as Acapulco.

LINES THAT CRUISE IN THIS REGION: American Canadian Caribbean, Carnival, Celebrity, Clipper, Crystal, Cunard, Holland America, Lindblad, Norwegian, Orient, Princess, Radisson Seven Seas, Regal, Royal Caribbean, Royal Olympic, Seabourn, Silversea and Windstar.

MAGICAL, MEMORABLE MOMENTS: Experiencing dawn on one ocean and the same day's sunset on another. What a neat trick! Quick, pass me a pina colada for a toast!

Cruising Regions

> Most cruise lines will give you maps of port cities including sites of major attractions and shops as well as practical information including currency details. One of the best is Royal Caribbean International, a line that gives you pocket-sized "port explorers" at each call.

Mexican Riviera Voyages

Fun-loving, laid-back, absolutely gorgeous, the Mexican Riviera is one of the Pacific's most popular playgrounds. Chic resorts like Puerto Vallarta and Acapulco, quaint fishing villages like Zihuatanejo, excursions from Mazatlan to colonial towns with cathedrals, shrines and handicrafts markets are all part of its allure—the rest is the fabulous beaches with all manner of water sports. You can visit on three—to seven-day cruises from Los Angeles year-round; longer cruises depart from San Diego in the winter, and Panama Canal voyages also include this corner of the world.

LINES THAT CRUISE IN THIS REGION: Carnival, Celebrity, Cunard, Crystal, Holland America, Norwegian, Orient, Princess, Radisson Seven Seas, Royal Caribbean, Seabourn and Silversea.

MAGICAL, MEMORABLE MOMENTS: The entrance into the port of Acapulco, always ranked among the three most beautiful harbors in the world (the other two being Rio de Janeiro and Hong Kong). At dawn, with music still floating in the air from waterfront clubs, and lights still on, shimmering like diamond necklaces, in the buildings is a never-to-be-forgotten experience. So is watching the world-famous cliff divers of La Quebrada in Acapulco (literally breathtaking). And so is sailing, happy as a clam, with something cool and bubbly in your glass, past Los Arcos (the much-photographed natural arch rock formation) in Cabo San Lucas.

> The U.S. dollar is widely accepted in Caribbean, Mexican, Panama Canal ports, but it isn't in Europe and other cruising regions. Many ships offer a bank/money exchange service while on European cruises and voyages in other corners of the world where you need to exchange your dollars for the local currency or, alternatively, they direct you to the nearest currency exchange offices ashore. Prior to the cruise, exchange dollars at home for enough of the embarkation port's currency to get you going (taxis, tips). At the ports of call, to obtain the best exchange rates, use credit cards whenever possible.

Mediterranean Cruises

Cradle of civilizations and religions, the Mediterranean beckoned to Homer's Odysseus in antiquity and it beguiles modern cruise passengers with as many charms as there are fish in the sea. A Med cruise -seven- and 14-night long voyages are popular—can take you to:

THE FRENCH RIVIERA -A jet-set playground, France's Cote d'Azur, with its magnificent golden light, cobalt-blue sea and dramatic mountains has inspired the likes of Matisse, Picasso, Renoir and Cocteau. Ports of call here include Nice with its bayfront Promenade des Anglais and colorful Flower Market; Cannes, of Film Festival fame, with its oceanfront La Croisette filled with designer boutiques; Monte Carlo, with its elegant casino and reminders of American film actress Grace Kelly, including a lovely rose garden and her tomb in the Cathedral where she wed Prince Rainier; and Villefranche sur Mer, with its incredible bay and frescoes by Jean Cocteau in the Chapelle St. Pierre.

ITALY AND THE ITALIAN RIVIERA -Just as beautiful as the French Riviera, with a tad warmer colors, the Italian Riviera welcomes passengers to tiny, jewel-like Portofino, with its pretty gold, rose, and ochre buildings (with green shutters that when opened look like the wings of birds in flight) hugging the bay and cobblestone piazza with cafes and shops. Other unforgettable spots in this region include Portovenere, a

Cruising Regions

charming Cinque Terre village, and poetic Sorrento (from where you can take the breathtaking drive to Positano and Amalfi) or a hydrofoil to Capri to explore the famous Blue Grotto.

If your ship calls at Livorno you can take all-day tours to the cradle of the Renaissance, Florence, where you can feast your eyes on Michelangelo's **David** in the Accademia and works by Leonardo da Vinci and other great masters in the Uffizi. Tours to Pisa, where the famous leaning tower was re-opened to the public in December of 2001 after a decade of restoration, are another option from Livorno. Some tours combine a brief stop at Pisa with Florence.

Other Italian must-sees include (if they are not on your itinerary this time, you have a great reason to return!): Venice, where St. Mark's Square, which Napoleon referred to as Europe's "drawing room" is a once-in-a-lifetime sight with St. Mark's Basilica, the Doge's Palace and romantic sidewalk cafes. Rome (port of Civitavecchia) with the glories of St. Peter's Basilica and the Vatican Museum including Michelangelo's Pieta and Sistine Chapel ceiling (I remember thinking the figures seemed to pop out of the paintings when I first saw the Sistine Chapel ceiling); the Colosseum, the Trevi Fountain and the Spanish Steps, to mention just a few of the attractions in the Eternal City. Sicily, with its ports of Palermo, Catania and Messina (for tours to Taormina where you will be able to visit a Third Century Greek Amphitheater with views of Mt. Etna) is another of Italy's multitude of treats for cruise passengers.

> Festivals and other special events add cultural insights to a European cruise. For a calendar of events and information on European countries, go to www.VisitEurope.com or write to The European Travel Commission, Donald N. Martin & Co, One Rockefeller Plaza, N.Y., N.Y. 10020.

ATHENS AND THE GREEK ISLES
If your ship calls or sails from Piraeus, the port for Athens, "musts" on your list will, of course, be the Parthenon on the city's Acropolis, the National Archaeological Museum, and the Plaka section of shops and cafes. When it comes to the Greek Isles, sailing into the volcano's sunken caldera in Santorini

(the result of an eruption in 1450 B.C. which many associate with the Lost Continent of Atlantis) is one of cruising's greatest moments. The water is a sapphire blue and, from a distance, the town's white buildings look like snow on the tops of the cliffs. From the pier at Skala Fira, you can ascend to Fira, the main town, 890 ft. above at the top of the cliff, via donkey (the romantics' way), via the cable car, or on foot via 587 steps. While in Santorini, spend the morning exploring Oia at the northern tip of the island (where the blue-domed church you see on so many posters and postcards of Santorini is located) and take a boat to the volcano's hot springs, where you can luxuriate in bathtub warm waters and put mineral-rich mud from the springs' bottom on your skin (the best facial I ever got!). Another option in Santorini is a tour of the excavations at ancient Akrotiri, a Minoan town buried in volcanic ash until recently. Other Greek Isles idylls include Mykonos (a photogenic island with windmills, a section called Little Venice, and, like Santorini, the greatest sunsets); Crete, where you can visit the restored Minoan Palace of Knossos associated with the legend of the Minotaur; and Rhodes, where the Colossus of Rhodes, one of the Seven Wonders of the World once stood, and where you can time-travel back to the Middle Ages in its Old Town with its cobblestone Street of the Knights.

SPAIN/PORTUGAL -
Ports in the Iberian Peninsula include Barcelona, Spain, where highlights are the pedestrian walkway of Las Ramblas, filled with shops and cafes, and Antoni Gaudi's unconventional Sagrada Familia Church; Malaga in the Costa del Sol, for tours of the white mountain village of Mijas and of the fabled Moorish palace of the Alhambra; and Cadiz, for tours of Seville, the queen of Andalusia, where the air is perfumed with orange blossoms in the spring, and where attractions include the 15th Century Cathedral with its Giralda Tower. In Portugal, Lisbon is the starting/ending point for many Mediterranean voyages. Like a fine lady with a past, Lisbon sits elegantly at the edge of the Tagus boasting such charms as the Jeronimos Monastery; the Belem Tower in honor of Portuguese seafaring prowess; and Castelo Sao Jorge, a fortress pre-dating Roman times, and built upon by the Moors. The Alfama neighborhood, is the oldest quarter of the city, a colorful area where every June 12-13 the feast of St. Anthony is celebrated with food, drink

Cruising Regions

and dancing and locals decorate with streamers and lanterns. Excursions include a trip to Fatima, as beloved a Marian Catholic shrine as Lourdes is in France; and a visit to Sintra, a summer hideaway for Portuguese royalty.

TURKEY - In addition to Istanbul, where the points of interest include the Blue Mosque, St. Sophia, the Grand Bazaar and Topkapi Palace (the residence of Ottoman sultans), Turkish ports of call on Mediterranean cruises include Kusadasi for tours to ancient Ephesus (with its amphitheater, Celsus library, mile-long marble street where you can still see the tracks of chariots of old) and the House of the Virgin Mary, where it is believed that Mary, the mother of Jesus, spent her last years.

Holy Land/Egypt

Back in 1922, British archaeologist Howard Carter, first peered into a hole on the wall of the tomb of Tutankhamon at Luxor, Egypt. When his assistants asked if he could see anything, he replied: "Yes, wonderful things."

Such is a cruise to Egypt and the Holy Land where visitors can explore the Pyramids at Giza, the Sphinx, the Nile, Jerusalem's Old City, Bethlehem's Church of the Nativity, the Wailing Wall and other marvels—and after a day of exploring in this exotic corner of the planet, return to their safe and comfortable home base aboard ship. Frequent unrest in this part of the world often forces cancellations of voyages. But if you are lucky that your trip plans coincide with a relatively peaceful period in this troubled corner, you will realize that on this itinerary wonders never cease.

LINES THAT CRUISE IN THIS REGION: Celebrity, Clipper, Costa, Crystal, Cunard, First European, Lindblad, Norwegian, Orient, Princess, Radisson Seven Seas, Royal Caribbean, Royal Olympic, Seabourn, Silversea, Star Clippers, Windstar.

MAGICAL, MEMORABLE MOMENTS: Tossing three coins in the Trevi Fountain in Rome. Sitting at a café while munching on a Greek salad on the lip of the caldera in Santorini. Taking an evening gondola ride in Venice's Grand Canal. Posing for photos in

129

the Court of the Lions at the Alhambra in Spain. Enjoying a gelato in a waterfront café in Portofino. Hearing a visiting choir sing carols in Bethlehem's Church of the Nativity. Going for a camel ride at the Pyramids in Giza and photographing the Sphinx with the backdrop of a pink and violet sunset. Helicopter flightseeing in dazzling Monaco and the French Riviera.

> Mixing with the locals at their houses of worship and shrines can be not only enlightening, but moving as well, as in Fatima, outside Lisbon where the faithful come every day (many approaching the basilica on their knees and big throngs making pilgrimages May 12-13 and Oct. 12-13) to this spot where three shepherd children reported visions of the Virgin Mary in 1917.

Northern Europe Cruises

Cruising's answer to the European "grand tour" (but having to unpack only once!), these voyages take you to explore the British Isles; French and German ports (from where you can take daytrips to Paris, the Beaches of Normandy and Berlin); the city of the czars, St. Petersburg, Russia and other Baltic cities; not to mention wonderful, wonderful Copenhagen and other Scandinavian capitals. These itineraries -two week voyages are popular-appeal to history buffs, art and architecture lovers, and people who want to enjoy the Continent's cornucopia of culture, dining, shopping and festivals. Cruising season is summer (Norwegian Coastal Voyage operates year-round).

LINES THAT CRUISE IN THIS REGION -Celebrity, Clipper, Costa, Crystal, Cunard, First European, Holland America, Norwegian, Norwegian Coastal Voyage, Orient, Princess, Radisson Seven Seas, Royal Caribbean, Seabourn and Silversea.

MAGICAL, MEMORABLE MOMENTS -Watching the fireworks in Copenhagen's Tivoli Gardens. Museum hopping including such world-renowned institutions like the Louvre in Paris, the Rijksmuseum and Van Gogh Museum in Amsterdam and the Hermitage in St. Petersburg, Russia. Taking in the Eiffel Tower and Notre Dame

Cruising Regions

in Paris. Visiting Anne Frank's House, where the young Jewish diarist hid with her family from the Nazis during World War II, in Amsterdam. Enjoying an evening of ballet in St. Petersburg, Russia.

> Walking on cobblestone streets and exploring fortresses require comfortable shoes. A woman wearing high heels while exploring in Tallinn, Estonia on one of my tours, tripped and fell. Wear conservative clothing when touring cities, particularly if stops will be made in houses of worship.

New England/Canada

Autumn in all its golden glory is the big draw in this cruising region with its quaint villages and natural scenery -not to mention the delicious lobster and other fresh seafood you can enjoy. Most cruises are seven- or 14-days in length and feature such ports as Newport, R.I., with the opulent turn of the century "cottages" of the rich and famous including Vanderbilts; Boston, where one of the highlights is the historic Freedom Trail. Other delightful ports include Bar Harbor, Maine, Martha's Vineyard, Halifax, Quebec City and Montreal. If the Saguenay River is in your itinerary, be on the lookout for Beluga whales.

LINES THAT CRUISE IN THIS REGION- American Canadian Caribbean, Carnival, Clipper, Crystal, Cunard, Holland America, Norwegian, Princess, Regal, Royal Caribbean, Seabourn and Silversea.

MAGICAL, MEMORABLE MOMENTS- Joe, the Lobster Man, coming aboard our Seabourn ship with buckets and buckets of live lobsters for our dinner. Spotting Belugas in the Saguenay River. Visiting Peggy's Cove with its picturesque lighthouse near Halifax. Listening to the noonday gun at the Citadel in Halifax, Nova Scotia.

Bermuda

You could say you are in the pink when you are in Bermuda: pink-sand beaches, pastel buildings, pink and violet sunsets. Put on a pair of Bermuda shorts (yes, they were invented here) and explore on mopeds and scooters—the preferred mode of transportation. Other pastimes include water sports, horseback-riding, glass-bottom boat rides, golf, tennis and walks around St. George's. Another popular port of call is Hamilton.

LINES THAT CRUISE IN THIS REGION- Celebrity, Cunard, Holland America, Norwegian, Orient, Princess, Radisson Seven Seas, Regal, Seabourn. Some lines call regularly from April to October; others during transatlantic voyages or in combination with Colonial America coastal voyages calling at such cities as Savannah and Charleston.

MAGICAL, MEMORABLE MOMENTS- Spending a glorious morning at a pink-sand idyll and wondering if the sand is blushing due to its contact with the beautiful blue waters.

South America

It's a case of toucans to tango: variety spices up South America voyages. The continent is a marvelous mélange of European style and native soul with sensuous rhythms and exotic flavors, cosmopolitan cities, and the breathtaking natural beauty of massive glaciers, incredible jungles and amazing waterfalls. True, the region struggles with poverty and bouts of political instability, but those shortcomings somehow make it more human and real.

Small, midsize ships and megaliners; moderately priced and ultra-deluxe-ply the waters of this region in the fall and winter seasons (spring and summer in South America). They offer a variety of voyages—including explorations of the jungles of the Amazon River, Atlantic and/or Pacific coastal voyages (many sailing around the rugged coast of Cape Horn and taking in Patagonia's glaciers), exotic Galapagos expeditions, circumnavigations of the continent and even combinations that take you to the White Continent of Antarctica. Ports of call on South America cruises include something to tempt every taste: exciting cities like

Cruising Regions

Buenos Aires and Rio de Janeiro (some cruises calling in Rio de Janeiro during Carnaval, a once-in-a-lifetime spectacle and opportunity to live it up at one of the planet's biggest bashes); fashionable seaside resorts like Punta del Este in Uruguay; and remote enclaves like the Falkland Islands. Some voyages also offer a chance to visit the Lost City of the Incas, Machu Picchu, perched more than 12,000 feet high in the Andes and pre- or post-cruise extensions to see spectacular Iguazu Falls.

LINES THAT CRUISE IN THIS REGION- Celebrity, Crystal, Cunard, Holland America, Norwegian, Orient, Lindblad, Princess, Radisson Seven Seas, Royal Caribbean, Royal Olympic, Seabourn, and Silversea.

MAGICAL, MEMORABLE MOMENTS - The entrance into Rio de Janeiro with the Serra do Carioca mountains seemingly doing a samba around Guanabara Bay is simply spectacular. Enjoying an evening of tango at Senor Tango, Vieytes 1653 in the Barracas section of Buenos Aires (brought me a flood of memories of my mother, who had been a tango lover). Spotting a gigantic Blue Morpho butterfly in the Amazon. Glimpsing mysterious, mystical Machu Picchu, the Lost City of the Incas. Sharing a beach with a colony of swimming and sunbathing sea lions in the Galapagos Islands—the curious pups coming up to greet you.

Baja and The Sea of Cortez

A paradise for nature lovers, the main attraction in Baja and the Sea of Cortez is wildlife watching, particularly whale-watching. Other popular activities during seven-day cruises include swimming, snorkeling, kayaking and hiking.

LINES THAT CRUISE IN THIS REGION- American Safari, Clipper, Cruise West, Glacier Bay, Lindblad.

MAGICAL, MEMORABLE MOMENTS- Spotting gray whales close to your ship and colonies of sea lions frolicking in beaches.

Hawaii

"Aloha!" The Hawaiian multi-purpose word that means hello, goodbye and love welcomes you on the lips of its friendly people seemingly everywhere in the Hawaiian Island chain. What else, other than a warm reception (including a kiss and a flower lei to wear around your neck) will you come across in this tropical eden? Well, spectacular beaches, mountains and volcanoes, lush vegetation, waterfalls, and a rich cultural heritage that you can taste in traditional feasts or "luaus" and hear in the bubbly music of these islands.

Among the main islands where most ships call are:

OAHU - The Gathering Place, where Honolulu is located, boasts world-famous Waikiki Beach with its backdrop of Diamond Head volcano, historical attractions including Pearl Harbor and the ***USS Arizona Memorial*** (always moving, during our visit a woman threw flowers into the waters as a tribute to an uncle of hers who had died in the Japanese attack), and heritage attractions like the Polynesian Cultural Center.

MAUI - The historic whaling port of Lahaina is one of Maui's charms -others include fabulous beaches, the moonscape crater of 10,000-ft. high Haleakala volcano, the Iao Needle, soaring 2,250-feet high, and whale-watching from November through April when humpback whales journey more than 3,000 miles from Alaska to breed in Maui's warm waters.

KAUAI - Considered by many one of the world's most beautiful islands, Hollywood seems to agree: this is where ***Jurassic Park, Raiders of the Lost Ark, South Pacific*** and other motion pictures were filmed. Its attractions include Waimea Canyon, the Grand Canyon of the Pacific, the rugged Na Pali coastline and the lush, romantic Fern Grotto, where tours are treated to a musical performance including the Hawaiian Wedding Song.

THE BIG ISLAND OF HAWAII - Black and gray sand beaches, Volcanoes National Park where you can see the lava spouts of Kilauea (one of the world's most active volcanoes) and the 442-ft. Akaka Falls are among the points of interest here. Ports of call include Kona and Hilo.

Cruising Regions

> Some "tasteful" souvenirs to bring back home from your Hawaii cruise include delectable Macadamia nuts and Kona coffee.

U.S. law prohibits ships not built in Hawaii from sailing exclusively among its islands (without calling at a foreign port) or from sailing directly from the U.S. mainland to Hawaii. Cruise lines go out of their way to comply so as to be able to offer this popular destination to their passengers: Norwegian Cruise Line's whose Norwegian Star is sailing year-round in Hawaii, for instance, calls at Fanning Island in the Republic of Kiribati in addition to the four major Hawaiian islands on its seven-day cruises. Holland America leaves from San Diego, calls in Mexico, and then does the Hawaiian chain on two-week sailings.

LINES THAT CRUISE IN THIS REGION- Carnival, Celebrity, Cunard, Crystal, Holland America, Norwegian, Orient, P & O, Princess, Radisson Seven Seas, Royal Caribbean and Silversea.

MAGICAL, MEMORABLE MOMENTS- Helicopter flightseeing over Kauai including its breathtaking Na Pali coast. Cruising by Kilauea Volcano at night and watching spouting bright orange lava glowing eerily in the dark. Whale watching—and seeing mothers and babies swimming together—in Maui. Learning to make fragrant leis and other Hawaiian crafts.

Australia/Pacific Islands

This corner of the world lured the likes of Paul Gauguin, Somerset Maugham and Robert Louis Stevenson and now it attracts modern-day tourists to its fabled golden islands surrounded by aquamarine waters: Tahiti, Bora Bora, Moorea, Bali, and more—quick, pass me a pareu and a flower for my hair!

As to Australia, well, g'dday, mate! Photograph kangaroos, pet a koala (they are fluffy and soft like the teddy bears they look like), snorkel the Great Barrier Reef, explore the

Outback, take in the panorama of the Sydney Opera House -such are the multiple and varied pleasures Down Under. In New Zealand, put on your hiking shoes and tour some of the world's most beautiful scenery.

LINES THAT CRUISE IN THIS REGION - Crystal, Cunard, Holland America, Orient, P & O, Princess, Radisson Seven Seas, Royal Caribbean, Seabourn, Silversea.

MAGICAL, MEMORABLE MOMENTS - Sailing into Sydney Harbor and posing for photos with the "white sails" of the Opera House in the background. Feeding kangaroos who eat daintily out of your hand and petting koalas in natural sanctuaries. Shopping for native handicrafts and watching ceremonial dances in Bali. Indolent days in the sun in Tahiti, Bora Bora and Moorea.

Asia

Exploring the exotic Orient from the comfort and luxury of a cruise ship is an unbeatable combination, particularly if you set out for developing countries like Vietnam and China. Singapore, one of Asia's most modern and cleanest cities, and Hong Kong, one of the world's most scenic harbors, are two popular embarkation ports.

LINES THAT CRUISE IN THIS REGION - Crystal, Cunard, Holland America, Orient, P & O, Princess, Radisson Seven Seas, Royal Caribbean, Seabourn, and Silversea.

MAGICAL, MEMORABLE MOMENTS - Entering Hong Kong harbor, considered by many one of the top three most scenic harbors in the world (along with Rio de Janeiro and Acapulco). Visiting Beijing's Forbidden City and the Great Wall of China. Sipping a Singapore Sling at the luxurious Raffles Hotel's Long Bar (where the drink was invented, and a setting worthy of a Somerset Maugham novel—the famous writer, we were told during our visit, did live at Raffles and worked under one of its casuarinas trees every morning).

Still Other Cruises

Still more, you ask? Yep. Other sailings you could take include the following:

TRANSATLANTIC CROSSINGS - Cunard's legendary **Queen Elizabeth 2** is the only ship still doing regular crossings from New York to Southampton, Great Britain. A "crossing," particularly on the QE2, is generally a more elegant experience than a "cruise" with several consecutive evenings calling for formal wear as the ship traverses the Atlantic. Crossings are leisurely, taking six days and longer—a great way to cross time zones and adjust to the change slowly arriving without jet lag. A variety of cruise lines including Costa, Crystal, Holland America, Princess, Royal Caribbean and Windstar offer transatlantic crossing repositioning cruises usually in the spring to launch the Mediterranean/northern Europe cruise season and in the fall at its conclusion.

RIVERS AND LAKES OF AMERICA - Exploring the Mississippi, Missouri and Ohio from a riverboat or barge is as pleasurable as sitting on a rocker and sipping a lemonade in your back porch on a hot day. The **Delta Queen** Steamboat Company, which filed for Chapter 11 bankruptcy protection in the fall of 2001, is back operating its national historic landmark Delta Queen—this steamboat is like a charming Victoria inn floating on American rivers—and its sister ships, the Mississippi Queen and American Queen. The RiverBarge Excursion Lines (888-GO-BARGE) offers sailings on the Mississippi, Missouri and other American rivers, and other lines including American Canadian Caribbean and Clipper offer cruises on the Great Lakes.

OTHER RIVERS - Or perhaps you'd prefer slowly gliding through European canals and other country waterways or navigating the Rhine or the Danube. Or even more exotic, perhaps you would like to sail the Nile, or the Yangtze. See Part C of Chapter Three in this guide for information on River & Barge Cruises.

EAST AFRICA/INDIA - Always wanted to borrow a page from Ernest Hemingway and go on safari? Or dreamed of seeing the Taj Mahal at sunrise? Cruise ships

have the ticket for you to such ports as Bombay and Goa in India; and Kenya (Mombasa), Tanzania (Zanzibar), and Cape Town (South Africa). Lines that can take you to India include Crystal, Cunard, Holland America, Orient, P & O, Princess, Radisson Seven Seas, Royal Caribbean, Seabourn, and Silversea. Lines that cruise to East Africa include Crystal, Cunard, Orient, P & O, Princess, and Silversea.

AROUND THE WORLD

The equivalent of a never-ending gourmet banquet, a grand voyage around the world is a feast of ports -usually around 50-over the space of more than 100 days. Lines that offer World Cruises include Holland America, Crystal, Cunard, P & O, and Silversea.

ANTARCTICA

If you are the adventuresome type, bent on exploring the ends of the earth and rubbing elbows with colonies of Emperor or Adelie penguins while you are there, you are not alone. Each year, some 12,000 people book passage on ships headed to the Great White Continent (or The Ice, as people who live in Antarctica refer to it). Orient Lines' **Marco Polo** alone brings approximately 2,500. More would come, but "people think it's colder than it really is—but I've been colder in New York and Chicago," David Lawton, a cruise director aboard Orient Lines, once told me. Temperatures can sometimes rise to 45-degrees. But to nature lovers, it does not matter how cold it gets—they concentrate on the dramatic vistas of icebergs in the Austral sun. Exploration is via zodiacs—be on the lookout for Blue, Fin, Humpback, Minke and Orca whales. Most cruises depart from Ushuaia, Argentina; Chilean ports and the Falkland Islands. Lines that offer these cruises include Orient, Radisson Seven Seas and Lindblad.

> Orient Lines operates the biggest ship in Antarctica, the 22,080-ton, 850-passenger, ice-strengthened hull, Marco Polo.

Test the Waters Tips

* Travel is a privilege. Thank your lucky stars that you can enjoy it -so many would love to, but can't for health, monetary and even political reasons (in such countries as Cuba, for instance). In your travels, be prepared to find things different than they are at home; be respectful of the differences you come across, and if you can't celebrate the changes then at least adapt to them gracefully (after all, if things were the same as at home what would be the point of traveling?).

* If this is your first voyage and you are concerned you may not like it, begin with a short cruise -maybe a three-day sailing to the Bahamas, that way if it turns out that you indeed do not like it, the end is near.

* Even if you are visiting ports where English is widely spoken, like Puerto Rico, for example, learn a few words in the native language. A "buenos dias" (good morning) and a "gracias" (thank you) in Spanish-speaking countries, for example, is a courtesy always very well received by the natives. When visiting France or French islands, greet the locals with a "bonjour" (good morning, afternoon)—this is the polite way to begin a conversation in France and your courtesy will be appreciated.

* When in Rome, as the saying goes, do like the Romans. Try to dress like the locals (it is a way of showing respect and it allows you to blend in and not attract the attention of pick-pockets) and dress conservatively (no shorts or bare shoulders) if you are visiting houses of worship.

Insider's Savings Insights

* If you decide to buy shipboard tours, consider what you will take carefully, as on many ships tours are non-refundable.

* Those friends you made at the shipboard culinary demonstration or wine tasting may like to share some of your adventures ashore. If two or more people are touring together, particularly in the major Caribbean ports where vans and taxis are plentiful, you will be able to arrange an island tour and/or trips to the beach at better prices than if each of you individually bought ship's tours.

* If you plan to dine ashore or if you will be doing pre- or post-cruise land stays, either as a package from the cruise line or independently, always check over your bills to see if gratuities have been automatically charged and ask at your ship's shore excursions office or at hotels' reception desk what the local custom is regarding tipping. In Singapore, for instance, it is 10 percent and it is generally added to your bill. In Australia, there is typically tipping as a token of appreciation when service has been exceptional (we were told by locals that if the service has been outstanding and their restaurant bill is AU$190, they round it out to AU$200, and that they do not tip other service personnel such as taxi drivers and barbers/beauticians).

* If you will be shopping during your cruise for jewelry, cameras, liquor and other merchandise, price the items you are considering to purchase at home before you set sail to be truly an informed consumer.

Chapter: 5
Itineraries

If, as we said in the beginning of this guide, a cruise is the travel equivalent of a piece of cake, your voyage's itinerary is like the recipe for that cake, telling you what its ingredients are and the order they are "prepared in." In other words, in the case of a cruise, what the ports of call are, how many days at sea you will have, and when each occurs.

So, if you looked over Chapter Four or you already knew where in the world you want to go all you need to do now is find an itinerary that takes you there, the way you wish to go there and when you want to get there.

Preliminary Planning

So let's start by getting some preliminaries out of the way. Ask yourself a bunch of questions: First, time is of the essence: How many days do you have for your vacation? Perhaps you just have a long weekend? A week? Longer?

From one-day party cruises to nowhere (no ports of call) to 100-plus odysseys around the world, calling at more than 50 ports and rivaling Odysseus' own fabled wanderings, itineraries abound out there—as plentiful as floating chunks of ice near the Alaskan glaciers—that can fit into most people's vacation time requirements.

What time of the year do you want to travel? Through the decades, I have cruised during every month of the calendar—several times—and when it comes to weather, well, it has been variable: I have run into both inclement weather and picture-perfect conditions the same month in the same itineraries, so what can I tell you? It's mostly just luck. Recently, to give you an example, I sailed in the Caribbean in October (right smack in the hurricane season, as "high risk" a period as any you could find) and enjoyed perfect weather: cloudless skies and seas smooth as silk. And when you sail on "high risk" weather periods, of course, you enjoy low fares.

"Season" fares, generally in effect during peak travel periods (most popular times of travel, generally during what is expected to be "best weather" times) are the highest fares, with "off-season" or "value" fares being the least expensive (sometimes $500 or more below "season" rates). In between, there are "shoulder season" rates—for periods sandwiched between the "season" and "off-season" (with savings of $100-$300 off "season" fares).

> **If you pick an itinerary in the off-season or shoulder-season, and can get your foot out the door quickly, last-minute bargains tend to be most plentiful and attractive.**

In Alaska, for example, lowest fares are usually in early May and mid-September (the off-season); next lowest fares are generally in late May and early September (shoulder season) and highest fares are usually June to August (season).

In the Caribbean, season or peak prices are usually encountered in the winter months and sometimes in the summer as well (as many families travel there during school holidays), off-season fares are usually in May and October, and shoulder season fares are generally available in April, September and November.

Timing considerations out of the way, your preliminary planning continues with the type of holiday you are looking for. Do you prefer a laid-back plan? Or do you want an active, sightseeing-intensive vacation? Some itineraries call for several days at sea (ocean crossings and repositioning cruises requiring ocean crossings). Others feature just one or two at-sea days, full-day stays in ports and sometimes overnights in a port or two.

Itineraries

SAMPLE ITINERARIES - (These are typical itineraries offered by cruise lines in 2001 and 2002 and listed here as examples of what will generally be out there, with slight variations, whenever you are ready to sail).

Sample three-day Bahamas Itinerary on Carnival's Fascination

	Arrive	Depart
Fri.- Miami, Fla.		4 p.m.
Saturday, Nassau	8 a.m.	
Sunday, Nassau		8 a.m.
Sunday, At Sea		
Mon.- Miami, Fla.	8 a.m.	

REMARKS ABOUT THIS ITINERARY: Short and sweet. Time for some sightseeing in Miami before and/or after the cruise if your transportation schedule allows, and time for evening activities in Nassau as the ship overnights there.

Sample seven-day Eastern Caribbean Itinerary on Royal Caribbean's Explorer of the Seas

	Arrive	Depart
Saturday, Miami, Fla.		5 p.m.
Sunday, Nassau/Paradise Island, Bahamas	7 a.m.	2 p.m.
Monday, At Sea		
Tuesday, St. Thomas, U.S. Virgin Islands	7 a.m.	6 p.m.
Wednesday, San Juan, Puerto Rico	7 a.m.	2 p.m.
Thursday, Labadee, Hispaniola	9 a.m.	5 p.m.
Friday, At Sea		
Saturday, Miami, Fla	8:30 a.m.	

REMARKS ABOUT THIS ITINERARY- Typical seven-day Caribbean itinerary from Florida ports (featuring two days at sea, one going, one coming). There is time for sightseeing in Miami before and after the cruise if your home-to-pier transportation arrangements allow it. Early departure from San Juan so you cannot sample its nightlife if that is your desire.

Sample 14-night Northern Europe & Scandinavia Itinerary on Celebrity's Galaxy

	Arrive	Depart
Saturday: Stockholm, Sweden		5 p.m.
Sunday: Helsinki, Finland	10 a.m.	6 p.m.
Monday: St. Petersburg, Russia	7 a.m.	
Tuesday: St. Petersburg, Russia		6 p.m.
Wednesday: Muuga (Tallinn), Estonia	7 a.m.	6 p.m.
Thursday: Visby, Sweden	7 a.m.	6 p.m.
Friday: Riga, Latvia	7 a.m.	6 p.m.
Saturday, At Sea		
Sunday: Gdynia (Gdansk), Poland	7 a.m.	5 p.m.
Monday: Rostock (Berlin), Germany	7 a.m.	11:30 p.m.
Tuesday: Copenhagen, Denmark	Noon	10:30 p.m.
Wednesday, At Sea		
Thursday: Oslo, Norway	8 a.m.	5 p.m.
Friday, At Sea		
Saturday: Amsterdam, Netherlands	6 a.m.	

Itineraries

REMARKS ABOUT THIS ITINERARY - Opportunities for sightseeing in Stockholm and Amsterdam before and after the cruise respectively if your flights allow it. Overnight in St. Petersburg so you can enjoy the ballet, opera, or a folkloric show.

Sample 11-day Ocean-Crossing and Hawaii Voyage on Crystal Cruises' Crystal Harmony

	Arrive	Depart
Sunday, Acapulco, Mexico		9 p.m.
Monday, Cruising the Pacific Ocean		
Tuesday, Cruising the Pacific Ocean		
Wednesday, Cruising the Pacific Ocean		
Thursday, Cruising the Pacific Ocean		
Friday, Cruising the Pacific Ocean		
Saturday, Cruising the Pacific Ocean		
Sunday, Cruising the Pacific Ocean		
Monday, Hilo, Hawaii	8 a.m.	5 p.m.
Tuesday, Lahaina, Maui, Hawaii	8 a.m.	6 p.m.
Wednesday, Honolulu, Oahu, Hawaii	8 a.m.	

Fell's Official Know-It-All: Cruises

REMARKS ABOUT THIS ITINERARY - Many say there is nothing like a relaxing Pacific Ocean crossing, everyone is settling in and contentedly enjoying shipboard pleasures including enrichment programs, but for many seven consecutive days at sea may prove to be too much of a good thing.

Sample seven-day Hawaii Voyage on Norwegian Cruise Line's Norwegian Star

	Arrive	Depart
Day 1 - Honolulu, Oahu, Hawaii		8 p.m.
Day 2 - Kona, Hawaii	7 a.m.	2 p.m.
Day 3 - At Sea		
Day 4 - Fanning Island, Kiribati	9 a.m.	3 p.m.
Day 5 - At Sea		
Day 6 - Lahaina, Maui, Hawaii	1 p.m.	10 p.m.
Day 7 - Nawiliwili, Kauai, Hawaii	8 a.m.	4 p.m.
Day 8 - Honolulu, Oahu, Hawaii	7 a.m.	

REMARKS ABOUT THIS ITINERARY - Opportunities to tour Honolulu before and after the cruise if your flights allow it. Late departure from Lahaina allows you to dine ashore if you like.

Sample Itinerary for seven-day Greek Isles Athens to Istanbul cruise on Windstar Cruises' Wind Song

	Arrive	Depart
Sat.- Athens, Greece		5 p.m.
Sun.- Mykonos, Greece*	8 a.m.	11 p.m.
Mon.- Santorini, Greece	8 a.m.	4 p.m.
Tue.- Rhodes, Greece	8 a.m.	11 p.m.
Wed.- Bodrum, Turkey	7 a.m.	6 p.m.
Thu.- Kusadasi, Turkey	8 a.m.	4 p.m.
Fri. - At Sea		
Sat.-Istanbul, Turkey	8 a.m.	

* weather permitting

Itineraries

REMARKS ABOUT THIS ITINERARY - The call at Mykonos is weather permitting (this port is generally listed like this due to wind conditions and other factors that may prevent a call there), but if all goes well, the ship is scheduled to stay there till 11 p.m., ample time to take in the glorious sunset.

Sample seven-day Alaska Inside Passage Cruise on Holland America ships

	Arrive	Depart
Day 0 - Vancouver, British Columbia		5 p.m.
Day 1 - Scenic Inside Passage Cruising		
Day 2 - Juneau, Alaska	2 p.m.	11 p.m.
Day 3 - Skagway, Alaska	7 a.m.	9 p.m.
Day 4 - Glacier Bay National Park	7 a.m.	4 p.m.
Day 5 - Ketchikan, Alaska	10 a.m.	6 p.m.
Day 6 - Cruising the Inside Passage		
Day 7 - Vancouver, British Columbia	8 a.m.	

REMARKS ABOUT THIS ITINERARY - Typical seven-day Inside Passage cruise, visiting Glacier Bay (entrance into Galcier Bay is by permit only, and not all Alaska ships visit this highlight). Late departure from Juneau allows you to take in a salmon bake for dinner and see the city lights from Mt. Roberts tramway.

Sample seven-day Alaska Gulf of Alaska/Glacier Route Northbound cruise on Holland America ships

(southbound itineraries do the reverse)

	Arrive	Depart
Day 0 - Vancouver, British Columbia		5 p.m.
Day 1 - Cruising the Inside Passage		
Day 2 - Ketchikan, Alaska	7 a.m.	3 p.m.
Day 3 - Juneau, Alaska	8 a.m.	6 p.m.
Day 4 - Sitka, Alaska	8 a.m.	6 p.m.
Day 5 - Cruising Hubbard Glacier	7 a.m.	1 p.m.
Day 6 - Valdez Cruising College Fjord	7 a.m.	Noon
Day 7 - Seward, Alaska	8 a.m.	

REMARKS ABOUT THIS ITINERARY - Gulf of Alaska/Route of the Glaciers voyage, combinable with land programs to Denali National Park. Does not visit Glacier Bay.

Itineraries

Sample Westbound Transatlantic Repositioning 16-night voyage on Costa's CostaAtlantica

	Arrive	Depart
Nov. 8- Genoa, Italy		5 p.m.
Nov. 9- Barcelona, Spain	1 p.m.	7 p.m.
Nov. 10-11 - At sea		
Nov. 12- Tenerife, Canary Islands	7 a.m.	1 p.m.
Nov. 13-Nov. 16 - At sea		
Nov. 17- Barbados	1 p.m.	Midnight
Nov. 18- St. Lucia	8 a.m.	6 p.m.
Nov. 19- St. Maarten	8 a.m.	6 p.m.
Nov. 20- Tortola	8 a.m.	6 p.m.
Nov. 21- Catalina Island/ Casa de Campo*	8 a.m.	5:30 p.m.
Nov. 22- At sea		
Nov. 23 - Nassau	8 a.m.	6 p.m.
Nov. 24- Fort Lauderdale	8 a.m.	

* Port of Call is Catalina Island. Only passengers participating in the onboard shore excursion program may disembark at Casa de Campo.

REMARKS ABOUT THIS ITINERARY - This is a repositioning voyage combined with a Caribbean cruise—the days at sea are spaced out, but there is still a four-day block at sea while crossing the Atlantic.

Chapter Five

Finding The Right Itinerary For You

The preliminaries out of the way, you can concentrate on finding the right itinerary for you. Browse through as many cruise line brochures as you can get your hands on, and/or visit cruise line Web sites (for addresses, consult this guide's appendix). You can generally access itineraries by clicking on "destinations," "itineraries" and/or "cruise calendar" icons on the cruise lines' Web sites). Other resources at your disposal include, of course, experienced travel agents who can recommend several itineraries for the vacation you have in mind that are available for the time you wish to sail.

As you look over itineraries (and study them carefully) these are some things to look out for:

* If there are two cities mentioned in the port name, and one is in parenthesis, the city in parenthesis is usually not the one the ship will dock in, but there will optional tours available to take you there. For example if the itinerary reads: Day 2: Le Havre (Paris), France—it means that the ship will be docked in Le Havre and that there will be optional tours for sale to Paris.

* If it is not obvious by reading the itinerary, ask your travel agent or the cruise line whether the ship will be tendering at any of the ports of call. Tendering (anchoring off shore at small ports and bringing passengers ashore in launches at a port of call) is time-consuming: you may have to obtain numbered passes for the launches to disembark at peak times (upon arrival and shortly thereafter when everyone wants to get off to start exploring at once). And you may have to wait for a launch when you are ready to return to the ship. If you have mobility problems, you may want to steer clear of ships that have to tender in ports, as you will have to negotiate gangways—steep in many cases—to board the tender and to return to the ship, and board and disembark the launches from platforms that bob up and down with the waves. Crewmembers do assist passengers on and off launches, but if you are mobility impaired, it can be a tricky procedure.

Itineraries

> If you have mobility problems, ask your agent and/or the cruise line specifically what is there to assist you if your ship tenders at some ports. Holland America, for example, has begun a process of installing lifts on its ships so mobility-impaired passengers can bypass gangways to board tenders.

As you study itineraries, check to see if the ports that are important to you are included within a particular destination. For instance, if you have always associated the Greek islands with a sunset in Mykonos, check to see if it is one of the ports in a Greek Isles itinerary and that enough time is allowed there for you to do and see what you want—you won't be sorry: I was privileged to enjoy a sunset while in Santorini (one of my sailings there stayed late into the evening; another did not) and it was just glorious: with the island's white houses blushing as the sun kissed the water.

Read the fine print associated with asterisks and other notations next to port names in itineraries, if any. For example, if there is an asterisk next to a port, it could be that the ship will be making a service call only to let off passengers on a shore excursion (independents will not be allowed off if that is the case). An asterisk, or similar notation may tell you that a call is "weather permitting," and so forth.

Check the itinerary for embarkation time (usually in the afternoon of sailing date, often at 5 p.m. or later) and disembarkation time at the end of the cruise (generally early morning). If your transportation arrangements get you to the port in the morning prior to embarkation, you may be able to get some sightseeing done before you set sail. Likewise, if you have an afternoon flight on disembarkation day, the cruise line may sell tours that let you see some of the disembarkation city and take you directly to the airport afterwards (much better than sitting around in the airport for hours awaiting your flight). One word of warning: if you do decide to tour independently in the embarkation port (or any of the ports, for that matter) make sure you get back to the pier in time (cruise lines stick to schedule) so you can board the ship or you will be waving goodbye to it, instead of sailing on it. This happened to a couple on one of our steamboat cruises and they had to arrange for a launch service to call the boat and then bring them up to rendezvous with it at their own expense: $150.

Pre-And Post-Cruise Hotel Stays

Whenever your time and budget allows a pre-cruise hotel stay is a good idea, particularly if you have to fly from home to meet the ship. Arriving a day early at the port city means no worries about airline delays causing you to miss the boat literally. It also allows you to rest, relax and do some sightseeing after your flight and/or other travel to the pier, and in the case of travel across time zones, it gives you an extra day for your body to combat jet lag and adjust to the new time. So you can board your ship and start your cruise fresh and ready for the fun to begin. Post-cruise packages are good too, if your budget and time allow - giving you an opportunity to explore the disembarkation city and relax after leaving the ship and before beginning your journey home.

Test the Waters Tips

* Does the itinerary have the right ratio of days at sea to port days for your taste? If it has too many days at sea, you cannot do anything about it, but if it has too many port days to suit you, you can always stay onboard one or more days and relax (at ports least important to you) -you will have the ship's facilities practically all too yourself.

* When looking over Alaska itineraries, check to see if Glacier Bay is included. One of Alaska's most spectacular sights, the National Park Service each year issues a limited number of permits for ships to enter.

* Check the days/hours your ship is in port if you have a special agenda in a particular locale: for example, if you want to see the fireworks at Tivoli in Copenhagen, check if the ship will be there on a day when they are presented, and if the stay in port allows you to take them in.

Insider's Savings Insights

* Repositioning itineraries (when the cruise line needs to take a ship out of one area of the world to cruise in another) are usually some of the best bargains at sea. They do generally include a good number of days at sea, but if this suits you fine, you will enjoy excellent savings, sometimes of 50 percent or more over regular cruises. Examples of repositioning voyages include fall and spring transatlantic sailings when lines like Celebrity and Royal Caribbean deploy their ships from Europe to the Caribbean (in the fall) and from the Caribbean to Europe (in the spring).

* Cruise line pre- and post-hotel packages are good buys as they usually also include transfers and in some cases, sightseeing. They also save you time as the cruise line can package it all for you: air, pre- and/or post-cruise hotel stay, sightseeing and transfers.

"*Carnival Pride*" Photo courtesy of Carnival Cruise Lines.

Chapter: 6
Shore Excursions

In my travels, I have come across some passengers who consider the ship their destination and seldom, if ever, get off at the ports of call. They particularly love the feeling of "having the ship all to themselves" when everyone else gets off to explore.

For me, and most cruise passengers, however, the allure of exotic ports of call is like a siren's song -simply irresistible. You will find me disembarking early, touring, sampling cultural offerings and local cuisine, and in general, making the most of each stop the ship makes.

Options for Touring

On a cruise, passengers have three touring options: independently, via optional shore excursions purchased through the cruise line or a combination of both (independently in some ports, on organized tours in others, or maybe a little of both in each stop). Let's take a look at the advantages and disadvantages of each method.

Optional Tours from the Line

These organized excursions are generally extra (not included in the cruise price) unless you are on certain expedition or adventure ships, where programs of tours—naturalist-led if appropriate—are included in the cruise fare. And that is why, by the way, prices on expedition/adventure ships are often higher than on mainstream ships where tours are extra.

When you receive your cruise documents, a booklet describing the shore excursions available for purchase on your sailing (and listing their prices) is generally enclosed. Cruise line Web sites often also have shore excursion information and cruise brochures often touch on the highlights of available activities ashore too (for cruise lines' Web sites, consult this guide's Appendix).

Shipboard excursions range from walking tours to a nearby fortress or historic quarter (in the $25-per-person-price-range) to ambitious programs ($200-$300-plus-range) including train or bus rides (with meals) to Paris or Berlin from ports like Le Havre and Rostock respectively while on Northern Europe voyages; flights to Mayan ruins on the Yucatan (with a meal) from Cozumel on Western Caribbean itineraries; helicopter flight-seeing over glaciers/and dog sledding combinations while in Alaska; hot-air ballooning in Africa, Europe and other scenic locales.

Some lines, including the Disney Cruise Line, Royal Caribbean and Celebrity, offer advance purchase of shore excursions, so if you know what places you want to tour you can pre-order the excursions through your travel agent or the cruise line and thus have one less thing to do during the voyage. Tickets for the tours you pre-ordered are delivered to your stateroom and usually charged to your onboard account—neat and easy.

If you are not sure what tours to pick or have questions about them, the Shore Excursions Desk on your ship generally has a tour talk early in the voyage to describe the programs. These lectures, often including a slide or video presentation, also have a question-and-answer period so you can get all the information you need. In your cabin and/or at this talk, shore excursion order forms are available. You fill out your name, cabin number and the number of tickets you want for each tour, drop it in the box at the ship's shore excursions office and the tickets are delivered to your cabin and charged to your onboard account.

> Some shipboard tours (particularly those involving submarines, helicopters, floatplanes, yachts and the like) are very popular and have a limited capacity. Order yours as soon as possible after boarding (or pre-order them) to avoid disappointment.

Shore Excursions

Pros & Cons Of Buying Tours Through The Line

Buying shore tours through the line has advantages and disadvantages. Weigh them both to see what is best for you.

Advantages

* Easily arranged.
* Admission fees to museums and attractions are generally included.
* The shore tours are operated by local companies, not by the cruise lines, but since the companies want to keep the cruise lines' business, they generally do furnish them with well-maintained equipment and English-speaking guides.
* A member of the cruise staff generally accompanies the tours and counts heads to make sure nobody is missing after a stop to visit a site (the cruise staff escort also lends an ear if you have any complaints). And another member of the cruise staff generally stays on the pier counting returning buses to make sure nobody is left behind in a port of call on one of their tours.
* Often cruise lines can make arrangements to get you into places you might normally not be able to get into: an artist's home/studio in the Caribbean island of St. Martin; a dance school in Bali; the Hermitage Museum before opening hours, and historic Yusupov Palace where Rasputin was murdered (open only by arrangement to groups) in St. Petersburg, Russia; a working ranch in Helsinki, Finland—to name a few.
* Cruise lines generally give you "difficulty ratings" for each tour, often listing the number of steps you have to climb to visit a palace or fortress, and the quality of the terrain you will be walking on (steep hill, cobblestones, etc.), so you have an idea how much walking/strenuous activity you are in for.
* Safety in numbers. This is a big plus when touring in exotic or troubled areas of the world. You may feel safer going with a big group from the ship. This was the case when we went to the Pyramids in the Giza Plateau from Alexandria, Egypt while on a cruise to the Holy Land and Egypt aboard Cunard's ***Vistafjord*** (now ***Caronia***) 10 years ago. A convoy of a half-dozen buses left the ship together escorted by military personnel

armed with rifles (one of their jeeps in the front, two on each side and one in the rear). Even so, in the dark of night during our return to Alexandria, our bus was hit by a thrown rock that shattered its windshield with a thunder-bolt-like crash. Our driver kept on going and we were very happy to have our military escorts and to be returned to our ship safe and sound.

Disadvantages

* Many excursions are bus tours, pretty passive, and sold to big groups (time is lost, loading, counting, and unloading the bus, and you may sit around if someone is late returning to the bus after a visit to a site).

* Organized excursions may allow more time than you want for shopping -this was the case on a recent tour we took in Bali where out of the four hours available for touring, one full hour was spent in a shop selling woodcarvings. On full-day tours where a meal is included, more time than you wish might have to be spent lunching (while the whole group gets served) than you might spend if you were on your own and grab something quick.

* Shipboard tours are generally more expensive (particularly if two or more people are touring) when compared to independent touring. You are paying for the convenience of having someone else do the homework, make the arrangements, pick you up at the pier, take you to see the sights and return you to the ship.

* When it comes to organized tours, it's of course the luck of the draw when it comes to the guide you get. While the guide will be English-speaking, he or she may have a heavy accent, or might not be a local (that happened to me recently in Brisbane, where the guide was from Germany and not Australia as I would have preferred). And other problems you might encounter: the guide might not speak loudly enough, might not discuss what you are seeing (as it happened to me while on a tour of the Egyptian Museum in Cairo when the guide passed by King Tut's bejeweled throne without a word).

Shore Excursions

Things To Ask About Ship's Tours

* Always ask, if not spelled out in the tour's description, how much time is spent commuting from the pier to the attraction or activity. Say it is a river rafting tour -find out how far it is to the river so you do not wind up spending more than two hours going to, and returning from, the river and a mere half hour actually rafting.

* Are there refreshments, snacks or meals included or available for purchase?

> Bring a bottle of water with you on shore excursions -particularly in the tropics where the heat tends to be intense.

* Ask, if it is not included in the description, what actual stops (and their length) are made during the tour. If you always wanted to visit a particular monument, attraction or historic site you will not be happy just photographing it from the bus as you drive by.

* Ask if there are opportunities to mingle with the locals -like during visits to marketplaces or crafts fairs, for instance.

Mixing with The Locals

Shipboard tours that let you mix with the locals more than just briefly, like in a crafts fair, tend to be the most memorable port time you spend, as they yield valuable insights as to how people live in the regions you are visiting: what problems they face, how they go about their daily lives, what they enjoy doing in their free time. Tours that let you visit them in their homes, perhaps for a home-cooked meal, are wonderful: as you not only taste the local cuisine and beverages, but you can see how they decorate their homes and relax while you talk to them about their daily lives: how they work and play.

Oh, yes, there is no place like home—the locals' homes-for cruise holidays (as well as other types of travel). Mixing with families in the places you visit in their own homes, farms, ranches and schools or visiting historic mansions and palaces enriches a voyage much more than all the umbrella-pointing a sightseeing bus tour guide can muster during a typical bus excursion.

Having lunch with a family in a ranch outside Helsinki, for example, allows for conversation and getting to know various generations. The opportunity also gives you a peak into typical Finnish décor and a taste of Finnish cooking—perhaps moose stew or baked salmon washed down with homemade beer.

Visits to historic mansions are rewarding as well. The extra-long drapes in Colonial-era mansions, you learn, were to show off the stature of the residents: fabric was very expensive, so by making the drapes extra long, the owners were showing off their wealth. And the fireplace face guard by the mantelpiece tells tales of the wax-based makeup ladies used in the 18th century to cover their smallpox scars (and scarring from other diseases they were faced with prior to vaccines—the fireplace guard shielded the ladies' faces from the warmth of the fire so their makeup would not melt).

These types of tours that offer opportunities to mix with the locals in their homes and that visit historic mansions are "like an open book filled with details about the people of the places you visit," said Donatella Braghieri, a shore excursions manager aboard a cruise ship my husband and I recently took in Northern Europe. Details that go beyond mere sightseeing and that tend to become the most memorable aspects of a voyage.

If you would like to be "at home" ashore during your next voyage, here are some noteworthy shore excursion programs available from a variety of cruise lines. I list them as examples of what, in my opinion, are the most memorable types of shore excursions. Consider taking similar programs when you sail—they are a wonderful investment of your port time and shore excursion dollar. (As with all other prices quoted throughout this book, they are current as of the time I wrote the book, and subject to change without notice).

SUDI DANCE SCHOOL, BALI - The heart and soul of the Balinese is in their religious beliefs: a form of Hinduism imported from Java in the 15th century. There are some 20,000 temples in Bali and the Balinese also express their religion through art: woodcarving, painting, music, stone carving and above all, dance. Passengers of Orient Lines' *Crown Odyssey* have a wonderful opportunity to visit a dance school in the village of Blah Batuh during the Artistic & Cultural Bali half-day excursion ($35). Upon arrival, children

greet the passengers with a welcome dance and a procession of balenganjur traditional music. The school's headmaster, Tari Terondong, invites the passengers to watch a dance lesson that is followed by a performance of traditional Balinese dances. Established in 1997, the school also teaches gamelan and angklung bamboo playing (Balinese musical instruments) as well as mask-making (demonstrations are given). Additionally, there is a visit to a foundry to see the complete process of making the gamelan (which is similar to the xylophone). Passengers who wish to participate, also receive an angklung bamboo musical instrument lesson and play a piece together with the students (the result is not really concert-caliber, but it is fun!). The tour also includes a stop at the Marka Gallery in the village of Kemenuh where master woodcarvers' works are offered for sale.

SAVIJARVI HOMESTEAD - Helsinki, Finland.

Royal Caribbean International offers this program on its ships that call on Helsinki during Northern Europe voyages. It includes a visit to a horse ranch outside Helsinki where three generations of the Savijarvi family live and work -grandma in her apron, her children tending to the horses, her grandchildren helping serve a welcome berry drink and greeting visitors with scrubbed, smiling faces. A friendly German shepherd on the geranium-bedecked front porch keeps a vigilant eye over the lush grounds.

Upon arrival, guests have an opportunity to tour the ranch with one of the family members and see its 67 horses and ponies and its flock of geese (watch out: the geese are like guard dogs and can bite) as well as learn about the workings of the ranch. Back in the house, the dining room table is set with fresh flowers and lit candles and lunch is served: hearty, creamy nettle (a spinach-like vegetable) soup, garden salad, moose or salmon, and homemade beer. A special cake with strawberry filling from a favorite family recipe for birthdays and special occasions is also served, accompanied by fresh berries, rhubarb, and a warm caramel sauce for toppings. After the meal, guests are free to enjoy their coffee in the parlor, where a photo of the family's oldest son is surrounded with flowers and a lit candle. The young man, our hosts told us, died in an accident at 33 years of age while helping a neighbor dig a well. Also included in the full-day tour, which costs $130, are a visit to quaint Porvoo, a town on the Baltic Sea and the mouth of the Porvoo River with 16th century wooden buildings, and highlights of Helsinki, including the Tempelli Aukio Church famous for its design hewn into rock.

BEAUTIFUL BARBADOS AND COLONIAL PLANTATION HOUSE - Barbados.
This is a three-and-a-half tour offered by Celebrity Cruises that takes in highlights of Barbados including Holetown, where the British first landed in 1625, Farley Hill National Park, Bathsheba (stopping at St. John's Church for panoramic views) and the "Lion" on Gun Hill. Best of all, it makes a stop at the Francia Plantation House, nestled in a wooded area and surrounded by landscaped gardens. The resident Sisnett family welcomes visitors with a drink, shares its ancestral heritage and shows off its collection of old maps of the Caribbean and antiques. Price is $39.

ARTISTIC KONAVLE AND CAVTAT - Dubrovnik.
A drive to a location providing panoramic views of Dubrovnik and its Riviera is followed by a visit to the fertile Konavle Valley with its numerous small villages. At the village of Mihanici, guests stop at the gallery of artist Mijo Sisa, located in his family home. Sisa, a primitive painter, welcomes passengers of Radisson Seven Seas' vessels to his studio with a glass of homemade grape brandy and shows them his work, discussing his paintings as proudly as a father does his children. The four-hour tour ($42) also takes in Cavtat, 10 miles from Dubrovnik, and built on the ancient Roman town of Epidaurus, destroyed in the 7th century during an invasion of Avar tribes.

GAUCHO FIESTA WITH LUNCH - Buenos Aires, Argentina.
Passengers of Celebrity's **Mercury** in South America get a taste of Argentina's pampas (grasslands) during this shore excursion that takes them to a ranch northwest of Buenos Aires. Along the way, guests get to taste the "mate" (Argentina's tea-like national drink) prepared in a gourd and shared by families and friends. At the ranch, the family greets the group with trays of "empanadas" (little meat pies) and drinks, and the gauchos (cowboys) show their riding skills. Then an "asado" (barbecue) is served with beef, chicken, sausages, salad and local

Shore Excursions

wine and beer. Afterwards a musical show, including tango selections, is presented and guests are free to visit the ranch, ride the horses or go for a horse-and-carriage ride, and tour the ranch house. Price is $79.

AN EVENING AT YUSUPOV PALACE - St. Petersburg, Russia.
The closest thing you will probably come across to time-travel in your lifetime. Hosts dressed in 18th century apparel greet Royal Caribbean International's guests by the grand staircase and a string quartet plays classical music as guests enter Yusupov Palace. The palace, open only by special arrangement, was the home of Prince Felix Yusupov and Princess Irina Romanov, niece to Tsar Nicholas II, and the place where the madman Rasputin was murdered in 1916. Overlooking the Moyka, the yellow, colonnaded building dating back to the 1760s was designed by Vallinde la Mothe (the same architect who designed the Small Hermitage). A guided private tour of the palace takes in its opulence, including the Moorish Room complete with fountain, mosaics and horseshoe arches' the family quarters including the room were the tsar was received; and the basement where wax figures of Yusupov and Rasputin and exhibits document the murder of the eccentric who befriended the Romanovs. After the tour, guests sip champagne and caviar in the ballroom while listening to balalaika music. Then -are we feeling like royalty yet?- it is on to the exquisite Rococo-style private theater of the palace with its red velvet and gold leaf boxes, for an evening of opera presented by members of the St. Petersburg Opera Company. Cost is $230 and if your budget allows it, you will not regret it for a minute.

VENETIAN VILLAS - Venice, Italy.
Available on Radisson Seven Seas' vessels, this full-day tour ($175) leaves by private coach to Fanzolo and visits Villa Emo, built by the Emo Family between 1561 and 1566 and designed by Andrea Palladio. Frescoes inside the villa were painted by G. Battista Zetolli. Lunch is at the Villa Cipriani Hotel in Asolo. Afterwards, the program visits another of Andrea Palladio's masterpieces, the Villa Barbaro, located in Master and built by the Barbaro Family in 1550. Inside, guests can admire the frescoes painted by Paolo Veronese, the 16th century master.

AUSTRALIAN HOMESTEAD - Orient Lines offers a full day tour to the Gledswood Colonial Farm ($85) on calls to Sydney. Participants get a taste of country life as they watch farm hands performing chores including cow milking, sheep shearing and animal feeding. Boomerang and sheepdog demonstrations are among the highlights, plus a traditional Aussie barbecue lunch.

ESTANCIA LA RABIDA & CITY ORIENTATION - Montevideo, Uruguay. Featured on Silversea Cruises, this six-hour program provides a brief introduction to Montevideo and spends time at a 2,900-acre cattle and sheep ranch along the impressive Plate River. The owners welcome guests, who have an opportunity to observe farm hands going about their daily chores. A traditional meal is served with a side of folklore. Cost is $126.

HOMES & GARDENS OF HAWAII - Honolulu. This three-hour tour available on Cunard Line, provides an opportunity to visit a select showing of Honolulu's privately owned homes and gardens. Members of the Garden Club of Honolulu take guests to view some of their superbly landscaped homes set in a variety of natural locations. These range from tropical valleys to hillsides with sweeping ocean vistas. Other uniquely Hawaiian homes open directly onto the island's shoreline. Guests also are afforded a glimpse of the Hawaiian style in which the garden becomes an integral part of the home. Club members acting as hostesses answer questions about the lush tropical plants as they escort guests through their gardens. Refreshments are served at the last of the three homes scheduled on this program. Price is $65.

HOME HOSTED DINNER - Auckland, New Zealand—The people of New Zealand are famous for the warmth of their welcome to visitors. This evening excursion, available on Cunard Line, enables passengers to experience local hospitality and to learn about New Zealand and its lifestyles while enjoying dinner at a local home. Hosts meet guests shipside in the early evening and transfer them in their private vehicle. Cost is $84.00.

Shore Excursions

A MEXICAN COUNTRY FIESTA - Puerto Vallarta. Silversea Cruises offers this tour, an included program, when in Puerto Vallarta. This is a traditional fiesta in the foothills of the Sierra Madre, 30 minutes north of this Mexican Riviera port. While driving through plantations and small towns, the local guide provides information into the villagers' way of life. Upon arrival, guests discover that the village has donned a festive atmosphere including strolling musicians, colorful piñatas and paper flowers adorning the Zócalo or town square. Guests are free to wander and browse in the village, among the artisans' stands, and watch Mexican fair games. Margaritas and other beverages are served, accompanied by a selection of hors d'oeuvres. Tables and chairs have been arranged in the festive setting of the Zócalo and guests enjoy a buffet-style luncheon with such local delights as seafood, grilled meats, yellow saffron rice, tropical fruits and such. After lunch, the villagers present a folkloric show with a mariachi band. Afterwards, guests may join the dancers and show off their own dancing skills to the tunes of a marimba band.

Other Worthwhile Ship's Tours

Other shore excursions good to purchase from the cruise lines are activities and programs that might be difficult for you to arrange on your own during the limited time you have in port, like for instance, helicopter flightseeing or floatplane sightseeing in Alaska (often all available helicopters and floatplanes are booked by the cruise lines), and sports programs like golf and snorkeling/diving. Cruise lines that offer excellent golf programs at the ports of call include Silversea and Royal Caribbean; snorkel/diving programs are great on Norwegian Cruise Line and Princess. Princess is the only line on which you can actually get scuba certification during a seven-day cruise.

Usual tip to your tour guide is $1 per person for a half-day tour; $2 per person for a full-day excursion.

Tips for Touring Independently

If you prefer to tour independently at all or some of the ports of call, here are some tips:

* Seeing the sights on your own can be very rewarding, if you begin by doing your homework. Read up on your destination. Resources include Chapter Four in this guide, the line's own shore excursions booklet (to get ideas about what places to see) and travel literature: narratives about the destination to give you a sense of the place and its culture. Take some language lessons if you do not speak the destination's language.

* Contact Visitors' Bureaus—often they have information desks with complimentary maps and brochures at cruise terminals or near the pier (your ship's own shore excursions office can direct you). For instance, in Montevideo, Uruguay, I have picked up a free walking tour map at a tourist office right at the cruise terminal. Near the pier, at the entrance to Old San Juan, Puerto Rico, there is a Visitors Bureau that dispenses free maps and brochures and answers any questions you might have. In Oranjestad, Aruba, I have obtained free brochures and maps right in the cruise terminal—to name a few examples.

* Tell staff in the shore excursions office of your ship that you plan to tour independently and ask if you should avoid certain areas of the port or if it is safe to walk around everywhere.

* Ask your shore excursions staff if there are any free or nominal fee shuttles or trolleys that leave from, or near, the pier to the center of town or its attractions. We have taken free shuttles from the ship's pier in such cities as Copenhagen and Brisbane and from the center of town, toured independently. The shuttles/trolleys are also a good, inexpensive way to get your bearings.

* Ask at the shore excursions office how much a taxi is to the place you want to go, and if taxis are plentiful and available at the pier. Is public transportation good and reliable? Before getting into a taxi, agree with the driver on a rate and if you are having the driver wait for you, say at a remote beach (a very good idea), negotiate a round-trip-plus-wait-time rate and do not pay him until you return to the pier.

* Most important of all: before you set off on your own check at what time you need to be back at the pier to re-board the ship so as not to be left behind. Plan your touring,

Shore Excursions

taking in attractions that are close together whenever possible, and take care not to overload your schedule. As the day progresses, check your watch often—and always allow extra time for traffic jams and the unforeseen.

When It Is Not A Good Idea To Tour Independently

There are times when it is not advisable to go exploring on your own. These include the following situations:

* If you have heard, either from the shore excursions staff, or other sources that it is not safe to tour alone.

* If you do not speak the language and are completely unfamiliar with the port.

* When attractions you wish to visit are distant from the pier and local transportation is unreliable.

Test the Waters Tips

* Everyone, but particularly independents, should take the ship's daily activity log with them ashore. This log generally has the ship's port agent's phone number printed on it. The port agent can assist you in an emergency or if you return late and miss the ship.

* Want to do more background reading on your ports of call? Ships' libraries usually have travel narratives about the destinations they visit right on their shelves. But visit the ship's library early—the first afternoon of the voyage, if possible—for the best selection, as most of the volumes are checked out by the second day.

* Go to your public library at home and check out language tapes for your destination if you do not speak the language. Or if you prefer, sign up for language lessons at your community college or other institution.

* Interested in visiting a museum or other attraction on your own? Check with the shore excursions office to make sure it will be open that day—they will certainly know if they are running an organized shore excursion there. National holidays and/or regular closures may coincide with your visit.

* Always dreamed of enjoying a particular sight or activity during your cruise? Don't make opportunity come knocking twice before you enjoy it—do it the first chance you get.

167

On a recent cruise to Australia, for example, there were two opportunities listed for snorkeling on the Great Barrier Reef—the first was an optional shore excursion to Agincourt Reef in the Outer Great Barrier Reef and the second one was an included trip to Hardy Reef near the Whitsunday Islands. Without thinking twice, we immediately signed up for the paid shore excursion, went on it and snorkeled among Technicolor fish in a fantasy of coral gardens -a once-in-a-lifetime opportunity. When windy conditions prevented the trip to Hardy Reef later on in the cruise, many passengers who had not taken the earlier snorkeling opportunity were kicking themselves.

* If you have never gone in for water sports and other strenuous activities, know what you are in for and prepare for it. My husband and daughter went for a banana boat ride for the first time in their lives in the Greek Isles without even at least observing a ride. It turned out the program, on Star Clippers, was organized by two young people who drove the banana boat in such a way as to ensure riders were overthrown into the cold Aegean at least two or three times. My daughter did not know so she did not remove her sunglasses and lost them; my husband fell directly under the banana boat and had a few panicked moments before he could surface again. He had not taken off his wedding ring, but luckily it did not slip out. Had they observed the ride at least once I do not think they would have gone on it -or they would at least have known what to expect and prepared for it.

Insider's Savings Insights

* As the saying goes, if a deal seems too good to be true, it probably is. Once at the Pyramids near Cairo, Egypt, a woman from our ship believed the camel man when he said the camel ride would be "free"—and then learned it was $25 to get off!

* Complain to the shore excursions office if you feel your shipboard-bought tour left something to be desired -for instance, places listed on the tour's itinerary were not covered; the guide's English was bad and you could not understand him; the driver drove too fast and you could not properly see the sights. If the cruise staff escort corroborates your complaint or others on the tour speak up, they generally will credit your shipboard account for the full amount or at least part of what you paid for the excursion.

Shore Excursions

* If your tour does not offer refreshments and snacks, take little cereal boxes and yogurt containers from the ship's breakfast buffet before you set out in case you get hungry (but make sure this is not forbidden by local regulations). Also fill up an empty water bottle at the ship's lemonade, juice, punch, iced tea and/or water dispenser so you have something to drink during the excursion or purchase bottled water from the ship (often sold right near the gangway).

" Outdoor Pool "*Crown Odyssey*" Photo courtesy of Orient Lines.

"Top of Crown Lounge "*Crown Odyssey*" Photo courtesy of Orient Lines.

Seven Continents Restaurant "*Crown Odyssey*" Photo courtesy of Orient Lines

Chapter: 7
Shipboard Cabins

You may have intended only to use your cabin for showering, changing and sleeping, but once you board, you will find that that ship has sailed. The reality, nine times out of 10, will be that you wind up spending more time in your stateroom than you anticipated, particularly if you are on a seven-day or longer cruise.

You will most certainly find yourself enjoying a good amount of time in your cabin, especially on at sea days, perhaps having breakfast in bed, planning your day and evening, writing postcards to family and friends back home, taking a nap, relaxing while reading, listening to music or watching television—not to mention romantic interludes (or marathons, in the case of honeymooners).

Your cozy home at sea, your cabin is your private domain—like a mini-castle with the ocean as its moat. You can be comfortable and ecstatic, or uncomfortable and unhappy in it, so the choice of accommodations can color your entire cruise vacation—hopefully not blue as in miserable.

Picking the right cabin for you is therefore as important as finding the perfect spot for your deck chair so as to catch just the right number of rays and thus return home from your vacation with the perfect tan.

Let's start at the beginning. What are standard shipboard cabins like? Well, generally, they are bigger than train compartments and smaller than rooms on land-based resorts. Standard cabins typically measure between 120 sq. ft. to 180 sq. ft. depending on the cruise line—140 sq. ft. and over is a comfortable size, and if you tend to be claustrophobic, it is advisable to go for 180 sq. ft., or more if you can afford it -perhaps even a suite (typically 250 sq. ft and larger).

Shipboard accommodations are generally attractively decorated -often in pleasant earth tones and with art on the wall-and usually feature two beds that can be converted to queen size, wall to wall carpeting, individually-controlled air conditioning/heating, telephone, television (with CNN International and sometimes ESPN International, two to four movie channels, local channels when close to land) radio channels (with taped music including classical, jazz, and pop), private bathroom with shower, closet and chest of drawers, night table and chair. Bathrooms, though functional, are typically tiny (I have heard many a passenger exclaim that they have closets at home bigger than their cabin's bathroom and with reason: I do too!). Bathrooms generally have a small shower (you may find yourself getting more intimate with your shower curtain than you wished), wash basin, medicine cabinet or shelves to put your toiletries) and a vacuum toilet that often makes a noise on a par with the ship's horn (never put anything other than toilet paper in your toilet if you want to keep using it without problems). Bath amenities typically include soaps and shampoo—with ultra-deluxe lines like Crystal, Seabourn and Silversea providing designer soaps, lotions and more.

Most bathrooms usually also have a removable clothesline in the shower (very handy for hand-washables, bathing suits and such, and if your ship does not have a self-service launderette). And typically there is a high threshold separating the bathroom from the rest of the cabin—make a mental note not to trip over it the first few days of the cruise (particularly if you get up in the middle of the night to use the bathroom) until you get used to it. I always leave the bathroom light on all night in my cabin as a night-light (a practice I began when we were sailing with our young daughter).

Families will find a good number of triples and quads as well as adjoining cabins. Some ships, including Royal Caribbean's latest mega-liners and ultra-liners also have family suites accommodating up to eight persons (with two bedrooms with twins that convert to queens, two bathrooms—one with tub—, living room with sofa-bed and Pullman bed, refrigerator, vanity area and balcony).

Shipboard Cabins

When looking at cruise brochures you will notice often there are more than a dozen cabin categories -sometimes more than two dozen-with names like "standard," "superior," "deluxe" for variations of four basic types: inside (no window), ocean view (with window or porthole), veranda and suite. Generally, higher deck locations (closer to the pool and public areas) command higher prices.

Standard staterooms on newer vessels may also feature such conveniences as personal safe, hairdryer, mini-fridge, loveseat or sofa (often convertible to an extra bed), table, desk and stool and Internet access. Other amenities, usually available in higher categories, may even incorporate a bathtub and a veranda.

A balcony is one of two ways—the most expensive of the two-to be able to enjoy an ocean view from your shipboard accommodations. The other way is a window or porthole. Staterooms without windows are referred to as "inside cabins" and they are the cheapest accommodations at sea -less expensive than "outside cabins" (with windows). Though they are good deals, inside cabins are not good choices for the claustrophobic. I am not, and neither are my family members, so the first cabin we booked was an inside stateroom, lowest category: it worked fine for us, particularly homey, once we decorated it with plush toys and souvenirs bought at the ports of call. Through the years some people who have mild cases of claustrophobia have told me they are able to book inside cabins if they decorate them with big posters showing expansive beach scenes and the like -one painted a picture of a window through which you could see a pretty landscape and put it on her wall to sail successfully in an inside cabin.

Windowed cabins are a good middle-of-the-road value, as the views of the sea and ports -the reason most of us do set sail in the first place-are a great feature. In the case of a cabin with a veranda—the more expensive of the two ocean view options—the balcony is generally furnished with two chairs and a table and has a sliding glass door separating it from the rest of the cabin. The glass door usually ensures that you can see the sea from any point inside the stateroom—in many cases, even while resting in bed. So veranda cabins are a wonderful splurge because these are rooms with a view -make that a View with a capital "V."

The advantages of a veranda are as pleasurable as the gentle and sparkling sea breezes you will enjoy every day from it, so if you can afford the extra cost you will not be sorry, particularly if you are doing scenic cruising in such areas as the Caribbean, the Panama Canal and Alaska. You will thank your lucky stars as you watch a Panama Canal crossing from your balcony, with the sides of the canal so close you can almost reach out and touch them, or when you witness a glacier calving in Alaska—listening to the roar of the ancient ice breaking off and falling on to the sea-all from the comfort of your private perch. You can have breakfast served on your veranda and delight in the early morning light and fresh breezes while you linger over your coffee, or nibble on a snack al fresco while savoring the passing panoramas.

> Cabin stewards clean your stateroom, and bring you fresh towels, supplies of shampoo and soap, as well as a chocolate for your pillow with nightly turndown service. Some make bunnies, elephants, snakes and other fanciful creatures out of hand towels to amuse you. They are typically efficient and unobstrusive so much so that shipboard comedians often quip that they got up to go to the bathroom in the middle of the night and when they returned their steward had already made their bed. Another often-heard joke: that you hardly ever see your room steward—except the last night of the cruise, when tips are traditionally given.

Yet other balcony bonuses: reveling in the sounds of the ocean as you drift off to sleep, leaving your sliding glass door ajar to breathe the fresh sea air all night long, stargazing in privacy and comfort, and waking up to the natural light flowing in through your sliding glass door.

In fact, at sea the only thing better than a cabin with a veranda is, of course, a suite with a veranda. I have had the pleasure of occupying suites on several ships, and what can I tell you? They're simply great with plenty of room to spread out during your vacation.

Suites are the roomiest and hence the most desirable accommodations at sea, and

Shipboard Cabins

generally come in a variety of sizes from 200+ mini-suites to several categories of suites climaxing in palatial accommodations featuring up to more than 5,000 sq. ft. as in the case of the two fantasy suites aboard NCL's **Norwegian Star**. These lavish suites and those on Royal Caribbean and Celebrity Cruises, to cite two more examples, feature everything from entertainment centers with baby grand piano and flat-screen televisions to luxurious marble baths with whirlpool tubs and separate glass-enclosed showers. Typical suite perks include VCR, personalized stationery, and coffee tables that can be adjusted for meal service.

> Your travel agent, the cruise line and/or the line's brochure will tell you exactly what pieces of furniture there are in the cabin you are considering, as well as such amenities as sitting area and mini-refrigerator.

But whether you book a cabin or a suite, the old real estate adage of "location, location, location," applies at sea too. Always keep the following in mind:

* Locations amidships are desirable for two reasons: they are generally the most stable (where least motion is felt) particularly those cabins in the ship's lower decks; and if they are near the vessel's main bank of elevators (those serving the heart of the ship or atrium in newer vessels) they also save you steps as the atrium is surrounded by many of the public areas like restaurants, shops, casino, Internet Café, lounges, reception/shore excursions desk and the like.

* Avoid locations too close to the disco, show lounge and dining rooms as people tend to gather and chat around these areas. In the case of the lounge and disco the music may be loud enough to be heard in your cabin.

* Steer away from locations over the engine room or near the anchor (these areas may be noisy). I had a fellow passenger tell me she was awakened several mornings with a grinding noise that felt like they were hoisting the anchor's chain around her ears several mornings—her cabin was, you guessed it, situated near the anchor.

* Locations near the children's playrooms may be a bit too lively during the day (when you may be trying to take a nap).

* Cabins next to elevator shafts may be noisy -try to be near elevators to save steps, but not in so close proximity that you would hear the elevators going up and down, and/or people talking as they get on and off, from your bed. As a rule of thumb, book a cabin at least two or three staterooms away from the elevator shaft.

* Find out from your agent, cruise brochure or the line itself, if the windows or portholes are angled, overlooking parts of the ship that aren't particularly attractive. Also, ask if one of the beds is positioned against the window and thus obstructing your access to it.

* Always check that your window does not open to a promenade or your views will often be of a parade of joggers and walkers.

> A cabin situated at either end of the ship will be less stable (more motion will be felt) and it may be a long walk to public areas on the opposite end of the vessel.

* Stay away from cabins located directly under jogging/walking tracks -as you may hear stomping from runners above. Often there are posted hours for the use of jogging/walking tracks, but some passengers may disregard them and wake you up earlier than you wished.

All cabins and suites come with a steward and an assistant steward who clean and tidy up the room (picking up after you when necessary), turn down your bed at night, and leave a chocolate on your pillow. Suites also boast a butler who serves you tea, sandwiches and cookies in the afternoon, and hors d'oeuvres before dinner. You will want to pack this gentleman up and take him home with you at the end of the voyage—I did after I had one of them taking care of my suite on a Celebrity ship—as his pampering services also include getting you newspapers at the ports of call, delivering your shore excursion order form and tickets, delivering your laundry/dry-cleaning and getting your dress shoes shined. You'll

Shipboard Cabins

exclaim, "the butler did it!" when he sets up a romantic dinner for two on your terrace—serving you course by course-or makes perfect arrangements for a private cocktail party for your new-found friends right on your veranda or in the living room of your suite.

Test the Waters Tips

* Before deciding upon a particular cabin category, first of all consider what use you want to get out of your accommodations. Are you on a short (one- to four-day sailing) and plan to join in a lot of shipboard activities and do plenty of sightseeing in port? Then you may want to steam past the higher priced accommodations to one of the lowest (and cheapest) categories of cabins. On longer voyages, or if you plan to spend a good amount of time in your room, or if it is a special occasion -such as a honeymoon or anniversary- you may want to splurge on a higher cabin category.

* Look at the ship's deck plans carefully noting what is over, under, to the side of, and in the immediate neighborhood of the cabin you are considering. If there is any area that could conceivably be noisy, look for a better location.

* When you are ready, book the actual stateroom by specific cabin number, not just by category, as usually there are location differences within a particular category.

* Book early for the best cabin locations to be available (other people are reading this guide too and as a result, know a good cabin when they see it!). Cheapest cabins and those with the best locations typically sell first.

* Normally you can get exact cabin dimensions from the cruise line's brochure, from the cruise line itself or from your travel agent. You can also request specific facilities and amenities in your cabin from your travel agent and/or the cruise line before booking a stateroom. Do not make your decision based merely on brochure photos—these may have been taken with wide angle lenses that can distort size, and as the brochure is the cruise line's advertising tool, the photos will certainly have been taken from the most advantageous point to make the stateroom appear as large and attractive as possible. Cabin sketches usually yield more and better information than photos—generally showing you what furniture and amenities are in the stateroom. One quick way to get an idea about cabin dimensions if

there are sketches in the line's brochure is this: most shipboard beds are three feet by six and a half feet or 19.5 square feet. So, looking at the sketch, you can estimate how many more beds could fit in the cabin, and then multiply that number by 19.5 to get an idea of the square footage.

* If you have any questions at all about the cabin you are thinking of booking and its facilities and amenities, ask your travel agent and/or the cruise line. The only dumb question, as the saying goes, is the one left unasked.

* If in spite of all your care you find there is a problem with your cabin—noisy location or neighbors, for instance, it may be possible to change it (our daughter once did when she found herself in a noisy location on a sailing vessel) if the ship is not full. Take your case, as soon as possible, to the reception/guest relations' desk and if they cannot help you, write a letter to the hotel manager.

Insider's Savings Insights

* On newer ships, generally most cabins are identical in dimensions—with the lowest prices available on the lowest decks (as you do have a longer elevator ride to the pool deck, spa and other public areas, but, guess what? You will be laughing all the way to the top as you pocket the savings!).

* Reserve your cabin early for best locations and to benefit from early booking discounts and also to be eligible for a complimentary upgrade if a subsequent group booking demands a block of cabins that includes your stateroom.

* Ask your agent and/or the cruise line if there are any special deals or discounts available on the cabin you are thinking of booking or on similar ones for the dates you are planning to travel.

* If you are flexible and can leave quickly, check with short-notice agencies (see Insider's Savings Insights section in Chapter One) to see if there are special deals you can take advantage of.

* Sometimes cruise lines offer specials that allow you to book a cabin category instead of a specific cabin, and you are guaranteed a cabin in that category or one better for a good discount. Check with your agent or the line to see if there are deals like these and if they are attractive enough you may be willing to take your luck with cabin location.

Photo courtesy of Norwegian Cruise Line.

Chapter: 8
Shipboard Lifestyles

I have often thought that a ship passenger is very much like a crab, which carries his home on his back as he wanders. The ship's hull is like a gigantic shell with the amenities, facilities and activities to suit a variety of lifestyles.

Life aboard a modern cruise ship is pretty much what a passenger wants to make it: days filled with a whirlwind of activity or a laid-back, indolent interlude, whiling away the hours by the pool. Or perhaps it can be something in between.

Let's take a look at some lifestyles/personal preferences that can be enjoyed/accommodated on today's ships.

Active/Social Cruiser

You love lots of activities and lots of interaction with other people. Well, you will find it is very easy to make friends aboard ship with organized get-togethers galore so you can meet your fellow passengers. There is a wonderful camaraderie at sea, with everyone feeling as if they are sharing a great adventure together—all on the same boat, so to speak—and thus more prone and amenable to talk to perfect strangers.

And, what is more, you can help the process along considerably. Here are several ways of making friends aboard ship that have never failed me through the years:

* Go a few minutes early to the lifeboat drill (usually the first afternoon, shortly after you set sail) and strike up a conversation with others there (talk about the life jacket you are attempting to put on, or the drill itself, or ask if this is their first cruise). It is easy to make a friend or two: everyone is wearing their life preservers, looking silly, and feeling adventuresome and talkative as their holiday begins.

* Go to lots of organized activities (you cannot meet people if you stay in your cabin) and arrive at the functions a little early, that way you can strike up a conversation with others who are waiting too—begin by asking: is this the place for trivia (or the culinary demonstration, or crafts, etc.) and take it from there.

* Offer to lend someone at the railing your binoculars if you spot wildlife, or your ship is doing scenic cruising in Alaska's Inside Passage, Australia's Great Barrier Reef and other such locales.

* Offer to take people's photos with their cameras at points of interest at the ports.

* Attend the captain's welcome aboard cocktail party and any other get-togethers that apply to your situation (singles, grandparents' bragging parties, honeymooners, etc.).

Active/Social Cruisers will generally be happiest in mega-liners and ultra-liners like those of Royal Caribbean, Celebrity, Carnival, Norwegian and Princess.

Here is a sample daily activities' schedule from Celebrity Cruises. Your cabin steward brings this log to your stateroom every evening so you can read about the following day's activities and entertainment events and plan your day. These daily programs also list the next evening's dress code and include meal times at the various restaurants, hours of operation of the guest relations' desk, bank, shore excursions desk and other offices and facilities. Often, daily drink specials are also listed, along with navigational information/port of call details. The port agent's phone number (who can assist you if you miss the ship or other emergency) is generally also included when the ship will be in port.

So this daily sheet is pretty much your bible while on your cruise—write all over it (marking things you are interested in), fold it, and put it in your pocket or purse and carry it with you always so no matter where you are on the ship or ashore you have all this great information with you and you know what is going on, where, and when.

Shipboard Lifestyles

Sample Daily Activity Program on Celebrity's Infinity

8 a.m. Catholic Mass, Cinema/Conference Center, Deck 3
8:30-9 a.m. Walk-A-Mile with your Cruise Staff, Meet in the Mast Bar, Sunrise Deck 11
9 a.m. Getting Started: Windows. Join Computer Trainer Todd in the Alpha Meeting Room Deck 3
9 a.m. Sit & Be Fit, Constellation Club, Deck 11
9-11 a.m. Future Cruise Sales, Samira is available to answer any questions in the Grand Foyer Deck 3
9:30 a.m. Morning Quiz available in the Library, Decks 8,9
9:30-11 a.m. Books may be checked out in the Library Deck 8
9:45 a.m. Celebrity Enrichment Series on Close Encounters with Alaska's Wildlife, Celebrity Theater, Decks 4,5
10 a.m. Napkin Folding with Social Hostess Liz, Rendez-Vous Lounge, Deck 4
10-10:30 a.m. Bingo cards go on sale for today's game, Celebrity Theater, Decks 4,5
10:30 a.m. Passenger Talent Show Rehearsal, Constellation Club, Deck 11
11 a.m. Five-Minute Makeover, AquaSpa Deck 10
11 a.m. Informal Bridge Games, Tower Card Room, Deck 6
11:15 a.m. Culinary Demonstration with the Executive Chef, Rendez-Vous Lounge, Deck 4
11:15 a.m. Minimum $2,000 Giant Jackpot Bingorama, Celebrity Theater, Decks 4,5
12 noon Service Club meeting with the Cruise Staff, Cova Café Deck 5
1:30 p.m. Movie Time, Cinema, Deck 3
1:30 p.m. Slots Tournament, Fortunes Casino, Deck 4
1:30 p.m. Table Tennis Open Tournament, Sports Deck 12
1:30 p.m. Celebrity Enrichment Series - Astronomer John Miller features a Starlab Planetarium presentation, Celebrity Theater, Decks 4,5

Chapter Eight

2 p.m.	Scavenger Quest for prizes, Constellation Club Deck 11
2 p.m.	Afternoon Bridge play, Tower Card Room Deck 6
2:15 p.m.	Darts Tournament with the Cruise Staff, Sports Deck 12
2:30-4 p.m.	Redeem your Frequent Fitness cards for prizes, Grand Foyer Deck 3
3 p.m.	De-stress for Wellness, AquaSpa Deck 11
3 p.m.	Passenger Talent Show, Celebrity Theater Decks 4,5
3:15 p.m.	Celebrity Enrichment Series. The Nature Conservancy's Dan Quinn speaks about his visit to the Titanic, Celebrity Theater, Decks 4,5
3:30 p.m.	Art auction, Rendez-Vous Lounge Deck 4
3:45 p.m.	Volleyball with the Cruise Staff, Sports Deck 12
4 p.m.	Junior Cruiser's Talent Show, Constellation Club Deck 11
4 p.m.	Bingorama, Celebrity Theater, Decks 4,5
4 p.m.	Friends of Lois & Bill W. meet in the Beta Meeting Room Deck 3
5-6 p.m.	Piano melodies in the Constellation Club Deck 11
5-6 p.m	Harp music in the Cova Café Deck 5
5:30-6:30	Dance music in the Rendez-vous Lounge Deck 4
6 p.m.	Movie Time, Cinema Deck 3
7 and 9 p.m.	Showtime (Broadway-style revue),Celebrity Theater Decks 4,5
7-8 p.m.	Party band plays in the Constellation Club Deck 11
7:30-8:30 p.m.	Informal discussion on Global Conservation, The Conservancy Deck 11
7:30-9 p.m.	Port and Shopping Guide with the Cruise Staff, Grand Foyer Deck 3
7:45-8:45 p.m.	Harp music in the Cova Café Deck 5
7:45-8:45 p.m.	Music for dancing in the Rendez-Vous Lounge Deck 4
8-8:30 p.m.	Piano with a view in the Constellation Club Deck 11
8:30 p.m.	Movie Time, Cinema Deck 3
9-9:45 p.m.	Piano Music in the Atrium, Deck 4
9:30-10:15 p.m.	Dance Music, Rendez-Vous Lounge Deck 4

Shipboard Lifestyles

9:30-10:15 p.m.	Dancing in the Constellation Club Deck 11
9:45-11:30 p.m.	Harp Music in the Cova Café Deck 5
10 and 11:15 p.m.	Stargazing with astronomer John Miller, Sunrise Deck 11
10:15 p.m.	Team Trivia with the Cruise Staff, Rendez-Vous Lounge Deck 4
10:30 p.m.-Midnight	Party time - Constellation Club Deck 11
10:45 p.m.	Movie Time, Cinema Deck 3
10:45 p.m.-12:15 a.m.	Dance music in the Rendez-Vous Lounge Deck 4
Midnight-???	D.J. Drew plays the hits for your dancing pleasure, Constellation Club Deck 11

Whew! And that is just one single, solitary day! What do you think? Will you be busy or what? And don't forget, on top of all this, you will probably want to spend some time by the pool, visit the gym/spa, shops, and you also know that somehow you will want to sandwich in several meals and snacks—this same program lists the following Dining Hours:

6:30-7:30 a.m.	Sunrise Breakfast, Oceanview Grill
6:30-10 a.m.	Continental Breakfast in stateroom on request
24 hours	Coffee and Tea available, Oceanview Café
7:30-10 a.m.	Breakfast Buffet, Oceanview Café
7:30-10 a.m.	Light & Healthy Breakfast, AquaSpa Café
7:30 a.m. & 8:45 a.m.	Main and Late Seating Breakfasts in the Trellis Restaurant
10-11 a.m.	Late Risers' Breakfast, Oceanview Grill
10 a.m.- noon	Croissants, Danish, Muffins available Cova Café
10:30-11:00 a.m.	Bouillon, Oceanview Grill
Noon and 1:30 p.m.	Main and Late Seating Lunch in the Trellis Restaurant
Noon - 2 p.m.	Buffet Luncheon, Oceanview Café
Noon - 2 p.m.	Light & Healthy Luncheon, AquaSpa Café
Noon to 2:30 p.m.	Hot Dogs & Hamburgers, Breezes Pool Grill
12:30-2:30 p.m.	Specialty of the Day, Oceanview Grill
3-5 p.m.	Pastries available, Cova Café

Fell's Official Know-It-All: Cruises

> **3-7 p.m.** Homemade Pizza, Breezes Pool Grill
> **4-5 p.m.** Afternoon Tea, Oceanview Café
> **4-6 p.m.** Frozen Yogurt available, Oceanview Café
> **6:00 p.m & 8:30 p.m.** Main and Late Seating Dinner, Trellis Restaurant
> **6:30-9 p.m.** Specialty Restaurant Dinner (reservations and fee venue) SS United States Restaurant
> **10 p.m.-1 a.m.** Homemade Pizza, Oceanview Grill
> **11:30 p.m.-12:30 a.m.** Gourmet Bites, Martini Bar, Casino, Champagne Bar, Cova Café, Constellation Club and Rendez-Vous Bar

On many ships, you are generally assigned to a large dinner table (usually six or eight diners). Your tablemates are newfound friends to discuss your day and activities with and exchange information about the ship and the ports.

* Passive/Just-wanna-get-away-from-it-all Cruiser - If you just want to decompress - relaxing, taking each day as it comes, with a minimum of involvement in organized activities and little, if any, contact with others, you too will be happy aboard ship. Best for this cruiser group are small, yacht-like vessels like those of Silversea, Seabourn and Windstar, where less is more when it comes to organized activities and passengers are pretty much left to entertain themselves and they kind of like it that way.

But even if you decide to sail on mid-size ships and mega-liners and ultra-liners, there is never any pressure to participate in any of the multitude of events and activities available: you take them or leave them—it is strictly up to you and nobody will ever bother you about participating in this or that. You can find a quiet corner up on deck or in your favorite among an array of intimate spaces such as libraries, card rooms and some lounges (you will find these and plenty of other intimate spaces even on mega-liners and ultra-liners -for instance, some of Royal Caribbean's and Celebrity's ships have cozy music libraries too) and enjoy peace and quiet and as much solitude and tranquility as your heart desires.

Shipboard Lifestyles

> Ships with the best libraries include Cunard's Queen Elizabeth 2 (where there are full-time librarians on duty) and the vessels of Holland America, Celebrity and Royal Caribbean.

* Special Interest Cruiser -Say you have come onboard with a special interest: perhaps you want to continue a health/exercise plan you began at home or launch a new one; or maybe you have shopping or gambling on your mind—well, today's cruise ships have it all right there for you, the health-conscious/spa enthusiast, shopper or gambler.

When it comes to health clubs, cruise lines boast spas that would make many of those on land-based resorts mud-green with envy. To name a few: the 25,000 sq. ft. AquaSpa on Celebrity's Millennium-Class ships features holistic spa treatments in 16 treatment rooms, an ocean-view state-of-the-art gymnasium and a free thalassotherapy pool with neck massage pipes, two airbeds and jet massage stations. A Café poolside offers light and healthy dishes for breakfast and dinner (at no extra charge) for those who wish to continue a diet regimen (and the main dining room features "Lean & Light" and vegetarian dishes).

Another great example of floating spas is the ShipShape Spa found on Royal Caribbean ships. These facilities feature a themed Solarium—on **Radiance of the Seas**, for example, the theme is exotic Africa—with a pool, spas and fountain covered by a retractable glass dome and adorned by an abundance of vegetation, three life-sized, sculptured stone elephants and stone relief art panels depicting gazelles and antelopes. The ShipShape Spa also features a beauty treatment area with hair salon, massage rooms, hydrotherapy bath room, Rasul Oriental Ceremony Suite (I thoroughly enjoyed this treatment with its variety of muds to apply all over your body), thermal suite, gentle steam room, mild sauna, aromatic room with tropical and fog showers and relaxation area with sea views. The spa's ocean view gym has an aerobics area and gymnasium equipped with 18 treadmills, 10 Reebok Recumbent Cycles, eight Reebok Body Peaks, four Reebok Ridge Rocker Cycles, four Reebok Body Treks, extensive free-weights area, television monitors and stereo sound system.

> If you have some free time on port days, hit the gymnasium (you will generally have it almost to yourself).

On Royal Caribbean's Voyager-Class ships—the biggest ships in the world—the health club facilities are colossal, with more than 15,000 sq. ft. of workout, aerobics and spa areas and 10,000 sq. ft. of Solarium relaxation space. The spa area features 14 multi-purpose treatment rooms complete with shower cubicles, vanity and adjustable massage couches; a relaxation area; hydrotherapy bath room, sauna, steam and shower areas, changing area, and full service beauty salon. The gym on Voyager-Class ships provides 20 treadmills (all with ocean view), 14 Reebok cycles (recumbent and upright), eight Reebok Body Peaks, 18 Reebok strength units, six Reebok Body Trecs and a free-weights area with multiple benches, abs crunchers, etc. Plus television monitors and full stereo system. And, recreational facilities on the Voyager-Class ships include an outdoor sports deck; full-length sports court for basketball, paddleball and volleyball; rock climbing wall; in-line skating rink; ice-skating rink and miniature golf.

To further tempt you many lines (including Norwegian, Royal Caribbean, Holland America and Celebrity) offer activities programs—everything from dance lessons to exercise classes to sports tourneys. When passengers participate in these programs, they receive stamps or "dollars" and the like that can be traded for free sports apparel and logo souvenirs at the end of the cruise.

Sample Schedule of Sports Afloat Activities from "In Motion on the Ocean" Program on Norwegian Cruise Line

Each activity gives those who participate one Sports Afloat credit. Participants can trade the credits they earn for a free Sports Afloat T-shirt. All activities are free unless otherwise indicated. Note that there are also some fitness activities ashore at the ports of call.

Shipboard Lifestyles

Sunday	At Sea
8 a.m.	Step It Up! Advanced Step Aerobics
9 a.m.	The Belt and Below Lower Body Muscle Toning
9:30 a.m.	Walk A Mile With A Smile
10 a.m.	Sit and Be Fit
10 a.m.	Beginning Spinning Program ($5)
11 a.m.	Energy Stretch
3 p.m.	Tribal Beats Spinning Program ($5)
4 p.m.	Kick-Box Aerobics
4:30 p.m.	Basketball Free Throw Contest
5 p.m.	Back to Abs! Total Torso Conditioning
5:30 p.m.	Beginning Yoga
Monday	Norfolk, Va.
3 p.m.	Beginning Spinning Program ($5)
3:30 p.m.	Golf Putting Tournament
4 p.m.	Speedy Walk A Mile
5 p.m.	Beginning Step Aerobics
5:45 p.m.	Quick Abs Torso Conditioning
6 p.m.	Evening Siesta Stretch
Tuesday	Charleston, S.C.
8 a.m.	Morning Walk A Mile
8:30 a.m.	Morning Stretch
9 a.m.	Basketball 3 pt. Contest
9 a.m.	Spinning Program ($5)
9:30 a.m.	Sit and Be Fit
10:30 a.m.	Jump 'N Jump - Jump Rope Aerobics and Body Tone
Wednesday	At Sea
8 a.m.	Beginning Step Aerobics
8:45 a.m.	Morning Stretch
9:15 a.m.	Quick Abs Torso Conditioning
10:30 a.m.	Beginning Spinning Program ($5)
11:30 a.m.	Energy Stretch
3 p.m.	Step It Up Advanced Step Aerobics
3:30 p.m.	Golf Putting Tournament
3:45 p.m.	Jump 'N Jump - Jump Rope Aerobics and Body Tone

4:30 p.m.	Spinning Program ($5)
5:30 p.m.	Beginning Yoga
Thursday	**At Sea**
8 a.m.	Low Impact Aerobics
9 a.m.	The Belt and Below Lower Body Muscle Toning
10 a.m.	Sit and Be Fit
10:30 a.m.	Beginning Spinning Program ($5)
11:30 a.m.	Energy Stretch
3 p.m.	Spinning Program ($5)
4 p.m.	Aerobics and Body Tone
4:30 p.m.	Speedy Walk A Mile
5 p.m.	Back to Abs! Total Torso Conditioning
5:30 p.m.	Beginning Yoga
Friday	**San Juan, Puerto Rico**
8 a.m.	Beginning Spinning Program ($5)
9 a.m.	Back to Abs! Total Torso Conditioning
9:30 a.m.	Intermediate Yoga
10 a.m.	Volleyball
10:30 a.m.	Morning Walk A Mile
1 p.m.	Fitness Walk ashore through Old San Juan to the Fort (1.5 miles)
Saturday	**St. Thomas, U.S. Virgin Islands**
8 a.m.	Fitness Walk to Shop St. Thomas (2 miles)
5:30 p.m.	Basketball
6 p.m.	Quick Step Aerobics
6:30 p.m.	Late Day Energy Stretch
Sunday	**St. Maarten**
8 a.m.	Seniors Young At Heart Aerobics
8:30 a.m.	Quick Abs Torso Conditioning
9 a.m.	Fitness Walk to the Fort (2.5 miles)
5:30 p.m.	Volleyball
5:30 p.m.	Flamenco Endurance Spinning Program ($5)
6:30 p.m.	Light Evening Stretch
Monday	**At Sea**
8 a.m.	Low Impact Aerobics
9 a.m.	Aerobics and Body Tone

Shipboard Lifestyles

9:30 a.m.	Sit and Be Fit
9:30 a.m.	Morning Walk A Mile
9:30 a.m.	Hypnotic Spinning Program ($5)
10:30 a.m.	Intermediate Yoga
3 p.m.	Spinning Program ($5)
4 p.m.	Seniors Young At Heart Aerobics
4:30 p.m.	Total Body Muscle Conditioning
5:30 p.m.	Back to Abs! Total Torso Conditioning
6 p.m.	Light Evening Stretch
Tuesday	Aruba
8 a.m.	Beginning Step Aerobics
8:45 a.m.	Back to Abs! Total Torso Conditioning
9:30 a.m.	Sit and Be Fit
10 a.m.	Spinning Program ($5)
10:30 a.m.	Walk A Mile With A Smile
11 a.m.	Energy Stretch
3 p.m.	Spinning Program ($5) 4 p.m.-Total Body Muscle Conditioning
4:30 p.m.	Trade your credits for your free Sports Afloat T-shirt
4:30 p.m.	Ping Pong Tournament
5 p.m.	Kick-box Aerobics
6 p.m.	Evening Siesta Stretch
Wednesday	At Sea
8 a.m.	Good Morning Walk A Mile
8:30 a.m.	Back to Abs!
9 a.m.	Step It Up! Advanced Step Aerobics
9:30 a.m.	Bring 18 credits and get your Sports Afloat T-shirt
10 a.m.	Morning Stretch
10:30 a.m.	Spinning Program ($5)
3 p.m.	Spinning Program ($5)
4 p.m.	Back to Abs! Total Torso Conditioning
4:30 p.m.	Bring 18 credits and get your Sports Afloat T-shirt
4:30 p.m.	Final Golf Putting Tournament
4:30 p.m.	Seniors Young At Heart Aerobics
5 p.m.	Beginners Yoga

Fell's Official Know-It-All: Cruises

> Everyone, but especially those of us who tend to be couch potatoes, should check with a physician before launching an exercise program.

Wow! I'm already pooped just reading this! Which goes to show you -you can be very, very, very (wait, let me mop up my brow) very, very active on a cruise!

> Make your spa treatment appointments early in the cruise for best time choices. For last-minute beauty salon or spa appointments your best bets will be a day when the ship is in a port of call (if you have time before or after your touring) or during meal times.

Here is a sample spa menu of a Steiner Transocean Ltd.—managed spa on a premium ship. Steiner is a company that operates more than 100 shipboard spas. (The same warning applies: All prices are current as of the time I wrote the book, but subject to change without notice).

Spa Rituals

Facial Treatments

La Therapie Facial (50 min.)...$99
The Biotherapie Facial (50 min.)...$99
Elemis Aromapure Facial (50 min.)...$99
Elemis Aromapure Facial for Men (50 min.)...$99
Hydrotherapy Facial (25 min.)...$50
La Therapie Back Treatment (50 min.)...$99

Detoxification, Anti-Cellulite and Slimming Therapies

Ionithermie Superdetox...$120
Course of three Ionithermie Superdetox...$300
Active Algae Wrap...$115
Course of three Active Algae Wraps...$285
Cleopatra Milk Wrap...$115
Wrap treatment with full body massage...$190
Wrap treatment with half body massage...$160

Aromatherapy, Massage and Holistic Treatments

Absolute Face and Body Treatment (105 min.)...$160
Body Blitz (50 min.)...$90
Full Body Massage (50 min.)...$99
Half Body Massage (25 min.)...$65
Couple's Massage (80 min.)...$220
Reflexology (50 min.)...$99
Reflexology and half body massage (80 min.)...$160
Reflexology and full body massage (105 min.)...$190
Sports therapy...$105
Shiatsu full body massage (50 min.)...$99
The Spa Taster (hydrotherapy facial and half body massage, 50 min.)...$99

Water Rituals

Aquameditation...$29
Hydrotherapy bath...$29
Hydrajet...$25
The Rasul/Serail Chamber...$75/$80

Fitness Rituals

Personal training (1 hr.)...$75
Lifestyle enhancement consultation with program...$35
Body composition analysis...$30

Additionally, this and other floating spas generally offer a complete menu of nail and beauty services in their full-service beauty salons. The suggested gratuity for spa and beauty services is 15 percent -check your bill, as it is sometimes automatically added. Most ships charge you if you cancel an appointment less than 24 hours in advance, so keep an eye on your schedule.

> The ship's spa may run specials in port, when it is less busy —perhaps a spa-taster treatment (mini facial and half-body massage) at a 20 or 30 discount.
>
> While in the spa, the therapist may pitch you some lotions and creams, sometimes even calling them a "prescription"—just smile, thank her, and tell her you'll think about it, if you are not interested.
>
> Some lines, including Princess and Celebrity, let you pre-order spa packages including a number of treatments (one less thing to do onboard). Check with your travel agent and/or the line.

Well, you say, all that is fine and dandy, but I am not a health-conscious cruiser—my special interest is shopping... or gambling. Don't worry, they've got you covered too.

* Gambling Anyone? Shipboard casinos go from small, understated areas, perhaps in a section of one of the lounges -like the one on Windstar's **Wind Surf** -to glitzy, Vegas-style establishments like those of Carnival and Royal Caribbean, two lines that boast the largest casinos at sea. These two lines, along with Princess, Celebrity, Holland America and Norwegian (except the **Norwegian Star** in Hawaii that due to local laws has no casino) are generally the best for people who want big casinos.

Floating casinos feature much the same games as their land-based counterparts: a variety of slot machines and tables for blackjack, dice, roulette, and poker. If you have never gambled, but would like to try it, the casino staff (who is generally very courteous and friendly) usually offers a casino get-acquainted session and gambling lesson early on the cruise.

Shipboard Lifestyles

I cannot recommend gambling at sea or on terra firma (note that if the casinos lost more than they won, there would be no casinos). If you want to try it as a recreational activity, put a fixed amount in your pocket—what you would spend on dinner and a show, perhaps-and leave the casino when you have lost that. If you find yourself a nice amount ahead during the course of the evening, that's another very good time to leave the casino.

However, all that said, if you are indeed contemplating a cruise primarily to tempt Lady Luck, note that shipboard casinos—like the ship's shops-are closed while the vessel is in port (but often you can gamble in casinos at the ports of call—as well as shop, of course). Also very important for you to consider is that certain ships do not have casinos -notable among which are the two Disney Cruise Line vessels (Disney did not think its clientele would go for gambling) and the already mentioned *Norwegian Star* (due to legislation in Hawaii, where the ship is based year-round).

> You must be 18 year old and over to gamble in the casinos.

Here is an example of what you will find at a large ship casino -in this case, the *Carnival Spirit:*

* Theming. The theme could be ancient Egypt, Greece or Rome or Caribbean Pirates executed with mummies, classical statues or cannons and treasure chests or the like respectively. In the case of the *Carnival Spirit*, it is a French accent with a Louis XIV (the Sun King) theme.
* 220 slot machines
* 13 gaming tables broken down as follows:

> One table for roulette/dice
> 10 tables for blackjack
> Two tables for poker

Other forms of gambling are available in addition to the casino games on a typical cruise, including the ever popular bingo—usually a daily session and sometimes two, particularly when the ship is at sea—plus "horse racing" with wooden horses that you can bet on and which are moved around at the throw of dice until one wins by reaching the finish line. You can also bet on mileage pools in which you try to guess the number of miles your ship will cover in a day.

> Progressive bingo, generally called "snowball jackpot bingo," is very popular with the jackpot (often enough for a free cruise for two) going to a lucky winner or winners by cruise end.

* Shopping, anyone? If you are the shop-till-you-drop type, mega-liners and ultra-liners are the best choice for you, as these ships generally have big shopping arcades. Because of space considerations, yacht-like ships may only have a couple of shops, usually a logo/souvenir shop (that also stocks toiletries and such) and a gift emporium with perfumes and designer gifts. Shops on ships, whether large or small, are usually run by concessionaires. They will often offer a price guarantee (if you find the same item ashore for less than what you paid for in the ship's shop, they will refund the difference in price).

Among large ships, arguably the absolute best for shoppers are the biggest ships in the world, Royal Caribbean International's Voyager-Class ships. These vessels have a shopping mall-like horizontal atrium longer than a football field right in their hearts. Called The Royal Promenade, it is four decks tall and punctuated by two atria. This incredible space (with a Mardi Gras atmosphere as there is street entertainment and even parades presented here) boasts an array of specialty shops selling perfume, jewelry, fashion, china, liquor, and a variety of designer-label gifts by Versace, Bvlgary, Lladro, Kosta Boda and Royal Copenhagen. There is a Sun Shop for suntan lotions, hats and beachwear, a General Store with sundry items, books, magazines and such, and a Logo Shop for souvenir t-shirts, jackets, sweatshirts, mugs and hats.

Shipboard Lifestyles

The shops on board on most ships usually advertise specials in the vessel's daily activities sheets -a perennial one in almost every cruise I have taken recently is a sale of imported watches for less than $70—sometimes for less than $50. Check the specials out every day and browse to your heart's content. Also often, like in voyages to Russia, the Far East and Australia—to cite a few examples—the ship's shops will bring aboard an array of local handicrafts, including lacquered boxes and the popular nesting dolls in Russia to sell to passengers after the ship leaves the ports. They will usually advertise these special sales of local port merchandise ahead of arrival in the port. So what all this means to you is that you have more time for sightseeing ashore when you can shop on board.

Other shopping opportunities on board ship include art auctions—Park West Gallery runs many of them, generally during at sea days. Usually, there is a viewing period during which you can look over the art and mark it with stickers furnished to you (if you'd like some pieces to come up for auctioning) followed by the auction itself. Champagne is usually complimentary and you generally also receive a gift (a poster or a small, unframed, print) for staying throughout all the proceedings. Bidding can start as low as $50 or so depending on the item. While prices are often below terra firma galleries, consider that in art auctions there is generally a buyer's premium of 15 percent over what you bid and there could be other fees and taxes (check before you bid). Also, some of the items you must take home with you, which might not be too convenient if you have to fly home after the cruise—once I ran into a woman who had purchased three paintings that were take home items in the airport in Copenhagen—her artwork had not been packed properly and it was unraveling (she was too, she was so furious at having to lug the stuff home on two flights).

But shopping on the shipboard emporiums and art auctions is only half the story while on a cruise. Shopping at the ports of call is, of course, the second half. Most ships feature a port shopping talk and give you maps with "recommended" shops marked on them. Prizes are often raffled during this talk to lure you to attend. Prices may be lower in other stores and in shops off the beaten path than in "recommended stores." The "recommended stores," which pay the cruise line for that recommendation, however, do offer a satisfaction guarantee to the cruise line's passengers, so you can return the item if it breaks or has a problem with it within 30 days for a refund.

Check the prices of articles you are thinking of buying back home before you set sail, so you have a basis for comparison. And why not also ask your waiter, or wine steward, cabin stewardess or reception/guest relations' clerk for their shopping recommendations? They often have visited the ports a number of times and may know where the good prices actually are.

Bargaining with the merchants, particularly street vendors, may be the way to go in many ports, but examine the merchandise carefully, and use your judgment: that "silver" bracelet you purchased in the street may turn your wrist green by the second time you wear it. Once a woman on one of our Caribbean cruises bought a "silver" chain from a street vendor that was stamped as sterling silver on the clasp—well, it turned out that only the clasp was silver; the rest of the chain was not. And, of course, if a "bargain" seems too good to be true, it generally is.

> Check the shipboard shops hours. They are always closed while the vessel is in port due to local regulations (so you will go shop ashore).

* You say you have other interests? Try a theme cruise. These voyages, themed to a variety of topics such as Big Band Music, Food & Wine, Films, Opera, Sports and the like are offered on a number of lines including Crystal, Cunard, Silversea and Holland America. These theme cruises offer an array of events including talks, demonstrations, films and concerts (whatever is appropriate to the theme in question) and opportunities to meet actors, musicians, chefs, vintners, lecturers and other VIPs.

The cruise lines do try to have it all for you, whatever your preferred shipboard lifestyle and interests may be, but what if something goes wrong? Here are some tips on complaining if you come across something that is not satisfactory.

* When To Complain: Right away -if you let someone know as soon as something goes wrong they can do something about it and remedy the situation quickly, so you can enjoy the rest of your vacation.

Shipboard Lifestyles

* How To Complain: First verbally, then if the situation is not remedied, in writing.
* To Whom Do You Complain: Well, first let's take a look at the people who work aboard ship and their responsibilities:

THE CAPTAIN - the master of the ship.
THE STAFF CAPTAIN - the second in command.
CHIEF ENGINEER - in charge of engines and machinery.
HOTEL MANAGER - oversees the "hotel" aspects (accommodations and dining) of the ship.
CRUISE DIRECTOR - supervises the cruise staff and oversees activities and entertainment; serves as emcee for shows and some shipboard activities.
CHIEF PURSER - handles financial matters.
CHIEF STEWARD - oversees maintenance and cleanliness of cabins and public areas.
CABIN STEWARD - cleans the cabin and provides turndown service.
CHEF DE CUISINE - in charge of the galley and all that delectable food.
MAITRE D' - oversees the restaurant.
DINING ROOM STEWARD AND BU BOY - wait on tables.
SHORE EXCURSIONS MGR. - in charge of tours ashore; gives talks about the excursions.

So, if the problem is with your accommodations, tell your room steward; if he or she fails to remedy the situation, tell the Chief Steward. In the unlikely event the Chief Steward does not help you, write a note to the Hotel Manager outlining the issue in detail and to whom you have complained, and deliver the note to reception/guest relations. They will see to it that the Hotel Manager receives it.

If the problem is in the dining room, tell your waiter. If he does not remedy it, complain to the dining room captain, and if he fails to solve the problem, tell the maitre d'. If he does not help you, write to the Hotel Manager and deliver the note to reception/guest relations.

If the concern is with other areas of the ship—say, the air conditioning is too strong in the lounges, report the matter to reception/guest relations. If that does not work, write a note to the Hotel Manager and deliver it to reception/guest relations.

If the problem is with your bill, complain to reception/guest relations/purser's desk. If they cannot help you, ask to talk to the Chief Purser.

If you have issues with the activities or entertainment—say, a cruise staff member does not show up at the scheduled time to organize the ping pong tournament—call reception/guest relations. If the problem is not solved, write a note to the cruise director and deliver it to reception/guest relations and they will route it to the cruise director.

If you are dissatisfied with a shore excursion, talk to, or write to, the Shore Excursions Manager, and so on.

If your problem never ever gets solved even after your complaint(s) (it can, of course, happen), do mention it on the comment card that your cabin steward delivers to your stateroom on the last full day of the cruise. And write to the cruise line's customer relations department upon your return home (see this guide's Index for cruise line addresses).

But if, on the other hand, all is well and you have had the time of your life on your vacation -as is so often the case on a cruise holiday-also do take a moment to give praise where praise is due. Name any staff members or entertainers that helped make your cruise special on the comment card. The cruise lines take these comment cards very seriously (we have seen suggestions we've made on some ships implemented on subsequent voyages (like for instance, we commented that there should be oatmeal for breakfast every day in the informal cafes on Royal Caribbean as opposed to every other day, alternating with grits; and that there should be a light alternative like grilled chicken breast available every evening on Delta Queen Steamboats) and they also take careful note of your kind words about staff members or entertainment and reward them with continued contracts, honors and so on.

Test the Waters Tips

* The more, the merrier. If you want to make friends during your cruise, participate in as many activities as possible.

Shipboard Lifestyles

* If your spouse or significant other is not too keen on the idea of a cruise, lure him or her with a theme cruise focusing on one of their special interests.

* There are so many activities on mainstream ships that even the most active cruiser will have to pace himself and pick some instead of others. If you wanted to watch a movie being shown on cabin television or in the ship's cinema, but it conflicts with something else you really want to do, ask at guest relations if the movie will be repeated later in the sailing -sometimes movies are presented twice.

Insider's Savings Insights

* Don't buy your souvenirs—earn them by competing in the pool games, Scrabble, chess and other game tourneys, trivia contests, and deck sports tournaments. Most lines give logo items such as coffee mugs, bookmarks, water bottles, coasters, canvas bags, etc. as prizes to the winners of the games and contests. I always compete in the Scrabble tournaments and have a travel alarm clock from Celebrity Cruises and a flashlight/reading light from Holland America to show for it, among other mementoes. My husband always participates in the chess tournaments and he has a personal organizer from Orient Lines and a world time travel clock from Holland America among other souvenirs. We have a great set of four Crystal Cruises' logo coffee mugs we earned for winning trivia quizzes. And think of the fun you'll have while earning your mementoes.

* Don't buy your souvenirs—sweat for them. Lines like Holland America, Royal Caribbean and Celebrity have sports/activities programs involving physical activity—things from dance lessons to advanced aerobics classes. Every time you participate you earn a stamp, credit or dollar and at the end of the cruise you can cash them in for sports apparel or souvenirs (You should see my closet: I have a t-shirt, baseball cap and jacket from Holland America; t-shirts, sun visors and fanny packs from Royal Caribbean; shorts and a t-shirt from Princess; a t-shirt from Norwegian—when I need clothes I'm tempted to skip the mall and just book a cruise to "earn" my sports apparel!).

* If you are shopping on board on your cruise, why not wait until the last day of the sailing (except, of course, in the case of advertised sale specials available only on a certain day). Not only can you then compare prices ashore, but also there seem to be a variety of sales at the

end of the voyage. On a recent Orient Lines' voyage, for example, the last day there were the following special offers: three ship's t-shirts for $24.95; souvenir bag on wheels (a frequent end of the cruise offer as people are getting ready to pack) for $25; a free album when you bought 22 scenic view photos for $39.95 (that same number of photos alone regularly sold for $86.90 earlier in the cruise); and French wine bottles for $12.50 per bottle.

* Staying in touch with family and friends during a cruise is important to many passengers. Here are some ways in order of cost, least expensive first: e-mail from the ports of call—I have come across such fees as $1 an hour (Bali) about $2 an hour (Australia) and about $2.50 an hour (Brazil); phone cards in the ports of call (10 cents a minute or less); e-mail from the ship (often .75 cents a minute) and phoning from the ship—on the last ship I was on, Orient Lines' **Crown Odyssey** it cost $5.95 a minute; and it was $12 a minute on Windstar's Wind Surf when I was on it recently (I only pick up the phone on a ship if there is an emergency). Ask the crew where to e-mail and/or phone home; generally they know the best places because they have been trying to stay in touch.

* Themed cruises are an excellent value -you get to rub elbows with celebrities, lecturers and experts and you get to enjoy special events like concerts, classes, demonstrations and the like as well as question and answer sessions, autograph sessions with chefs, musicians, actors and other VIPs, plus a wealth of information about a theme you enjoy—all included in the cruise fare.

Mercury Sky Suite "*Mercury*" Photo courtesy of Celebrity Cruises.

Chapter: 9
Culinary Delights

Food goes with cruising as sunshine goes with the tropics. In fact, the culinary delights of a cruise are so legendary (my mouth is watering already just thinking about them!) that they deserve an entire chapter in this guide all to themselves.

Food, glorious food! To give you an idea of exactly how many palate-pleasing pleasures there are to enjoy, here's a recent weekly shopping list from the chef on Royal Caribbean's ***Explorer of the Seas*** to feed this giant of the sea's 3,114 guests:

Ribs - 1,000 lbs.
Tenderloin - 1,500 lbs.
Leg of Veal - 326 lbs.
Pork Loin - 600 lbs.
Leg of Lamb - 261 lbs.
Chicken - 1,500 lbs.
Lobster - 3,000 pieces
Fresh Salmon - 500 lbs.
Other Fish - 1,275 lbs.
Eggs - 40,000 lbs.
Fresh Vegetables - 5,000 lbs.

Beer - 20,000 cans
Soda - 9,000 cans
Ice Cream - 700 gallons
Striploin - 2,500 lbs.
Veal Loin - 600 lbs.
Bacon - 2,000 lbs.
Smoked Ham - 600 lbs.
Rack of Lamb - 700 lbs.
Turkey - 761 lbs.

Shrimp - 1,500 lbs.
Smoked Salmon - 300 lbs.
Cheese - 500 lbs.
Potatoes - 2,000 lbs.
Fresh Fruit - 3,000 lbs.
Wine - 5,000 bottles
Liquor - 1,000 bottles

And after a typical week, guess what? it is all consumed—all gone!-and the chef has to write up a similar shopping list for the next cruise.

It is safe to say that no one goes hungry on a cruise. In fact, if you take advantage of the early risers' coffee and sweet rolls to get you started and the breakfast buffet to nibble on a little something, then have breakfast in the dining room, a mid-morning snack from room service, buffet lunch (to sample a few things), lunch in the dining room, mid-afternoon snack, teatime, dinner in the dining room, and late night snack—you are already into double-digit meals!

While many passengers will probably be judicious, rather than opportunistic (at least some days!) when it comes to food, the ship's galleys are kept humming day and night. And you can enjoy their handiwork with relish.

> On port days, if you are setting out on shore excursions, enjoy the ship's quick-and-easy breakfast and lunch buffets to get you out the door fast.

Dining At Sea

How many meals will you enjoy on any given day of your cruise?—a spokesman for Royal Caribbean once told me you could consume 15 meals daily if you wanted to (you'd almost need a stomach as big as a hull!)—due to 24-hour dining in some restaurants and room service and multiple venues for meals (three or more breakfasts and lunches served in various parts of the ships).

Traditional or Open Seating? That is the question du jour in cruising these days. Depending on the cruise line you are sailing on, the ship's main dining rooms will feature the traditional two seatings with passengers dining at the same table every evening (the vessels of Celebrity and Royal Caribbean are an example, where dinner is served at about 6 or 6:30 p.m. and 8 or 8:30 p.m.) or you will be dining at open seatings in which you dine anytime and with whom you wish between designated restaurant hours (Norwegian Cruise Line offers this type with the restaurants open from 5:30 p.m. to midnight, and calls it Freestyle

Culinary Delights

Dining). Some other lines have variations on these themes: Carnival offers four different seatings; Princess allows you to select from either open seating or traditional fixed seating.

Each system—traditional two seatings or open seating—has pros and cons. In the traditional two seating method, your wait team gets to know your tastes (bringing you the iced tea you like the minute you enter the dining room, the dressing you like with your salad, and pointing out if a dish is spicy and you have shown a preference for non-spicy foods, and the like). You sit with the same people every night and you can arrange your day without having to make decisions as to when and where you will eat.

Whom is the traditional two-seating dinner recommended for? People who enjoy structured days, who like to be catered to by the same wait staff and who enjoy the camaraderie of getting together with new-made friends (their tablemates) every night. This system is also good for single travelers who can request to be assigned to big tables and have people to dine with every night.

The open seating big advantage is, of course, the freedom, as you can eat when, where and with whom you choose. On port days you do not have to rush back to change and go to dinner as you may have to do if you are in the early seating dinner on a traditional two-seating format. And you do not need to finish dinner around 10 p.m. if you don't want to as you often do if you are on a traditional second seating. Additionally, generally, the ships that offer open seating—like the newest vessels of Norwegian Cruise Line, the **Norwegian Sun** and **Star** (that have nine and 10 restaurants respectively)—have more dining venues, so there is more variety for the guests.

Whom is the open seating dinner format recommended for? People who hate to be on a schedule while on vacation and who like variety.

Some say your wait staff is more attentive if you are on a traditional two-seating format, I have found that while the two-seating format is more personalized, I have enjoyed great service on both formats.

Whether you have traditional two-seating dinner or open seating, chances are very good that your ship also has one or more alternative dining venues. These restaurants provide both a delightful change of pace from everyday dining in the ship's main restaurant and a

207

great venue for special occasions or an intimate, romantic dinner. Some of these alternatives are free—outstanding among these are the specialty Italian restaurants on Holland America ships—the pizzas, the minestrone soup, the pastas, and the regional specialties like Scampi alla Luciano (grilled large butterfly shrimps on a bed of capellini with pesto and garlic salsa aurora)—are simply delicious, an incredible value at no extra charge (you would expect to pay upwards of $100 for a comparable five-course meal at an equivalent restaurant ashore). Others have fees that range from $5 to $25 and are usually worth every penny.

> It pays to listen to your waiter's recommendations—they are usually right on the money.

What's for dinner? Well, usually five- or six- course feasts. On Holland America ships, a premium, moderately-priced line featuring some of the most extensive menus at sea, for instance, dinner choices may consist of seven appetizers (usually six cold and one hot), three soups (generally two hot and one cold), three salads, six entrees, including a vegetarian selection and a low-fat one, cheeses and fruit, and six desserts including pastries, ice creams and light and sugar-free desserts. Quick, loosen your belt now! And your dinner is served on an elegant table adorned with fresh flowers, crisp linen, fine Rosenthal china, and gleaming silver.

> If you cannot decide between the Cherries Jubilee or the warm apple pie, order both! Your waiter will bring you two desserts, or two of anything, with a smile.

By the way, in the event you have not thrown your diet overboard by the second day at sea (many do and just resolve to go on a diet when they're back on terra firma), you will be glad to know that most mainstream ships feature low-fat selections in their menus as

Culinary Delights

well as vegetarian dishes and they can accommodate special diets if you notify the ship 30 days or more prior to sail date (you can ask your travel agent to notify the line at the time of booking). One ship, the ***Norwegian Sun***, actually has a no-fee, alternative restaurant serving exclusively light and healthy dishes, the Pacific Heights (sample menu below). And Celebrity's Millennium-Class ships feature no-fee cafes within their spa that serve solely delicious healthy cuisine for breakfast and lunch (sample menus below).

Here are some actual sample dinner menus from main and alternative restaurants at sea (fee, if any, is noted) to get you salivating, if you haven't started already.

Crystal Cruises' Crystal Harmony's The Crystal Restaurant Dinner Menu

Chef's Suggestions

Sauteed Sea Scallops on Pesto Risotto and Capsicum Beurre Blanc
Smoked Green Split Pea Soup with Champagne and Whole Wheat Croutons
Broiled Fillet of Fresh Alaskan Salmon with Wasabi Mashed Potatoes, on Honey-Mustard Sauce, Served with Steamed Vegetable Sticks
White Chocolate Brioche Pudding on Whiskey Flavored Caramel Sauce, Topped with Vanilla Ice Cream

Appetizers
    Chinoise Chicken Salad
    Asparagus en Fete - Marinated Green Asparagus with Olive Oil, Fresh Herbs, and Black Olives
    Chilled Fruit Cup with Raspberries, Marinated with Port Wine
Soups
    Chicken Consomme with Fois Gras Profiteroles
    Chilled Cream of Avocado with Snow Crabmeat
    Low sodium soups are available upon request
Salads
    Spinach Salad Served with Boiled Eggs, Crisp Bacon, and Creamy Mustard Dressing

Chopped Assorted Garden Greens with Tomato, Daikon, and Red Radish

Traditional favorite dressings available, plus today's specials and Fat-Free Mango-Passion Fruit or Low Calorie Chive Yogurt Dressing

Pasta Special

Farfalle Pasta with Assorted Forest Mushrooms, Tomato, Cream, and White Truffle Oil

Salad Entrée

Grilled Vegetable Salmon Salad - Spring Greens, Tomatoes, Fresh Herbs, Marinated Garden Vegetables, and Artichoke Hearts Tossed with a Truffle Vinaigrette, Topped with Grilled Salmon Fillet

Main Fares

- Macadamia Nut and Wasabi Crusted Lamb Loin - Served on Stir-Fried Vegetables with Balsamic Flavored Gravy and Roasted Red Skin Potato
- Cubes Roasted Free Range Chicken Breast - Filled with Sweet Corn and Shiitake Mushrooms, on Asparagus Risotto, with Slow Roasted Vegetables, and Rosemary Jus
- Grilled Black Angus Sirloin Steak - Topped with Grilled Onions, Served with Green Beans Wrapped in Bacon, Cauliflower Roses, Sauce Choron, and Baked Potato Filled with Sour Cream and Vegetable Ragout

Upon your request, these Traditional Main Fares are also available:

Filet Steak served with Baked Potato, Green Beans Wrapped in Bacon, and Cauliflower Roses or Grilled Fresh Tuna Medallion with Assorted Vegetables, Mashed Potatoes and Brandy Sauce

Vegetarian Selections

Asparagus en Fete

Chilled Cream of Avocado with Lime Filets

Golden Fried Pockets - Filled with Three Kinds of Cheese, Served on Tomato Butter with Broccoli Roses

Honey Glazed Pecan Pie

Side Orders

Cauliflower Roses, Slow Roasted Vegetables, Green Beans Wrapped in Bacon, Farfalle Pasta with Tomato Sauce, Baked Potato with Sour Cream and Chives

Culinary Delights

On The Lighter Side
- Chopped Assorted Garden Greens with Tomato, Daikon and Black Olives
- Plain Grilled Filet Steak Served with Steamed Vegetables, Oven Roasted Potatoes and Natural Gravy
- Passion Fruit Sherbet with Fruit Salad

Desserts
  Cinnamon Ice Parfait with Brandy Cherries
  Old Fashioned Honey Glazed Pecan Pie
  Sugar-Free Rice Pudding with Raspberry Sauce
  Sugar-Free Vanilla Éclair
  Homemade Cookies
  Assortment of Fruit in Season
  Ice Cream, Frozen Yogurt, Sherbet selections
  Cheese Trolley selections

Orient Lines' Crown Odyssey's
Seven Continents Restaurant Dinner Menu

Appetizers
  Country Style Pate with a Petite Salad, Cumberland Sauce
  Spicy Shrimp, Crab Meat & Fish Cake Cajun Style
  Caesar Salad, crisp salad leaves tossed in special Caesar dressing topped with focaccia croutons and shaved Parmesan cheese

Soups
  Consomme Julienne
  Cream of Sweet Maize, a rich cream of corn with bacon bits

Entrees
- Baked Fillet of Sea Bass Breval, sauce with white wine, mushrooms, shallots, tomato, natural potato and vegetables
- Slow Roasted Turkey Breast, complemented with sage stuffing, cranberry sauce, giblet gravy, broccoli, carrots and fondant potatoes

- Medallions of Veal, with ginger and asparagus sauce, green beans and chateau potatoes
- Prime Rib of American Beef, fresh market vegetables and Jackson potatoes
- Fettucine Pasta with Mushroom Cheese Sauce, pasta tossed in a light garlic, cream and Parmesan cheese sauce garnished with mushrooms

Cheeses
Selection of Cheeses

Desserts
Tropizian, caramelized almonds and fresh fruit coulis
Banana Burritos with cider butter sauce
Pineapple Upside Down Cake
Petit Fours
A selection of Ice Creams and Sorbets

Available Every Day
Steamed Vegetables - Baked Potato with Accompaniments

This Evening's Bread Selection
Sour Dough Rolls
German Beer Bread
Foccacia Bread

The Healthy Choice: Our Chef has adapted a selection of reduced fat & low salt dishes.
Caesar Salad
Consomme Julienne
Roasted Turkey Breast with steamed vegetables
Sugar Free Fruit Mousse
Choice of Diet Ice Creams
The Vegetarian Choice
Caesar Salad
Cream of Corn Soup
Wild Mushroom Risotto
Pineapple Upside Down Cake

Culinary Delights

Celebrity Cruises' Infinity's SS United States Alternative Restaurant (fee: $25)

Soups, Salads And Appetizers
    Iced Tropical Paradise - Chilled exotic fruit soup garnished with kiwi
    Lobster Veloute - A creamy lobster broth
    Caesar Salad - A classic; tossed and served at your table
    Russian Salad - A salad of diced vegetables, ham, tongue, a creamy mayonnaise, lobster and truffle
    Shredded Smoked Chicken with Oriental Salad - Sliced smoked breast of chicken served on ribbons of Chinese cabbage, toasted almonds and crispy rice noodles
    Tartare of Salmon Garnished with Quail Eggs
    Potted fresh and smoked salmon seasoned with herbs, lemon and fromage blanc
    Chilled Asparagus, Sauce Gribiche - Asparagus spears with a sauce of finely chopped capers, eggs, gherkins and parsley
    Stuffed Quail Glazed with Port Jelly - Boned quail with a forcemeat of veal, chicken and pork flavored with green peppercorns
    Goat Cheese Souffle with Tomato Coulis - Delicate warm goat cheese soufflé served with a creamy sauce and tomato coulis

Entrees
    Risotto Primavera - Risotto of baby spring vegetables
    Grilled Fillet of Sea Bass - Fillet of Sea Bass, brushed with tapenade and served with grilled vegetables
    Boston Scrod with Sauce Nantua - Medallions of young cod with a rich shellfish sauce
    Flambeed Scampi - Prawns, wrapped in pancetta, flamed in Armagnac and served on a bed of rocket leaves
    Long Island Duckling for Two - As was served on the *SS United States* in the Fifties and Sixties, crispy roast, apple and prune stuffing, citrus sauce
    Saltimbocca alla Romana - Escalopines of veal with prosciutto, pan fried and served with a Marsala sauce
    Rack of Lamb en Croute - Rack of lamb coated with a mushroom duxelle, wrapped in puff pastry and baked until golden

Steak Diane - New York steak cooked to your liking and served with garlic, parsley, Cognac and Worcestershire sauce
Cheese - A Selection of Cheeses served with Grapes and Apples

Desserts
Crepes Suzette - A classic dessert of fine crepes flavored with orange and Grand Marnier
Zabaglione flavored with Marsala - A fluffy delicate Marsala flavored sabayon
Waldorf Pudding - A creamy vanilla pudding flavored with a hint of nutmeg, diced apples and sultana grapes
Chocolate Souffle - The most classic and well known light soufflé
Michel Roux's Favorite Bite-Size Surprise Desserts
Selection of Ice Creams and Sorbets - Freshly churned ice creams and sorbets

Norwegian Cruise Line's Norwegian Star's Endless Summer Restaurant Menu

(Hawaiian alternative restaurant —the ship is based in Hawaii— no fee)

Pupus - Appetizers
Lomilomi Salmon
Salmon with Tomato and Spring Onion Salsa
Maui Opae Cocktail
Jumbo Shrimp on Island Greens with Papaya Salsa and Chervil Aioli
Hawaiian Caesar Lau'ai'ia
Caesar Salad Topped with Citrus Wedges and Crisp Pineapple Wafers
Kona Spring Rolls
Large Fried Chicken Spring Rolls Stuffed with Crisp Spaghetti Vegetables, Mild Green Coconut Curry Dip

Kupas - Soups
Mahi-Mahi Chowder
Chunks of Mahi-Mahi with Mushrooms and Potatoes, Spiced with Paprika
Makawao Portuguese Bean Soup

Culinary Delights

    Pork Hock Soup with Spicy Sausage, Kidney Beans and Chinese Cabbage

Nui Mea'ai'ai - Entrees
- Big Island Pulehu Ribs
  - Beef Short Ribs Glazed with Pineapple BBQ Sauce, Baked Taro
- Seared Ahi, Broke da Mouth Potato Salad
  - Seared Tuna on Potato and Olive Salad with Wasabi-Mango Dressing
- Lau Lau
  - Pork, Rock Cod and Rice Steamed in Wrapped Ti Leaves, Green Salad
- Chicken Adobo
  - Chicken Braised in Shoyu Scented Coconut Milk with Chilies and Herbs, Steamed Rice
- Hawaiian Mixed Plate
  - Crab Won Ton, Spicy Tuna Rolls, Sweet and Sour Chicken Wings, Gingered Wings, Gingered Tempura Swordfish, All Fried and Served with their own dip or salsa

Ono Mea'ai Momona - Desserts
- Pai Hala Kahiki
  - Golden Brown Meringue Atop Creamy Pineapple Pie
- Kope-Kokoleka-Macadamia Pai Palaoa
  - Coffee-Chocolate-Macadamia Nut Cake
- Pai Hua'ai
  - Tropical Fruit Tart with Island Coulis
- Kuawa Pai Waiupa's
  - Guava Cream Cheese Cake

Kope - Coffee
Ti - Tea

Breakfast Menu from Celebrity's Millennium-Class
Ships' AquaSpa Café
healthy breakfast alternative, no fee

Juices
    Orange, Grapefruit, Apple, Cranberry, Grape

Fruits
    Fresh Fruit Medley - A sampling of our fresh seasonal fruits
    Papaya with Lime
    Chilled Grapefruit and fresh Mint

Cereals Hot & Cold
    Whole Grain Oats Birchermuesli served with low-fat Yogurt and Berries
    Flax Seed, Pumpkin Seed, Raisins, Dates, Cranberries
    Organic Granola with Sun-dried Pears and Apricots Served with Milk and Bananas
    All Bran, Shredded Wheat, Oat Bran Flakes, Corn Flakes
    Apple Cinnamon Oatmeal with dried fruits and cinnamon apples

Low-fat Yogurt, plain or with Fruit
    Yogurt drink
    Low-fat milk, skim milk, buttermilk, soy milk Breads & Muffins
    Multi-grain bread, Whole Wheat bread, Banana bread, Muffin of the day, Wheat Bran Raisin Muffin, Spicy Cinnamon Apple Muffin, Bagels with low-fat Cream Cheese

Accompaniments
    Hard Boiled or Poached Egg
    Low-fat Cream Cheese
    Non-fat Cottage Cheese
    Margarine, Butter Spread, Fruit Preserves

Beverages
    Herbal Teas
    Decaffeinated Coffee

Culinary Delights

Menu from Norwegian Cruise Line's Norwegian Sun's Pacific Heights alternative restaurant, no fee
—All menu items feature healthy spa items and Cooking Light selections. All list nutrition facts and are low in salt, cholesterol and fat content

Appetizers

Steamed mussels with Chili, Garlic, White Wine and Tomato Sauce
Cal 220 (26% from fat), fat 6.2g (sat 1 g, mono 3.1g, poly 1.1 g), Protein 15.6g, Fiber 1.4g Chol 35 mg, Iron 5.8mg, Sodium 5.8mg, Calc 59 mg

Fresh Citrus Fruit Cocktail Crowned with Low-Fat Ricotta Cheese
Cal 150 (10% from fat), Fat 4.1g (sat 1.9g, mono 3.7g, poly 0.7g), Protein 5.8g, Fiber 2g, Chol 19mg, Iron .5 mg, Sodium 26mg, Calc 24mg

Pureed Brown Lentil Vegetable Soup
Cal 234 (30% from fat), Fat 7.8g (sat 2.9g, mono 3.7g, poly 0.7g), Protein 16.6g, Carb 26.6g, Fiber 7.3g, Chol 10mg, Iron 5.1mg, Sodium 729mg, Calc 260mg

Chunky Clam Chowder, Southwestern Style
Cal 218 (21% from fat), Fat 6.6g (sat 3.1g, mono 2.2g, poly 0.8g), Protein 6.4g, Carb 37.8g, Fiber 4.7g, Chol 37mg, Iron 3.2mg, Sodium 339mg, Calc 154mg

Pear, Blue Cheese and Walnut Salad with Smoked Turkey
Cal 151 (50% from fat), Fat 4.2g (sat. 1g, mono 2.2g, poly 1g), Protein 2g, Fiber 2g, Chol 28mg, Iron 0.7mg, Sodium 158mg, Calc 62mg

Grilled Chicken and Tabbouleh Salad
Cal 218 (21% from fat), Fat 5g (sat. 0.9g, mono 2.9g, poly 0.8g), Protein 14.9g, Carb 31g, Fiber 7.5g, Chol 26mg, Iron 1.5mg, Sodium 379mg, Calc 43mg

Entrees

Homemade Meat Loaf with Garlic Potato Mash, Light Roasted Gravy and Green String Beans
Cal 400.7 (22% from fat), Fat 11.7g (sat 3.21g, mono 4,8g, poly 1.54g), Protein 33.3g, Carb 45.4g, Fiber 3.57g, Chol 75mg, Iron 2.8mg, Sodium 334mg, Calc 92.7mg

Pike Perch with Fresh Garden Vegetables, Lime and White Wine "en papillote"
Cal 287 (37% from fat), Fat 22.8g (sat 2.1g, mono 6.4g, poly 2.3g), Protein 34g, Carb 10.4g, Fiber 0.7g, Chol 115mg, Iron 3.7mg, Sodium 171mg, Calc 194mg

Grilled Pork Chops, Apple Sauce and Roasted Cabbage Rolls
Cal 392.7 (22% from fat), Fat 12.7g (sat 3.43g, mono 4.8g, poly 1.54g), Protein 30.3g, Carb 41.4g, Fiber 3.57g, Chol 98mg, Iron 2.8mg, Sodium 684mg, Calc 98.7mg

Old Fashioned Spaghetti and Meat Balls in Tomato-Basil Sauce
Cal 437 (17% from fat), Fat 8.4g (sat 1.7g, mono 2.9g, poly 1.7g), Protein 37.9g, Carb 51.2g, Fiber 3.4g, Chol 79mg, Iron 5.6mg, Sodium 600mg, Calc 195mg

Calzone with Bell Peppers, Spicy Sausage, Mushrooms and Low-Fat Mozzarella Cheese
Cal 409 (26% from fat), Fat 11.7g (sat 4.9g, mono 4.2g, poly 1.4g), Protein 16.3g, Carb 58.9g, Fiber 3.3g, Chol 52 mg, Iron 5.1mg, Sodium 47.4mg, Calc 162mg

Roasted Shallots and Bell Peppers with Pesto-Flavored Tomato Pizza
Cal 285 (28% from fat), Fat 8.7g (sat 3.9g, mono 3.4g, poly 0.9g), Protein 14.2g, Carb 37.2g, Fiber 1g, Chol 12mg, Iron 2.7mg, Sodium 611mg, Calc 376mg

Culinary Delights

Grilled Vegetarian Lasagna
Cal 370 (25% from fat), Fat 7.3g (sat 1.6g, mono 3.9g, poly 1.1g), Protein 12.2g, Carb 57g, Fiber 6.1g, Chol 3mg, Iron 4.2mg, Sodium 295mg, Calc 138mg

Desserts

Cal 247 (25% from fat), Fat 6.8g (sat 2.1g), Protein 4.2g, Carb 43g, Fiber 0.4g, Chol 5mg, Iron 1.4mg, Sodium 102mg, Cal 131mg

Coconut Pavlova with Tropical Fruits
Cal 301 (14% from fat), Fat 4.8g (sat 3.5g, mono 0.6g, poly 0.2g), Protein 3.9g, Carb 60.4g, Fiber 3.7g, Chol 5mg, Iron 9.6mg, Sodium 80mg, Calc 73mg

Cinnamon Poached Fruits
Cal 132 (10% from fat), Fat 1.4g (sat 0.2g, mono 0.9g, poly 2g), Protein 1.1g, Carb 31g, Fiber 1.5g, Chol 0g, Iron 0.3mg, Sodium 4mg, Calc 9mg

Holland America's Marco Polo
Alternative Italian Dining Venue Menu (no fee)

Antipasti:
- Bruschetta - toasted Italian country bread topped with sautéed mushrooms, tomato and fontina
- Mozzarella alla Caprese - ripe sweet tomato with fresh Mozzarella cheese, extra virgin olive oil and basil
- Bresaola - cured beef served over marinated Italian-style pickles
- Frittura Mista di Mare - deep-fried assorted seafood served with a special green sauce of the house
- Specialita 'di Pasta del Giorno - our Chef's creation of the day
- Minestra Ribollita - traditional Tuscany vegetable soup
- Insalata alla Marco Polo - gourmet mixed greens with goat cheese and walnut dressing

Piatti Principali:
- Vitello alla Parmigiana con Pappardelle - sautéed breaded veal scaloppini with large wide noodles
- Petto di Pollo al Rosmarino e Limone - lemon rosemary marinated chicken breast with penne in four-cheese sauce
- Cotoletta d'Agnello alla Senape - grilled lamb chops on sautéed spinach with roast potatoes and herbs.
- Medaglionit di Manzo al Pepe Verde - Tenderloin of beef served with green pepper sauce on spinach fettuccini
- Scampi alla Luciano - grilled large butterfly shrimps on a bed of capellini with pesto and garlic salsa aurora
- Pizza Quatro Stagioni - artichokes, mushrooms, peppers, seafood, prosciutto and cheese
- Pizza Margherita - topped with tomato and Mozzarella

Dessert selection

Celebrity's Millennium-Class Ships' Alternative Restaurant
(no fee) AquaSpa Café Light & Healthy Lunch Menu

Soup
- Chilled Strawberry Soup with Apple Juice and Non-fat Skim Milk

Salads
- Sicilian Bean and Sprout Salad with Fresh Coriander
- Bulgur with Tofu, Ginger and Scallions

Light Fare
- White Tuna with spiced Plum Tomato, marinated Black Olives, Rosemary and Lemon Zest
- Mediterranean Tradition - Crunchy Heart of Romaine with Tabouli and sliced Lemon Garlic Chicken served with Hummus and Pita Bread
- Vegetable Sushi Rolls - Served with a bundle of Baby Lettuce and Cucumbers

Culinary Delights

> **A La Carte**
> Please allow 15 minutes preparation time for "a la carte" items to be cooked to order:
> - Broiled Lemon Garlic Chicken, Poached Chicken Breast or Farm-raised Tilapia, steamed or broiled.
>
> **Desserts**
> Apple Strudel, Chocolate Chip Cookies, Honey Cake with Lemon Sauce, Frozen Yogurt, Today's Ice Creams and Sherbets
>
> **Beverages**
> Herbal Teas, Decaffeinated Coffee

> Your ship may have a Captain's Table, where the master of the vessel dines. Usually, invitations are reserved for people who are taking several cruises in a row, or sailed numerous times with the line or booked expensive suites. It is a memorable experience with guests treated to two different wines and sometimes after dinner drinks—and of course, the captain's anecdotes about his life at sea. I recently dined at Captain Erik Bjurstedt's table on Orient Lines' Crown Odyssey and he regaled us with a story about how his mother got seasick when she sailed with him once and he recommended his favorite remedy: whiskey and peanuts, which she tried although she normally does not drink, and it worked so well for her that the next time she sailed with him, he said she always had a supply handy.

Here are some dining at sea superlatives:

* Best Alternative Restaurants (fee) - The nostalgic restaurants inspired in the great ocean liners of old aboard Celebrity's Millennium-Class ships. It is easy to imagine yourself on the legendary *Normandie* and other ships in those surroundings with memorabilia from those vessels and menu items faithfully recreated.

* Best Alternative Restaurants (free) - Holland America's Italian specialty venues—classy, delicious and with impeccable service.

* Best Restaurant Variety - Whatever you are in the mood for, you'll find it in the multiple dining venues on Norwegian Cruise Line's **Norwegian Star** and **Norwegian Sun**.

* Best Gourmet Fare (luxury ships) - Silversea, Seabourn, Radisson Seven Seas, Crystal, Windstar -all a gourmand's delight: go on a diet before you sail.

* Best Gourmet Fare (moderately-priced ships) - Celebrity's menus overseen by Michelin-starred Chef Michel Roux -truly delectable.

* Best Service (luxury ships) - Silversea, Seabourn, Crystal, Radisson Seven Seas, Windstar -all with impeccable service.

* Best Service (moderately-priced ships) - Holland America, Celebrity -both with attentive, friendly service.

* Best Spa Cuisine - Celebrity's Millennium-Class ships -it's so delightful, you don't mind being good to yourself, and the strawberry soup, grilled chicken breast and chocolate chip cookies are scrumptious.

* Best Lido Buffet - Holland America, with a bountiful variety every day of hot and cold dishes plus a delightful soup and salad express station, for when you want something light and out the door.

* Best Midnight Buffet (moderately-priced line) - Norwegian Cruise Line's Chocoholics Buffet (O.K., I'm a chocolate lover and everything in this lavish spread is made out of chocolate!).

* Best Themed Buffets (luxury line) - Crystal, with lavish and delicious special poolside spreads like Asia Café, with dishes from all corners of the Orient; Cuisine of the Sun, inspired in the Mediterranean and Provencale cooking; and The American Classic, with homestyle cooking from across the U.S.

* Best Afternoon Tea (luxury line) - Crystal's Mozart Tea with musicians in period dress and such goodies as chocolate fondue for chocolate-stemmed strawberries.

* Best Afternoon Tea (moderately-priced line) - Holland America's Royal Dutch Tea (try the almond cookies).

Culinary Delights

Test the Waters Tips

* If you are on a ship that has two traditional dinner seatings, arrive at your table on time. Your tablemates will appreciate it and so will the waiters.

* If your ship has two dinner seatings you can generally request not only early or late seating, but also table size at the time of booking. Tables for two are romantic, of course, but they are not plentiful so you may not get one; request one anyway -the cruise line will try to accommodate you particularly if you are on a honeymoon or anniversary celebration. Tables for four may not be the best situation as you can make conversation with two other people (assuming you are traveling with a companion) and if you do not like them, there is little you can do to avoid talking to them. Tables for six and eight provide the opportunity to talk to more people, so they tend to be more popular. Remember, if you have a problem with your table, go to the maitre d' as soon as possible and request a change. He will accommodate you unless the dining room is completely full -in which case he may suggest that you change your dinner seating. This happened to us during a seven-day Alaska sailing on the **Norwegian Wind** when the table next to ours had a one-year-old girl who constantly screamed, banged the table with her spoon and often threw rice, peas and other items like projectiles in our direction—the dining room was full, so the maitre d' suggested we change seatings which we did and from that moment on enjoyed blissful peace at meals, not to mention less soiled clothes.

* Follow the dress code of the evening -it is a courtesy your tablemates and everyone in the dining room will appreciate. One tip: on ships with traditional two dinner seatings, the second seating tends to be dressier.

* If you do not like your table or tablemates, ask the maitre d' to switch you after your first dinner. He will try to accommodate you.

Insider's Savings Insights

* Drink of the Day Specials are good buys (Yellow Bird, Apricot Fizz and such —a different drink every day—are $2.75 on Orient Lines and this and other lines also offer two-for-ones during Happy Hour in one of the bars). Check your daily activities sheet for daily specials and Happy Hours.

* Eating a meal ashore is an excellent idea to sample local flavors, but if you want to save money, eat all your meals onboard -they are included in the fare, and often your ship's restaurants will be among the best in some regions of the world.

* Save on snacks while on long shore excursions by taking something from the breakfast buffet ashore (like little milk containers, small boxes of cereal and such) if this is not forbidden by local regulations.

* Ships' tap water tends to be heavily chlorinated. Drink milk, juices, tea, coffee and other beverages included free of charge with meals in the dining room.

Show Lounge *Silver Shadow* & *Silver Whisper* Photo courtesy of Silversea Cruises.

Chapter: 10

Cruising Solo, With Your Significant Other, With The Kids, On Multi-generational Family Reunions, and Cruising for Free

Noah loaded his ark solely two-by-two, but, of course, modern cruise ship passengers come aboard in a variety of ways: solo, with a significant other, with the kids, and on multi-generational family reunions.

In my more than 100 voyages, I have sailed all those ways a number of times (alone, with my husband, with our daughter—at all ages: a child, teen, and young adult—with my aging parents, and on three-generational family reunions) so I can guide you from personal experience, whatever your case may be. In addition to my tips for each type of cruiser, I include a number of cruise lines/ships that are good for each case—that is, vessels that have the amenities/services that are important for singles, couples, and families (I give examples of good ships in a variety of price ranges), and have compatible clienteles for each group. While nobody in his right mind would try to predict with 100 percent accuracy who will be onboard on a ship on a particular voyage, ships do tend to attract a certain type of passenger: perhaps seasoned, well-educated, well-heeled travelers predominate; or middle-aged, middle class couples; or lots of families with children. Knowing that a ship mostly attracts seniors, for instance, might be a red flag for young singles ready to paaarty! Conversely, seniors looking for a gracious and sedate experience might want to avoid the party scene ship or a vessel that might attract more than 700 children per sailing in the summer.

> Do you want to avoid children on your cruise? Avoid school holidays periods. And/or try a luxury line -lines like Windstar and Seabourn do not encourage kids with special facilities for them.

Families with children and teenagers may be happier on ships that feature clubrooms, play pools and other facilities for kids, as well as programs of supervised activities. Couples will feel the allure of romantic ships, such as yacht-like sailing vessels; singles, depending on their age, may welcome a party atmosphere and/or such features as dancing hosts; people planning multi-generational family reunions may prefer a mega-liner or ultra-liner with a multitude of entertainment and activity options for every age group; and so on. For those who would like to sail for free, I give tips on how to get onboard as a dancing host, lecturer and the like.

Whatever your situation, find the right ship for you, and presto, change-o, you are in for a magical experience: the vacation of a lifetime. Here are some tips for families, couples, singles and multi-generational groups to help you navigate the wide, wide world of cruises.

SINGLES - Going solo? The chances are very good that you will not be lonely on a cruise. Cruising is my favorite way to travel if I am alone, simply because of its social nature (assigned communal dining tables on many ships; organized get-togethers galore). But while you will enjoy dining room companionship and social activities throughout the ship, it doesn't mean, however, that you can count on finding romance when you sail. In fact, finding your soul-mate at sea (or on any type of travel) is not generally as easy to do as you see in those "Love Boat" TV series reruns (usually couples outnumber singles, and often there are more women than men among the unattached passengers).

Cruising Solo, etc.

But cruising is, without a doubt, one of the most singles-friendly modes of travel. The problem of having to eat alone is left behind on the pier (along with everyday chores and cares) as unwanted passengers if you are on a traditional, two-dinner-seating ship (like those of Royal Caribbean and Celebrity) as passengers get assigned to big tables (usually of six or eight) in the dining room and they dine at the same table for the duration of the cruise. So instantly, solo cruisers have ready-made friends to share meals with, discuss their day, maybe even enlist for more activities, like participating in the trivia contest, or watching the nightly shows in the lounge, or touring in one of the ports together.

During the day, there are a number of organized get-togethers, including bridge tournaments, pool and deck games, and dancing lessons, which offer opportunities to meet other passengers, and in the evening, shipboard lounges are lively and fun. Most cruise lines feature a complimentary singles' cocktail party early in the voyage so unattached guests can get acquainted.

> If you want to meet others, attend the wine tasting seminar, cooking demonstration and any event that features tasting and sampling (people naturally turn to the people next to them to give their opinions).

In addition to being congenial, cruises provide a welcoming environment where most costs are covered with the one-time expenditure of the cruise ticket and where most needs from dining to entertainment are taken care of. Optional guided shore excursions, generally escorted by a member of the cruise staff and a local guide, are easily booked.

Many cruise lines also offer singles a "Guaranteed Share" program, whereby the line commits to finding a single passenger a same-sex roommate (same smoking preference and general age range) or if the line is unable to, the solo traveler uses the cabin without having to pay a single supplement (generally 125 to 150 percent of the per person, double occupancy fare on staterooms; 200 percent on suites and other high-end accommodations). Some lines also feature a "Guaranteed Single" rate, whereby the single passenger gets a stateroom chosen at the discretion of the line and assigned at the time of embarkation. The cost is usually more than the per person, double occupancy rate, but less than the standard single supplement.

All these reasons may be why, although the vast majority of passengers are couples, vacations at sea are growing in popularity with singles, who usually comprise 25 percent of ships' rosters, according to the Cruise Lines International Association.

What ships are best for solo travelers? Well, whenever I have to sail alone, I prefer ultra-liners, mega-liners or mid-size vessels that carry a respectable number of passengers (because I figure there is simply more of a chance of there being other compatible solo travelers when the ship carries greater numbers). Among my favorite lines for solo travel are Celebrity, Royal Caribbean, Princess and Norwegian. Small, yacht-like vessels tend to attract mostly couples and may be clubby as well, often with "cliques" of several couples getting together and socializing mostly among themselves.

Another consideration is age. Under-30 singles may wish to check out the Carnival fleet which seems to attract a good number of single men and women under 30. Under 30 singles may also wish to try Windjammer Barefoot Cruises' "singles cruises" offered about a half dozen times a year on designated dates. Mature singles, particularly women who like to dance, may feel more at home on lines which have dancing hosts. These are men over 50 who ask unescorted ladies to dance in the lounge, host dining room tables, play cards, attend afternoon tea and other social functions, and escort shore tours. Lines that offer these hosts include Cunard, Celebrity, Orient, Silversea, and Holland America (on longer cruises).

Here are some things to keep in mind when you sail solo:

* Mark your calendar to attend the unattached passenger cocktail party and take in a lion's share of general activities such as pool games, crafts, trivia, sports tournaments, and dance lessons. They are a great way to meet others and fun as well.

* Tell your travel agent to request a large table (eight or more if available) for you in the dining room. There is no doubt that the more the merrier and the greater the chance that you will meet people you enjoy to be with right there.

Cruising Solo, etc.

* When on shore tours, the cruise staff escort usually goes alone, and sits at the back of the bus -you may be able to share a seat with him or her, and if not, then certainly share conversation at the stops.

COUPLES
The romance of a cruise is as legendary as the ocean is deep. Let's face it: what could be more romantic than the sparkling salt air, the motion of a sapphire ocean, the endless horizons, and the exotic ports with idyllic beaches ready to be explored? These are just a handful of reasons for couples to take to the sea for a honeymoon, anniversary celebration or just a romantic getaway.

My husband Humberto and I have enjoyed a variety of cruises "a deux" and find there is no more relaxing, conducive way to get re-acquainted with a significant other and rekindle romance than on a cruise vacation—Noah definitely knew what he was doing.

In the pampered setting of a cruise, with staff to pick up after you, prepare delicious meals and snacks, and plan activities and entertainment, passengers do not have to lift a finger as they are whisked away from one exotic port to another. There is time for togetherness—not just to enjoy breakfast, but to linger over a second cup of coffee; not just to go from one place to another, but to promenade on deck; to read to each other from guides or literary narratives on the ports after lunch; to enjoy a cocktail before dinner, and dancing, a musical revue and stargazing afterwards.

> Romantic things you can enjoy on a cruise include ordering breakfast in bed (and, it is free too!), having a couple's massage in the spa, dancing under a canopy of stars up on deck after dinner and the show.

A very romantic, couples-oriented, choice is the cruise-sailers of Windstar (luxury category). Sailing on these chic vessels from one exotic port to another and participating in such activities as strolling under a canopy of stars, toasting dramatic sunsets on deck and enjoying complimentary water sports at pretty coves is an open invitation to romance. On our voyage to the French and Italian Rivieras we met many passengers who typify this line's clientele, mostly young and middle-aged, upper middle class, sophisticated couples looking to relax and explore.

Most were out on deck for our arrivals and departures from port, for hors d'oeuvres and drinks before dinner and for dancing after dinner. In port, many took the optional shore excursions or went sightseeing independently and opted for the fabulous program of included watersports (snorkeling, waterskiing, windsurfing, etc.). The cuisine, by Chef Joachim Splichal of Patina and Pinot Restaurants fame, was outstanding. The dress code is casually elegant.

Another big favorite of mine as a couples' cruise was a spring pilgrimage-themed vacation from Memphis to New Orleans on the Delta Queen Steamboat Co. This moderately-priced line that ran into financial straits in 2001 and filed for Chapter 11, is back in businesses and has several advantages for twosomes, particularly those middle-aged and older: first of all, most of its clientele is made up of just that, couples in that age range who are representative of Middle America, so it is easy to mingle and make friends out on deck, in the dining room and lounges. Secondly, this line (like some others) features theme cruises (gardens, music, culture, history, etc.). The themed activities are fun and are particularly handy if one member of the pair is not yet sold on the idea of cruising, but can be lured and entertained with lectures, demonstrations and activities on a special interest he or she cherishes.

Yet another plus for riverboats and barge cruises is that the boats and barges ride smoothly on rivers, usually within sight of land, which makes it appealing if one member of the couple is hesitant about trying cruising for fear of seasickness.

Other good choices for couples include the moderately-priced sailing vessels of Star Clippers, and premium, moderately-priced lines like Celebrity and Holland America; ultra-deluxe lines such as Crystal, Silversea, and Seabourn; and moderately-priced lines like Princess and Royal Caribbean. Celebrity, Holland America, Princess, Royal Caribbean and Crystal would appeal most to active couples as theirs are heavy-tonnage ships featuring a wide variety of activities and dining and nighttime entertainment

Cruising Solo, etc.

options. Crystal, for example, with its two 50,000-ton ships, offers two very romantic alternative restaurants (one Asian and one Italian) in addition to the formal dining room, and evening entertainment options include Broadway-style revues, dancing, movies, casino gaming and music at a variety of venues.

Seabourn's and Silversea's small vessels would appeal most to couples looking for a high-end, exclusive getaway, similar to spending a holiday on a rich friend's private yacht. On these ships, regimentation is minimal—guests dine when and with whom they wish—and organized activities are few, with passengers largely left to entertain themselves, and they prefer it that way.

My tips for couples on a honeymoon, anniversary, or simply enjoying a romantic getaway together at sea include the following:

* Check to make sure your cabin has a double bed or twins that convert to double. Some vintage ships have twins that cannot be pushed together.

* You may request a table for two at the time of booking, but these cannot always be guaranteed.

* Honeymooners and couples celebrating an anniversary who wish to be congratulated on board should notify their travel agent and they will be serenaded and presented a cake in the dining room or receive some other recognition from the line. Many lines also offer a complimentary cocktail party for newlyweds. If you want anonymity, keep mum and don't say anything to anyone, beginning with your travel agent (who may send you a bottle of champagne if you do speak up).

* Many lines offer complimentary renewal of vows ceremonies officiated by a clergyman or officer.

* If you are interested in celebrating in grand style, check if the line offers any special packages (available for an extra fee) including wedding, honeymoon, renewal of vows, and generic romance programs with amenities such as champagne, flowers, chocolates, bathrobes and the like.

* Couples wishing to be married aboard during their sailing have dedicated wedding chapels at their disposal on such vessels as the **Grand Princess** and on **Royal**

Caribbean's Voyager-Class ships. Princess is the only line offering marriage ceremonies officiated by the ship's captain.

FAMILIES -
Fun, fun, fun, not to mention, educational for the kids, and totally relaxing for the parents—it's a win-win situation that makes a family cruise hard to beat. Our daughter Veronica was only 4 years old when she first set foot on a ship for a Southern Caribbean cruise. Unlike other vacations we had taken her on (car and airplane trips), not once in the 10 days of the voyage did I hear her ask the proverbial, "Are we there yet?" She had a wonderful time, making friends in the children's playroom, going to ice cream parties, participating in everything from crafts to a masquerade. Her Dad and I sunbathed and read on deck, just outside the kids' playroom and told the counselors where we were in case Veronica wanted to leave -but, guess what, she never did!

Family cruising is like that: Mom and Dad can sunbathe and read by the pool, take in a wine tasting and a Broadway-style revue, and the children are happily entertained at supervised activities that are fun for their age group.

After that cruise, our daughter would accompany us on family vacations on a dozen cruise lines. Among her favorite ships, both as a young child and as a teenager, were those of moderately-priced Royal Caribbean. She loved the children's playrooms with crafts/games areas, the staff who organized activities, games and contests, the scavenger hunts, the "yummy" (her word) Make Your Own Sundae Bar by the pool, the masquerade and pizza parties, and the "cooool" prizes (also her word) awarded to participants including walkie-talkies, plush toys and the like as well as medals or trophies.

As a teenager, she enjoyed watching movies, playing trivia games, competing in sports and game tournaments like ping pong, basketball and checkers or chess, and just "hanging out," as she put it, at the teen center on Royal Caribbean's **Sovereign of the Seas**, complete with big screen TV and disco. And peeking into the high-tech teen centers on Sovereign-class and Vision-class ships with their video walls, dance floor, glitzy lights and soda bar makes many an adult (me definitely included!) long for a genie of the bottle to materialize and grant a wish for a return to youth, if only for a day at sea.

Cruising Solo, etc.

> Children's supervised activities programs are free on most ships (you may want to tip the counselors at the end of the voyage).Babysitting is available (arrange for it through reception/guest relations) for a nominal fee.

Royal Caribbean's Adventure Ocean program offers activities for children of four age groups: Aquanauts (3-5 years), Explorers (6 to 8 years), Voyagers (9-12 years) and Navigators (13-17 years). Supervised activities for children 3 to 12 are featured from 9:30 a.m. to 11:30 a.m., from 2 p.m. to 5 p.m. and from 7 p.m. to 10 p.m. at sea; and every morning and evening in port. Teen activities are from noon to 4 p.m. and from 10 p.m. to 1 a.m. at sea; from 3 p.m. to 6 p.m. and 10 p.m. to 1 a.m. in port.

Princess Cruises, another of our daughter's favorite lines as she was growing up, features an outstanding program, Princess Kids, for young sailors ages 3 to 17. The program features special activities designed by the California Science Center and the National Wildlife Federation including hands-on activities appropriate to each destination including launching rockets and squid dissection. Three age-specific programs are supervised by youth counselors: Princess Pelicans for ages 3-7 featuring crafts, games, ice cream socials, pizza parties and masquerades; Princess Pirateers for ages 8-12 with contests and such activities as stargazing and drawing; and Off Limits for ages 13-17 including movies, get-togethers in one of the dining rooms with photographs and a group night out to see one of Princess' stage productions, sports tourneys and language lessons.

The Princess Kids program offers a full schedule of complimentary activities both at sea and on ports days. The in-port program runs from 8 a.m. to 5 p.m. and includes complimentary dining room lunch. The at-sea days program runs until 10 p.m. Group babysitting is available each night from 10 p.m. to 1 a.m. in the Youth Center for $5 per hour per child.

Sample Daily Youth Activities Program for Ages 3-6
Celebrity's Summit

Wednesday

Morning Events:
- **9 a.m.** Pokemon, Pokemon, Pikachu! - Fun Factory
- **9:30 a.m.** Watercolor Masterpieces - Fun Factory
- **10 a.m.** Outdoor Sun Fun - Deck 12, aft
- **10:30 a.m.** Fabulous Great Ball Search - Fun Factory
- **11 a.m.** Wink Detective & Alien Attack Challenge - Fun Factory
- **12 noon** Activities conclude at Fun Factory - Parents, please pick up your Shipmates for lunch.

Afternoon Events:
- **2 p.m.** Four Corners & Musical Fun - Fun Factory
- **2:30 p.m.** Red Light, Green Light, Outdoor Play - Fun Factory Play-yard
- **3 p.m.** Create A Lazy Lion, Crazy Kitty or Slimy Snake Mask - Fun Factory
- **3:30 p.m.** The Shipmate Animal Masquerade Parade! - Shipwalk
- **4 p.m.** Ice Cream Break & Cool Down - Waterfall Café
- **4:30 p.m.** Color Bingo Bonanza - Fun Factory
- **5 p.m.** Activities conclude. Parents, please pick up your Shipmates for dinner.

Evening Events:
- **6 p.m.** Parents Night Out! Pizza Party! - Fun Factory (Please register for this event before 5 p.m.)
- **6:45 p.m.** Crafts, Card Craze and Playstation Madness - Fun Factory
- **8 p.m.** Wonderball & Circle Games - Fun Factory
- **8:30 p.m.** Starlight Ping Pong - Deck 12, aft
- **9 p.m.** Paper Bag Play and Team Imagination - Fun Factory
- **9:45 p.m.** Snacks & Dr. Seuss Riddlers! - Fun Factory
- **10 p.m.** Activities Conclude - Parents, please pick up your Shipmates.
- **10 p.m.** Complimentary Slumber Party Movie Time: The Little Rascals - Fun Factory
- **1 a.m.** Slumber Party ends at 1 a.m. or when the last child leaves.

Cruising Solo, etc.

Another superb choice for families is the Disney Cruise Line. This line features, in addition to extensive children's facilities -13,000 square feet of play space, including a themed playroom—activity programs for five different age groups. A nightly children's buffet is available as well as a restaurant featuring framed scenes from animated Disney classics that change from black and white to color (along with other room decor elements) during the course of a meal. Studio Sea is a family-oriented interactive television-themed entertainment lounge.

With increasing numbers of passengers bringing their children or grandchildren, according to the Cruise Lines International Association—and Carnival alone welcoming 350,000 children to its fleet wide Camp Carnival program annually—dedicated children's play areas are the norm on most cruise lines (Carnival itself has a two-level play area on the ***Destiny***).To respond to the numbers of families sailing, Norwegian Cruise Line has enhanced its Kids Crew program, offering it year round fleet wide (instead of just summers and school holiday periods) and including a new "tier" of supervised activities for 3 to 5 year olds. In addition to children's playrooms and pool, the line's newest ships ***Norwegian Sun*** and ***Star*** also boast a children's buffet with a special seating area with small tables and chairs.

Many lines also offer teenage clubs, electronic game rooms, splash pools and other facilities and features, including a kids' newsletter with daily activities. Most supervised club activities are complimentary. Babysitting (for a nominal fee) is usually available after hours and in port on most ships.

Carnival recently introduced a series of Alaska shore excursions specially designed for teens. Holland America likewise began offering "Just for Kids" shore excursions in Skagway for young passengers in Alaska. Princess and NCL have launched shore excursions for kids in Alaska too. And other lines, like Disney, also offer escorted shore tours for children on their itineraries.

Most ships boast a range of family-friendly accommodations including cribs. Among the lines offering quad cabins and/or family suites are Carnival, Celebrity, Costa, Disney, Holland America, Norwegian Cruise Line, Orient and Royal Caribbean. Most lines offer special rates for children sharing a cabin with adults. Sometimes special offers include children 17 and younger sailing free when sharing a cabin with two full-fare adults as was the case with Royal Olympic Cruises on selected Mediterranean cruises in 2001.

Here are some tips that have worked for our family and friends through the years:

* Begin with a short sailing (three or four days). You can combine the short cruise with a pre-or post-cruise land program available from most cruise lines if you want a weeklong vacation (On the Disney Cruise Line, for example, you can combine the sailing with a stay at Walt Disney World). Then you can work your way up to longer voyages.

* On today's well-stabilized liners, seasickness is rare. If your child is prone to motion sickness (has gotten sick in cars, trains or planes) consult your pediatrician for a remedy. The ship's own doctor and nurse are right there and available in case of any health problems, a very comforting thought for traveling families. Select an ultra-liner or mega-liner for a generally smoother ride.

* Prepare the child for the cruise by telling him or her about the ship and voyage so s/he knows what to expect. Read picture books about ships together, and if the child is old enough, books and brochures on the destination and the vessel. Let the youngster choose some of the activities ashore, and include beaches, parks, zoos, children's museums and other kid-friendly attractions in your sightseeing.

* Once aboard, encourage the child to go to the clubroom and activities, even if s/he is shy at first, or protests that a certain activity is "babyish," said Vicki Pokorny, a counselor on Royal Caribbean's *Sovereign of the Seas*. "By coming to the playroom and giving the activities a try, children will make friends," Pokorny said, "and before they know it, they'll be having fun."

* If you sail in the summer and other school holidays—when traditionally more families sail—your child will find more playmates and programs. One example of more activities: Royal Caribbean's children programs are available year-round, but summers and holiday periods they are supplemented with Mad Science, which makes learning fun with bubbling potions and the like.

* Many cruise lines, including Carnival, Royal Caribbean and Princess, feature special menus for children with such favorites as burgers, chicken fingers and hot dogs in the main dining rooms. Recently, Princess also began offering the children's menu in its 24-hour informal cafes, which have proven to be very popular for family dining, according to Rick James, senior vice president of customer service and sales for Princess.

* Check with the cruise line about age requirements, particularly if the child is

under 2 years old. Many lines have minimum age requirements. In 1998, Princess lowered the age requirements to six months aboard ships sailing in the Caribbean and Alaska. In all other Princess markets, children 12 months of age are welcomed, except on exotic cruises, where they must be at least 18 months old. Some lines, like Windstar, do not encourage children.

* Most mainstream lines youth counselors are trained to work with children. Inquire through your travel agent or directly through the line, what specific training the counselors have and if they know CPR, and what safety/security measures are in place in the children's clubroom (such as release of children to parents only, special kid's bracelets and so on).

MULTI-GENERATIONAL -
When it comes to family get-togethers, we have tried them on cruises and on land, and we prefer reunions at sea, by far. The main reason: on a cruise it is so easy (effortless, really) for all members to have a good time. The variety of activities and entertainment options readily available on cruises makes it possible for the whole family to find something they like. Another powerful reason: most details are already arranged when you board, so one person does not get stuck with making restaurant, daytime activity, evening entertainment and other arrangements during the vacation. And on a cruise your ticket covers most everything: lodging, activities, entertainment, food and snacks. Best of all, each traveler pays for the vacation ahead of time so the older folks do not feel they should be constantly reaching in their pockets to pay for everyone's meals, snacks and activities as the holiday progresses—as they might in other vacations.

We have enjoyed reunions in all types of vessels: small, moderately-priced (**Star Flyer**), mid-size, luxury (**Royal Viking Sun**) and big, moderately-priced (**Splendour of the Seas**). Our family prefers the ultra-liner and mega-liner experience because of the wealth of options. Our latest reunion was a 12-night British Isles and Norwegian Fjords voyage on Royal Caribbean's **Splendour of the Seas** in August of 1999—a success, from the comfortable one-hop flights on British Airways to meet the ship to the last crumb of baked Alaska during our last formal dinner onboard the ship.

We all had room to spread out on the 69,130-ton **Splendour**, and lots of options to suit all our varied tastes—quite a feat considering the span in our ages: our daughter, 26 and her husband, 27; my husband and me in our mid-50s, my mother, 80. During a typical day at sea, the younger members of our contingent chose from sports tournaments, aerobics and pool games; my mother browsed in the shops or enjoyed bingo or a cooking demonstration; my husband and I read in the well-stocked library, joined the walkathon, or attended an enrichment lecture.

> When planning family reunions, discuss with group members that it is O.K. for everyone to have some time alone (to relax or pursue their own interests) and some time to get together.

As a rule, we all went to some activities together, like port talks, and also gathered for meals—wonderful times to plan our days and catch up on each other. We had at our disposal four venues for breakfast and lunch and two for dinner: for the latter, the formal dining room (where we generally dined) and the alternative Windjammer Cafe (when the older generations wanted a light, casual supper after a full day of sightseeing).

The dinner menus in the restaurant had something to please everyone: a variety of soups and salads, top-grade prime steaks, excellent seafood including fresh Norwegian salmon, light ShipShape selections for my mother who was on a low-fat diet, a great array of fine breads, and delicious desserts, so we never had to argue about whether to go for Italian or Chinese (as we might have on a resort vacation) or compromise on what we ate.

To make our lives even easier, we could pre-order the ship's guided tours and city transfers—even before we left home—which we did, thus enjoying a paperwork-free vacation. Our tickets were delivered to our cabins and charged to our shipboard account. In most ports, we went sightseeing together; in others, separately, each generation following our own interests, and comparing lively notes during dinner.

After dinner and a walk on deck fanned by fresh sea breezes, my mother often called it a night, the youngest generation generally took in a movie or social activity and my husband and I usually enjoyed music in the atrium or one of the lounges.

Our mid-size ship experience on the **Royal Viking Sun** was outstanding as well, particularly because our group was made up of an older grandparent, middle-aged parents and older child. The ship, with its dancing hosts, was very appealing to my mother.

For family reunions with young grandchildren, however, ships like those of Princess, Royal Caribbean, Celebrity, Disney, Norwegian Cruise Line and Carnival might be more suitable as they have extensive children's and teens' activity programs.

Younger grandparents might also enjoy more our other family reunion choice: the soft-adventure of visiting the Greek Isles under sail aboard Star Clippers' ***Star Flyer***. Sightseeing and activity choices included something for each generation: an 11-mile bike ride and scuba lessons for the younger set, walking tours and a visit to a Byzantine monastery for the older generations. There is a red flag here, however, for people with mobility problems on account of the number of stairs and high thresholds on ***Star Flyer*** as well as the steep gangway we had to negotiate when we had anchor and disembark via launches in various ports.

So if someone in your party has mobility problems or tires easily, steer away from ships without elevators and book cabins near elevator banks, particularly on mega-liners where walks to some aft cabins can be long. If your budget allows, get a cabin with a veranda—they are wonderful for everyone, but particularly for people with mobility problems who can sit there and watch port entrances and departures, views of the sea, and also enjoy meals and snacks on the terrace.

Other tips for multi-generational cruises include the following:

* Discuss every aspect of the trip (itineraries, ship and cabin preferences, fares and sightseeing goals) with every member of the group well ahead of booking. When you communicate, it is easier to meet expectations.

* While togetherness is fine, spending a little time apart is also refreshing for all generations. Stress that it is O.K. to pursue different interests on board ship and even to sightsee separately on occasion.

* Put yourself in other members of your group's shoes. When planning days together ashore, take into account the varying degrees of stamina of various family members and plan accordingly, with sufficient rest periods: when we toured in Paris with my elderly mother and our daughter, for instance, we all enjoyed a stop at a sidewalk café for refreshments after a visit to the Louvre Museum, and a boat ride on the bateaux mouches on the Seine after walking up and down the Champs Elysees. Always alternate drives or boat rides with walking

stints; and sit down to people-watch at a café or park every so often.

* Check on pertinent discounts for your age groups. Carnival, for instance, offers discounts to members of the AARP. The discounts, available through December 2003, include $100 per cabin for most seven-day and longer voyages and $50 per cabin on three-, four- or five-day sailings (certain restrictions apply). Other lines offering seniors' discounts include American Canadian Caribbean Line (20 percent discount on winter Caribbean sailings); Costa ($100 per cabin to people over 60); and World Explorer Cruises (AARP members receive 10 percent off per person on lower stateroom categories, 20 percent in upper categories; other discounts on selected sailings).

* If this is your first family reunion, do not set impossibly high expectations. Instead of saying, "this is going to be the best trip ever," say "we are going to have a good time." And if it turns out to be the best trip ever (it may well be!) then it is a bonus.

Cruising for Free

Several years ago, I met a man who was making his fancy footwork (he had taken ballroom dancing lessons when he was young and he loved to dance) take him all over the Mediterranean on a luxury cruise—for free. He was a gentleman host on the now-defunct Royal Cruise Line.

Since then, on many occasions during my cruises (particularly on lines like Cunard, Orient and Crystal) I have come across people who, like that gentleman, are also sailing free: dancing hosts, lecturers giving two or three talks about art, history, and other cultural topics during the course of a voyage, or giving bridge instruction or even crafts instructions.

If you have a special talent and training, you may be able to parlay that into a free cruise yourself. Contact the cruise lines (see the Appendix at the end of this guide) for information on how to sail as a lecturer, crafts teacher, or bridge tournament director. For information on how to sail as a dancing host visit www.theworkingvacation.com (Lauretta Blake, The Working Vacation, Inc.'s Web site). Some lines, like Crystal, screen and hire their own dancing hosts, so in addition to checking the Lauretta Blake site, contact the cruise lines directly for details.

Cruising Solo, etc.

Test the Waters Tips

* If you are sailing solo, bring a guidebook or perhaps destination brochures obtained for free from tourist boards to share with tablemates or people you meet at organized activities. As a young adult, our daughter always made friends while sunbathing out on deck (it is easy to start up a conversation while lounging, particularly during pool games and crazy contests which you can comment about to your neighbors).

* When sailing alone or merely taking a full-day shore excursion by yourself that includes lunch, simply walk up to a table where some people you would like to meet are seated, and ask if you may join them.

* If you are cruising with elderly parents, book a cabin amidships (particularly near the elevators) to save them steps.

* The best piece of advice for anyone contemplating a cruise is this: whatever your age or circumstances, whether young or old, single, married, with kids or retired, try not to put it off for too long. If you do postpone it you may regret not having done it (should illness or some other cause prevent you from sailing). But if you do sail, the only risk you run is being thoroughly captivated by the experience—and hopelessly "hooked" on cruising.

Insider's Savings Insights

* If you are going on a multi-generational family reunion, inquire if your contingent qualifies for special group rates or even a free ticket. KD River Cruises of Europe, for instance, in 2002 is offering group rates to parties of 10 paying passengers and one free passage for every 20 passengers in a group (you can reduce everyone's passage proportionately, raffle the ticket or invite someone who would otherwise not be able to come).

* If you are cruising solo, see if you can lure a relative, friend or co-worker to come along -that way you avoid single supplements. Other places you may be able to enlist a cabin-mate, if you wish to, include your church or clubs/organizations you belong to.

* When booking a cruise, always ask if there are any special discounts pertaining to your situation: seniors, group, third/fourth person in cabin, children's, etc.

Appendix

Nautical Lingo

I never knew how important nautical lingo really is until one day, when the voice over the ship's public address system announced: "Ladies and gentlemen, there are whales on our starboard side." One woman who did not know her port from starboard later told us she missed the glorious sight of a pod of humpback whales in Alaska's Inside Passage. To make sure this never happens to you, here is a list of nautical terms that may come in handy during your cruise:

- Aft - toward the back of the ship.
- Forward - toward the front of the ship.
- Starboard - the right side of the ship when you are facing forward.
- Port - the left side of the ship when you are facing forward.
- Bow - the front end of the ship.
- Stern - the back end of the ship.
- Bulkheads - the ship's interior walls.
- Galley - the ship's kitchen. Tours of it may be offered during the cruise.
- Navigational Bridge - manned by the captain and his officers, this is where the navigational equipment is located. Tours of it, previously a staple activity on most cruises, were stopped post-Sept. 11, 2001 by Crystal and other cruise lines. Orient Lines is among the lines still offering them.

Tender - a launch that takes passengers ashore when the ship anchors off a port instead of docking at it.
Gangway - Detachable stairs that go from the ship to the pier or the tender platform.
Embark - Board the ship.
Disembark - Get off the ship.

Cruise Line Addresses, Phones and Websites

Abercrombie & Kent, Inc., 1520 Kensington Road, Oak Brook, Ill. 60523-2141; 800-323-7308; www.abercrombiekent.com.

American Canadian Caribbean Line, P.O. Box 368, Warren, RI 02885; 800-556-7450; www.accl-smallships.com.

American Safari Cruises, 19101 36th Avenue, W., Suite 201, Lynnwood, Wash. 98036; 888-862-8881; www.amsafari.com.

American West Steamboat Co., 2101 Fourth Avenue, Suite 1150, Seattle, Wash. 98121; 800-434-1232; www.columbiarivercruise.com.

Carnival Cruise Lines, Carnival Place, 3655 NW 87th Ave., Miami, Fla. 33178-2428; 800-327-9501; www.carnival.com.

Celebrity Cruises, 1050 Caribbean Way, Miami, Fla. 33132; 800-437-3111; www.celebrity-cruises.com.

Clipper Cruise Line, Windsor Building, 7711 Bonhomme Avenue, St. Louis, Mo. 63105-1956; 800-325-0010; www.clippercruise.com.

Costa Cruise Lines, 200 South Park Road, Suite 200, Hollywood, Fla. 33021-8541; 800-462-6782; www.costacruises.com.

Cruise West, 2401 Fourth Avenue, Suite 700, Seattle, Wash. 98121; 800-888-9378; www.cruisewest.com.

Crystal Cruises, 2049 Century Park East, Suite 1400, Los Angeles, Calif. 90067; 800-820-6663; www.crystalcruises.com.

Cunard Line, 6100 Blue Lagoon Drive, Suite 400, Miami, Fla. 33126; 800-728-6273; www.cunard.com.

Delta Queen Steamboat Co., Robin Street Wharf, 1380 Port of New Orleans Place, New Orleans, La 70130; 800-543-7637; www.deltaqueen.com.

Disney Cruise Line, 210 Celebration Place, Suite 400, Celebration, Fla. 34747; 800-939-2784; www.disneycruise.com.

Appendix

European Waterways, 140 E. 56th Street, New York, N.Y. 10022; 800-217-4447; www.ewaterways.com.

First European Cruises, 95 Madison Avenue, Suite 1203, New York, N.Y. 10016; 888-983-8767; www.first-european.com.

Fred Olsen Cruises, P.O. Box 342, N.Y., N.Y. 10014; 800-688-3876; www.fredolsencruises.co.uk.

French Country Waterways, P.O. Box 2195, Duxbury, Mass. 02331; 800-222-1236; www.fcwl.com.

Glacier Bay Cruise Line, 226 Second Avenue, W., Seattle, Wash. 98119; 800-451-5952; www.glacierbaycruiseline.com.

Global Quest (formerly OdessAmerica), 50 Glen Street, Suite 206, Glen Cove, N.Y. 11542; 800-221-3254; www.globalquesttravel.com.

Holland America Line, 300 Elliott Ave. West, Seattle, Wash. 98119; 877-724-5425; www.hollandamerica.com.

Imperial Majesty Cruise Line, Gateway Drive, Suite 200, Pompano Beach, Fla. 33069; 800-511-5737; www.imperialmajesty.com.

KD River Cruises, J.F.O. CruiseService Corp., 2500 Westchester Avenue, Suite 113, Purchase, N.Y. 10577; 800-346-6525; www.rivercruises.com.

Lindblad Expeditions, 720 Fifth Avenue, New York, N.Y., 10019; 800-762-0003; www.expeditions.com.

Mediterranean Shipping Cruises, 420 Fifth Ave., New York, NY 10018; 800-666-9333; www.mscgeneva.com.

Norwegian Coastal Voyage, 405 Park Avenue, New York, N.Y. 10022; 800-323-7436; www.coastalvoyage.com.

Norwegian Cruise Line, 7665 Corporate Center Drive, Miami, Fla. 33126; 800-327-7030; www.ncl.com.

Orient Express Cruises, c/o Orient Express Hotels, 1155 Avenue of the Americas, New York, N.Y. 10036; 800-524-2420; www.orient-expresstrains.com.

Orient Lines, 1510 S.E. 17th Street, Suite 400, Fort Lauderdale, Fla. 33316; 800-333-7300; www.orientlines.com.

Peter Deilmann EuropAmerica Cruises, 1800 Diagonal Road, Suite 170, Alexandria, Va. 22314; 800-348-8287; www.deilmann-cruises.com.

Princess Cruises, 24305 Town Center Drive, Santa Clarita, Calif. 91355-4999; 800-774-6237; www.princess.com.

Radisson Seven Seas Cruises, 600 Corporate Drive, Suite 410, Fort Lauderdale, Fla. 33334; 800-285-1835; www.rssc.com.

Regal China Cruises, 57 W. 38th Street, New York, N.Y. 10018; 800-808-3388; www.regalchinacruises.com.

Regal Cruises, P. O. Box 1329, Palmetto, Fla. 34220; 800-270-7245; www.regalcruises.com.

RiverBarge Excursions Lines, 201 Opelousas Avenue, New Orleans, La. 70114; 888-456-2206; www.riverbarge.com.

Royal Caribbean International, 1050 Caribbean Way, Miami, Fla. 33132-2096; 800-327-6700; www.royalcaribbean.com.

Royal Olympic Cruises, 805 Third Ave., New York, N.Y.; 10022-7513; 800-872-6400; www.royalolympiccruises.com.

Seabourn Cruise Line, 6100 Blue Lagoon Dr. Suite 400; Miami, Fla. 33126; 800-929-9391; www.seabourn.com.

Sea Cloud Cruises, 32-40 North Dean St., Englewood, N.J. 08631; 888-732-2568; www.seacloud.com.

SeaEscape Ltd., 3045 N. Federal Highway, Fort Lauderdale, Fla. 33306; 800-327-2005; www.seaescape.com.

Silversea Cruises, 110 East Broward Blvd., Fort Lauderdale, Fla. 33301; 800-722-9055; www.silversea.com.

Star Clippers, 4101 Salzedo Ave., Coral Gables, Fla. 33146; 800-442-0551; www.starclippers.com.

Swan Hellenic Cruises, 631 Commack Road, Suite 1A, Commack, N.Y. 11725; 877-219-4239; www.swanhellenic.com.

The Barge Lady, 101 W. Grand Avenue, Suite 200, Chicago, Ill. 60610; 800-880-0071; www.bargelady.com.

Windjammer Barefoot Cruises, P.O. Box 190120, Miami Beach, Fla. 33119; 800-327-2601; www.windjammer.com.

Windstar Cruises, 300 Elliott Ave. West, Seattle, Wash. 98119; 800-258-7245; www.windstarcruises.com.

World Explorer Cruises, 555 Montgomery St., Suite 1400, San Francisco, Calif. 94111; 800-854-3835; www.wecruise.com.

Appendix

Other Resources

Major Cruise Travel Agencies

Cruise Planners, 3300 University Dr., Suite 602, Coral Springs, Fla. 33065; 800-683-0206; www.weplancruises.com.

The Cruise Shoppe, 1525 Lapalco Blvd., Suite 4, Harvey, La. 70058; 800-392-3639.

CruiseMasters, 200 Corporate Point, Suite 150, Culver City, Calif. 90230; 800-242-9444; www.mytravelco.com.

Cruises-N-More, 725 Primera Blvd., Suite 215, Altamonte Springs, Fla. 32746; 800-733-2048; www.cruises-n-more.com.

Cruises-Only, 1011 Colonial Drive, Orlando, Fla. 32802; 800-395-3593; www.cruisesonly.com.

Cruise Specialists, 221 First Avenue W., Suite 210, Seattle, Wash. 98119; 800-544-2469; www.csiseattle.com.

Liberty Travel, 69 Spring Street, Ramsey, N.J. 07446; 877-442-7847; www.libertytravel.com.

Travel Services International/Cruises Only, 220 Congress Park Drive, Delray Beach, Fla. 33445; 800-683-7447; www.mytravelco.com.

The Vacation Store, 1556 Laskin Road, Virginia Beach, Va. 23451; 800-825-3633; www.takeoff.com.

World Wide Cruises/American Express, 8059 W. McNab Road, Tamarac, Fla. 33321; 800-882-9000; www.wwcruises.com.

Worldwide Travel & Cruises, 8784 S.W. Eighth Street, Miami, Fla. 33174; 800-441-1954; www.worldwidecruises.com.

Online Cruise Agencies & Auction Sites

www.icruise.com - This user-friendly site features "Pack & Go" hot specials and a live agent so you can talk online with a cruise expert.

www.cruise411.com - Rosenbluth Travel of Philadelphia's Web site. It features a large last minute database, hot deals, a Book It Now! Reservation System, cruise reviews and cruising tips.

www.uniglobe.com - You can chat with an agent live through this site and browse through last-minute offers, ship reviews and tips.

www.cruise.com - Omega World Travel's Web site, it features a large cruise inventory, lots of specials, ship profiles, reviews and stats.

www.bestpricecruises.com - Cruise Holidays' discount cruise agency site, it has specials, quotes and online booking.

www.allcruiseauction.com - In addition to a half-dozen featured cruise auctions, this site has promotions, cruise information and message boards.

www.SkyAuction.com - This site has a "Cruises" section with pages and pages on voyages up for bids.

Useful Internet Sites

www.towd.com - Tourism Offices Worldwide is a site featuring Internet addresses, information (and links) on Tourism Offices worldwide including Caribbean islands.

www.VisitEurope.com - The European Travel Commission's Web site, it has information on European countries including events calendars.

www.Caribbean.com and www.CaribbeanTravel.com are sites with information about Caribbean islands.

www.travelalaska.com is the Official Tourism Marketing Organization's site for the State of Alaska. Features include a Trip Planner, Virtual Tours, History & Culture and more.

http://travel.state.gov/ - U.S. State Department's information on travel abroad.

Appendix

www.cdc.gov/travel - Centers for Disease Control's site, it has information on Vessel Sanitation.

www.astanet.com - The American Society of Travel Agents' site is a good place to go to if you are looking for a travel agent.

www.cruising.org - The Cruise Lines International Association (CLIA), the cruise industry's marketing arm, has information about the cruise lines and travel agents on this, its site.

www.theworkingvacation.com - Lauretta Blake The Working Vacation Inc., site has information on cruising for free as a gentleman host (dancing with unescorted ladies).

www.CruiseCritic.com - (AOL keyword Cruise Critic) offers ship reviews, "virtual cruises" (day to day cruise diaries written by expert writers) tips and other features.

www.CruiseMates.com - This online cruise magazine features reviews, articles, advice and more.

Your Personal Cruise diary

Cruise Line:

Ship:

Sailing Date:

Port of Embarkation:

Port of Disembarkation:

Pre- or Post-Cruise Land Program:

Cruise Itinerary:

Captain:

Cruise Director:

Stateroom Number and Description:

Cruise Diary

Cabin Steward's Name:

Favorite Activities Onboard Ship:

Most Memorable Moments Onboard Ship:

Favorite Shore Excursions/Port Activities:

Favorite Port Shops/Souvenirs:

Most Memorable Moments Ashore:

Things Best Forgotten:

Tablemates:

Names Of Dining Room Personnel:
Maitre d':
Section Captain:
Waiter:
Busboy:
Wine Steward:

Favorite dishes/snacks:

New Friends Made During the Cruise:

Name_____Address & Phone Number

Cruise Diary

Shipboard Expense Diary:

Item_____Expense_____

Miscellaneous Notes:

Fell's Official Know-It-All Guide™

Check out these exciting titles in our Know-It-All™ series, available at your favorite bookstore:

- Fell's Official Know-It-All™ Guide: Advanced Hypnotism
- Fell's Official Know-It-All™ Guide: Advanced Magic
- Fell's Official Know-It-All™ Guide: A Kid's Guide to Surviving Braces
- Fell's Official Know-It-All™ Guide: The Art of Traveling Extravagantly & Nearly Free
- Fell's Official Know-It-All™ Guide: Budget Weddings
- Fell's Official Know-It-All™ Guide: Career Planning
- Fell's Official Know-It-All™ Guide: Contract Bridge
- Fell's Official Know-It-All™ Guide: Coins 2003
- Fell's Official Know-It-All™ Guide: Easy Entertaining
- Fell's Official Know-It-All™ Guide: ESP Power
- Fell's Official Know-It-All™ Guide: Getting Rich & Staying Rich
- Fell's Official Know-It-All™ Guide: Health & Wellness
- Fell's Official Know-It-All™ Guide: Let's Get Results, Not Excuses
- Fell's Official Know-It-All™ Guide: Magic For Beginners
- Fell's Official Know-It-All™ Guide: Money Management for College Students
- Fell's Official Know-It-All™ Guide: Mortgage Maze
- Fell's Official Know-It-All™ Guide: No Bull Selling
- Fell's Official Know-It-All™ Guide: Online Investing
- Fell's Official Know-It-All™ Guide: Palm Reading
- Fell's Official Know-It-All™ Guide: Relationship Selling
- Fell's Official Know-It-All™ Guide: Secrets of Mind Power
- Fell's Official Know-It-All™ Guide: So, You Want to Be a Teacher?
- Fell's Official Know-It-All™ Guide: Super Power Memory
- Fell's Official Know-It-All™ Guide: Wedding Planner